We Love You Yeah, Yeah, Yeah!

The Story of Liverpool's 1963-64 Title Triumph

Steven Horton

VERTICAL EDITIONS
www.verticaleditions.com

First published in the United Kingdom in 2014 by Vertical Editions, Unit 4a, Snaygill Industrial Estate, Skipton, North Yorkshire BD23 2QR

www.verticaleditions.com

ISBN 978-1-904091-82-0

A CIP catalogue record for this book is available from the British Library

Cover design by HBA, York

Printed and bound by CMP (uk) Ltd, Poole, Dorset

Contents

Acknowledgements

In no particular order I'd like to thank Rob Gowers and Hyder Jawad for their memorabilia, Chris Wood for the fact checking and proof reading, Arnie Baldursson and Gudmundur Magnusson for their brilliant website lfchistory.net and the players and coaching staff of Liverpool FC that season for making it so special.

Introduction

The inspiration to write this book came in part from having enjoyed the research and writing of my book *Ending the Seven Year Itch*, brought out during the 40th anniversary of the 1972-73 season. Looking at 2014, there were two obvious seasons to commemorate – 1963-64 and 1983-84. The latter would have been the easiest as I personally attended just about every home game as a 13 year old, but instead I could not resist the idea of researching Bill Shankly's first title.

Having heard older relatives and fans talk about the special bond that existed between players and fans and the rise of singing on the Kop it was something I wanted to learn more about. I had been fascinated about this era ever since I watched the excerpt from the Panorama programme on the BBC's Official History of Liverpool FC, released in 1987. I was used to seeing Liverpool win the league every year, it was incomprehensible to me to think of the club in Division Two. But I was old enough to imagine the euphoria that must have been felt after eight years in the doldrums, to emerge as Champions just two years after promotion. Add to this the nearly full employment and rise of the Merseybeat and the city must have been one special place to be if you were a Red.

1963-64 was a season that was played out before even televised highlights were common, let alone live games and social media. Local newspapers were the main source of information about favourite teams and even then they could go three or four days without a story. This added to the fascination of researching this book, the thought that fans would telephone Anfield to confirm a game hadn't been postponed due to the weather, and sometimes wouldn't know if a player was injured until they didn't appear in the starting line-up.

However there were so many similarities with this season and today. Disgruntled fans wrote to the newspapers bemoaning Liverpool's failure to sign a player before transfer deadline day, despite having just receiving a club record £50,000 for Jimmy Melia. The FA seemed to do all they could to disrupt clubs, with players inexplicably being called up for three day training camps as the season entered its closing stages. While in the ground itself, the fans in the Kemlyn Road (now Lower Centenary), left well before the end of the game even back then.

The tale of Liverpool's title winning side of 1963-64 is a remarkable one.

The side remained settled all season, with the starting eleven effectively picking itself when all were fit. Only 13 players played 10 or more games and 9 played 35 or more. In the second half of the season Jimmy Melia made way for Alf Arrowsmith and during the first half the versatile Phil Ferns covered for injuries involving Willie Stevenson, Ronnie Moran and Gerry Byrne, playing 18 times in the league. For a short time Moran looked to have lost his place to Ferns, who had been captain of the reserves, but in the end Shankly went for experience and the veteran got back in.

The side was on the whole a young one, with only Moran having played in the side that was relegated in 1953-54. There were no big name signings in the team compared to title challengers, such as Everton who splashed out £85,000 on Fred Pickering in March. This was more than double the £37,500 Liverpool had paid for Peter Thompson at the start of the season, which matched the club record fee that had been paid for Ian St John in 1961. Nine of the principal thirteen players had played in Division Two, while Ferns and Tommy Lawrence had joined the club during those years but only made their debuts after promotion. Only two of the thirteen had signed whilst the club was in Division One – Thompson and Willie Stevenson, who cost just £20,000 from Rangers. But these raw young men were moulded by Shankly into a side that won the title with three games to spare, then proved it was no one off by winning the FA Cup and reaching the semi-finals of the European Cup the next year, then winning the title again in 1966.

Some of the early indications of success in much later years could be seen in the events of 1963-64. Bob Paisley was the trainer/physio and being manager was the furthest thing from his mind, but a taste of his acumen was evident when he advised Ron Yeats to run onto the ball at corners rather than wait for it to come to him. This paid dividends at Old Trafford when he ran and connected with the ball to score with an unstoppable header. Chris Lawler, a mainstay of the team for nearly a decade, showed his ability in that season when he came in for Ron Yeats during injury and suspension. His performances in these games went a long way to ensuring there was no need to open the cheque book for a successor to Moran.

This book tells the story of the season on a match by match basis but rather than simply being a repetitive report of each game, I have written about the circumstances surrounding them with respect to training, internationals and the thoughts of players, with the local newspaper columns of St John and Yeats providing excellent insight. Some long forgotten Shanklyisms have been uncovered such as his comment on a particularly cold day at Melwood that it was cold enough to have frozen an Eskimo. Little quirky stories are also present, such as Arrowsmith getting married and then playing for the reserves the same afternoon and St John having his summer holiday at a caravan park in Morecambe.

The period was an eventful one nationally and internationally, with the assassination of Kennedy, Great Train Robbery and resignation of the Prime Minister all taking place that season, with the world also still suffering the fallout from the Cuban Missile Crisis. It was also the period that Beatlemania took off and chanting of 'Liv-er-pool' on the Kop expanded to full repertoires of their songs and those of other Merseybeat groups. It was the season that *You'll Never Walk Alone* was first sang at Anfield and it was one that will remain in the minds of those who were there forever. I hope this book can recapture that.

1

First Post War Champions, Decline and Promotion

When Liverpool became the first team to be crowned Football League Champions after the Second World War, they joined an elite band of just five clubs who had won five or more titles – the others being Aston Villa and Sunderland with six each, and Arsenal and Everton who also had five. There followed a steady decline however that saw the club relegated just seven years later, and whereas on the two previous occasions that Liverpool had gone down they had bounced straight back up again, this time fans would have to wait eight years before they were back in the top flight.

After winning the title in that first post war season in 1946-47 the Reds then finished a disappointing eleventh and twelfth in the next two campaigns. They had a great start to 1949-50, avoiding defeat in their first nineteen games, and leading the table between early November and the middle of February, except for one week in January when they fell to second after a defeat at Bolton. However, a 4-1 loss at Middlesbrough on 25th February was the first of four defeats in five league games that saw them slip to third behind Blackpool and Manchester United.

It was extremely tight at the top and the Reds won their next three matches to move back up to first place with five left to play, but Blackpool, Portsmouth and Sunderland could overhaul them if they won their own games in hand. Even though the Reds needed favours from others, they did themselves none at all by picking up just one point from their remaining fixtures to eventually finish eighth as Portsmouth won the title for a second year running.

Although the league ended in disappointing fashion there was still hope in the FA Cup as the Reds reached only their second ever final and their first at Wembley. After lower division sides Blackburn, Exeter and Stockport were beaten, Liverpool were paired with fellow title chasers Blackpool in the quarter finals. Billy Liddell's goal nine minutes from time took the Reds to the semi finals after Stan Mortensen had cancelled out Willie Fagan's opening goal in the first half.

The semi final draw paired Liverpool with Everton and many pubs in Manchester were literally 'drunk dry' on a day that saw the Reds triumph 2-0 at Maine Road, the opening goal being a lob just before half time from

Bob Paisley. For the final against Arsenal though, Paisley was left out of the side to accommodate the fit-again Laurie Hughes and the Reds fell to a 2-0 defeat.

The average age of that FA Cup final side was almost 29, and over the next few years there would be many changes to the team with players such as captain Phil Taylor, keeper Cyril Sidlow, and centre forward Albert Stubbins phased out. However those that came in weren't as good quality, with forwards Sammy Smyth, Arthur Rowley and Louis Bimpson being nowhere near as prolific as those of the late 1940s, namely Stubbins and Jack Balmer.

No keeper was able to firmly establish themselves between the sticks either, with Charlie Ashcroft and Russell Crossley vying for the number one slot for three seasons between 1951 and 1954. Billy Liddell remained the one shining light for the fans while there were promising youngsters coming through in the shape of defender Ronnie Moran and winger Alan A'Court. However, they alone couldn't halt the slide of a team now managed by Don Welsh who had taken over from title-winning manager George Kay in 1951 following his resignation due to ill health.

In 1952-53 only a last day defeat of Chelsea saved the Reds from relegation but the following season they rarely looked like staying up. A 3-1 opening day victory over Portsmouth was a false dawn and they failed to win any of the next eight games. Oddly, when Liverpool did win they won comfortably, with Aston Villa and Sheffield United being beaten 6-1 and 3-0 in home games during October, but away from home the Reds were dire, losing their opening thirteen fixtures on the road with the first point being picked up at Burnley on 6th February. By then they were five points adrift from safety and the inevitable relegation was confirmed in the third from last game when Cardiff won 1-0 at Anfield.

1954-55 was to be the worst season in Liverpool's history as they slumped to eleventh in the Second Division. Five defeats in their opening seven games left fans fearing another relegation and the dismal away form continued, culminating in a 9-1 humiliating loss at Birmingham on 11th December, still the club's all time record defeat. That was their eighth defeat in ten away games and the Reds didn't pick up their first win away from home until they beat Fulham 2-1 at Craven Cottage on 5th February. This came a week after a shock 4-0 derby win at Everton in the fourth round of the FA Cup, but any hopes of a run to Wembley were dashed in the next round when Huddersfield won 2-0 at Anfield.

The board retained faith in Welsh and the following season a concerted effort for promotion was made with the Reds being well placed at Easter. A 2-1 home win on Easter Saturday, 31st March, lifted them into second place on goal average but with a game in hand. Then they went and blew it by losing their next two games to eventually finish third, four points behind Leeds who went up along with Sheffield Wednesday.

A few days after the end of the season Welsh's resignation was accepted by the board who may well not have renewed his contract anyway. He was replaced by former captain Phil Taylor, who had been on the coaching staff since his retirement two years earlier. Taylor, a former England international and professional cricketer who had been at the club since 1936, was a popular appointment but a poor start in his first campaign, with just three wins from the first ten games, left them playing catch up. By New Year they had climbed to third but then lost three in a row to fall away to ninth. Although they had a strong finish, winning nine out of the last twelve, it wasn't enough and they missed out by just one point.

The strong finish from the previous campaign continued into 1957-58 and Liverpool were top at Christmas, only to fall to a shock 6-1 defeat at mid-table Cardiff on 28th December. It was the start of a run of just three wins from nine that saw the Reds drop to third and although they had another good finish, winning six and drawing two of their last eight games, they finished fourth. Another year in the Second Division was as good as confirmed in the penultimate game, when a 1-1 draw at West Ham United meant the Hammers were on the brink of promotion while Liverpool's goal average meant that some unthinkable scorelines were needed on the last day for them to go up.

1958-59 saw the Reds start disappointingly and they were tenth at the end of September after ten games. They were then well-beaten 5-0 at Huddersfield but this sparked a reaction and fourteen victories from the next sixteen games saw them enter the promotion positions for the first time on 7th February when Bristol City were beaten 3-2 at Anfield.

Yet again though the Reds imploded and won just six of their remaining fifteen fixtures, finishing fourth, seven points behind the promotion places. There was humiliation in the FA Cup too, as non league Worcester City beat the Reds 2-1 in a 3rd round tie and fans were now becoming impatient with Taylor after the club were handily placed for promotion on three occasions only to fall away.

The great Billy Liddell was nearing the end of his career and Alan A'Court, who represented England in the 1958 World Cup, remained loyal to the Reds despite their Second Division status. But on the whole, the team frustrated the crowd with inconsistency being a major problem as the likes of Jimmy Harrower and Fred Morris regularly incurred their wrath.

When Liverpool registered just five wins from their opening fifteen games in 1959-60, leaving them in the bottom half of the table, it was evidence that new blood was needed. Reserve striker Roger Hunt had been given a chance and scored on his debut, a 2-0 win over Scunthorpe on 9th September, but more experience was needed to get Liverpool out of the Second Division.

However the player who arrived was not what the fans envisaged, for in one of the most sensational transfers ever to occur in Merseyside football,

Dave Hickson crossed Stanley Park in a £12,000 deal. It outraged fans of both clubs with Evertonians believing he still had something to offer them, and Liverpudlians being aghast that their club had taken a player deemed surplus to requirements by the Everton board. In front of 49,981 fans, Hickson won over the Reds' faithful with both goals in a 2-1 win over Aston Villa on his debut on 7th November.

Within weeks of Hickson's arrival Taylor resigned, a 4-2 defeat in the next game at Lincoln City being the final straw for him. His replacement had already made his mark on the Reds board as Bill Shankly had been approached regarding the managerial vacancy in 1951, but declined the position as the manager didn't have the final say on team selection. He was then at Carlisle, but via Grimsby and Workington was now in charge of Huddersfield, making a further impression on the Reds board after overseeing that 5-0 hammering of the Reds in October 1958.

Ironically Shankly's last match in charge of Huddersfield was when they beat the Reds 1-0 on 28th November 1959, a game that saw Bob Paisley and Joe Fagan look after the team. Shankly's first two games in charge of Liverpool ended in 4-0 and 3-0 defeats but he managed to lift them up the table to eventually finish third, although there was never any realistic prospect of promotion.

Shankly had seen that the squad he inherited were on the whole not good enough, and at the start of his first full season in charge he broke the club transfer record to sign midfielder Gordon Milne for £16,000 from Preston. He joined other new arrivals in Alf Arrowsmith, a promising seventeen-year-old centre forward who joined from Ashton United for a nominal fee, and winger Kevin Lewis, a £13,000 signing from Sheffield United.

Yet again though, the Reds blew promotion after being well placed for much of the season. They were second on Boxing Day and remained in contention until the end of March, but just two wins in their last seven games saw them fall off the pace to finish a distant third again. The crowd made their dissatisfaction felt for the last home game of the season against Stoke with the attendance just 13,389 being less than half the season's average.

By now, even Shankly was getting annoyed with a Board who were unwilling to put their hands in their pockets to sign the players who would take the club into the First Division. Luckily he had on hand Eric Sawyer, appointed by the Moores family to oversee the club's finances and he could see that given the right players, Shankly could do great things for Liverpool.

Shankly identified Ron Yeats and Ian St John, two players who would give the side a great spine, as the final piece in his jigsaw. Sawyer told the other directors that Liverpool couldn't afford not to sign them, and the £37,500 paid to Motherwell for St John was more than double the previous transfer record set a year earlier when Milne had arrived.

Liverpool began the 1961-62 season like an express train, winning ten out of their first eleven games with Hunt finding the net eleven times. The new signings had adapted extremely well. St John never stopping running to make space for Hunt as well as being magnificent in the air despite his small height, while Yeats was a rock at the back. Even after the unbeaten start came to an end with a 2-0 defeat at Middlesbrough Kopites needn't have worried as the Reds responded by hammering Walsall 6-1 at Anfield in their next game.

Although the Reds had lost five games by the halfway stage they were eight points clear of third place Sunderland and had hit five goals at Anfield on four occasions. There was a slight blip over Christmas when they lost successive games in Yorkshire against Leeds and Rotherham but they bounced back in style, remaining unbeaten until the end of March when they lost 1-0 at Luton. This unbeaten run had opened up a nine point gap on third place Plymouth with a game in hand and by now it was just a case of when, and not if, promotion would be secured.

On East Saturday, 21st April, even a miserable wet day couldn't dampen the spirits of the crowd as 40,410 turned out to see the Reds play Southampton, knowing that a win would secure their return to the First Division with five games still to go. Mid-way through the half Lewis, playing at centre forward instead of the suspended St John, opened the scoring by firing in a rebound after his first effort was blocked. On the half hour he added another, netting from close range after the keeper could only parry a Hunt header.

Due to the appalling conditions the rest of the game was a scrappy affair but it didn't stop the crowd's enthusiasm and at the end most of them stayed in the ground after the players had disappeared down the tunnel, demanding their return. They did so for a lap of honour, accompanied by St John. With many having invaded the pitch the players then appeared in the Directors' Box, leading to the crowd beginning a rhythmic chanting and clapping of 'Liv-er-pool'. After eight long years Liverpool fans could finally look forward to playing in the top flight again.

Two days later the players were back at Anfield for a home game with Stoke, a 2-1 win confirming they would be promoted as champions with Leyton Orient joining them. The Reds said goodbye to the Second Division on 4th May with a 4-2 defeat in a re-arranged game at Swansea but by then nobody cared.

2

League Consolidation and FA Cup Heartbreak

1962-63, Liverpool's first season back in the 1st Division after an eight year absence, was one of consolidation that saw them recover to finish eighth after a slow start. They also went agonisingly close in the FA Cup, reaching the semi-finals only to lose 1-0 to Leicester.

Bill Shankly stuck with the players who had served him so well during the promotion season making no major close season signings and the Reds started slowly, picking up just one point from the first three games. Successive home wins took them into the top half of the table but inconsistency returned. Results at Anfield were good with the Reds remaining unbeaten in five games after an opening day defeat to Blackpool. However, away from home they were struggling and a 1-0 defeat at West Bromwich Albion on 27th October was their sixth loss in eight games on the road.

That day though football was far from everyone's minds as the Cuban Missile Crisis left the world on the brink of nuclear war. Shortly after the game ended an American air force re-fuelling plane was shot down near Cuba by a Soviet commander acting without authority. Thankfully, that didn't stop the negotiations and the following day it was announced that the USSR had agreed to withdraw their missiles from Cuba if the United States pulled theirs out of Turkey.

On 3rd November a 2-1 home defeat to Burnley left the Reds just one place above the relegation zone, however Shankly had already begun to make the changes that he knew were needed if the Reds were to climb the table. This game marked the debut of left half Willie Stevenson who had fallen out of favour at Rangers and looked set to quit Britain for Australia before Shankly stepped in to sign him. He took the place of Tom Leishman, and another player who lost his place was keeper Jim Furnell who suffered a broken finger in training. He was replaced by 22-year-old Tommy Lawrence who had waited patiently since being signed from Warrington Town in 1957, and he came into the side for the first time in the West Bromwich game.

The changes to the team soon invigorated them, and on 10th November the Reds were involved in a thrilling 3-3 draw at Old Trafford, a game which saw them come from 2-1 down with five minutes to go to lead 3-2, only to concede a last minute equaliser. Four days later though they beat

Arsenal 2-1 at Anfield, the first of nine wins in succession that lifted them up to fifth place by mid February, just five points behind leaders Tottenham.

The Reds failed to maintain the momentum and their title chances took a serious dent with a 2-0 home defeat by second placed Leicester followed by four successive draws in five games. By the time Easter came around the title race looked to be a three-way battle between Leicester, Tottenham and Everton and the Reds played their part in its destiny that weekend.

On Good Friday, Spurs came to Anfield and led 2-0 at half time only to capitulate as the Reds hit back after the break with five goals without reply in front of over 54,000 fans, including quite a few Evertonians. Three days later on Easter Monday, Jimmy Greaves opened the scoring only for Roger Hunt to equalise, but Spurs stormed to a 7-2 victory which remains Liverpool's heaviest defeat since they returned to the top flight. The Reds hadn't actually played that badly as Hunt hit the post and bar and Ian St John had an effort cleared off the line, but Greaves was unplayable and struck four of his side's goals.

The Spurs defeat left Liverpool in sixth place but they still had dreams of FA Cup glory. The third round had seen a comfortable 3-0 victory over at Wrexham, and then in the next round they were paired with Burnley, league champions in 1960. After a 1-1 draw at Turf Moor the replay was postponed several times due to the severe winter weather before it was eventually played on 20th February. This was three weeks after the first game and four days after the scheduled date for the 5th round.

With the sides locked at 1-1 deep into extra time, Burnley keeper Adam Blacklaw's clearance struck St John on the back and rebounded goalwards, and as the Reds forward raced to help the ball into the net Blacklaw brought him down. A penalty was awarded although Blacklaw received only a yellow card. The crowd of 57,906, a figure that has not been matched at Anfield since, remained silent as Ronnie Moran stepped forward to take the kick, sending the Burnley keeper the wrong way and setting up a fifth round tie with Arsenal at Highbury.

The Reds beat Arsenal 2-1 in a game that saw Moran again on target from the penalty spot, and in the sixth round they overcame West Ham United 1-0 at Anfield, Hunt scoring the winning goal nine minutes from time. In the semi final the Reds' opponents would be Leicester City in a game that was to be played at Hillsborough on 27th April 1963. Mike Stringfellow put Leicester ahead in the eighteenth minute and despite dominating the rest of the game, the Reds couldn't find a way past an inspired Gordon Banks.

The semi-final defeat knocked the stuffing out of Liverpool and the season ended unspectacularly as they won only one of their last six games to eventually finish eighth, casting envious glances across Stanley Park where Everton clinched the championship with a 4-1 win over Fulham on 11th May.

The Reds were quick to congratulate their neighbours but had a warning for the following season with chairman T.V. Williams, who was at Goodison Park on the day they clinched the title, telling the *Daily Post*: 'I do sincerely compliment them on a wonderful season. They have been a wonderfully consistent side and well deserve the honour. But I warn them now, one club which will press them all the way next season will be Liverpool.' Williams was right, the following April it would be the Reds half of Merseyside that would be celebrating the league championship.

3

Contract Uncertainties, Transfer Market Frustration and a New Stand

The close season of 1963 was far less eventful than those of today, with very little coverage in the newspapers about what was going on football-wise as they devoted most of their sports pages to cricket and tennis. During the whole of June for example, the *Daily Post* carried just three news items in relation to Liverpool FC. What news the local press did carry though was of great interest to fans as they learned of rapid progress with ground developments, potential new transfer targets and held their breath as current playing and management contracts were sorted out.

The eighth place finish and run to the semi-final of the cup had led to optimism amongst Liverpool's players and fans that they could build on this in the 1963-64 season. Even though the Reds had fallen away after looking like they could mount a title challenge at one stage, this had to be put into context against the fact they had just endured eight long years in the Second Division. On 10th May the *Daily Post* published a letter from a Mr F. Gill who lived in Crosby, paying tribute to Bill Shankly which read:

> 'I am sure I speak for many thousands of supporters when I say thank you very much for giving us such wonderful entertainment and great, thrilling football in our first season back in top grade soccer. When the season started we were known as the poor relations of Merseyside, the team that would have to play second fiddle to our neighbours and struggle through the winter. Admittedly things did not go too well earlier on, but you kept faith with the boys who topped Division II and suddenly you pounced on the season's bargain to bring the vital link to the club and we never looked back. We took over the title of team of the year for many weeks and for poor relations we became to the supporters the millionaires, not only of Merseyside but the whole of England. You, Mr Shankly, deserve our thanks because it was your determination, your will to win, your faith in entertaining football, comradeship with the players and your attitude to us all that has made this season so successful. The honours that have come to the players proves that your policy has brought the best out of the boys, including the reserves. Admittedly we have heard the slow handclap at Anfield and the odd boo but those that carry out such practices are not the true supporters and we ignore such actions. No-one can say that he

has not had his moneys worth, for the season has made us proud to be Liverpool supporters. Even at Sheffield when we were denied Wembley and possibly the cup, nobody had anything but praise for your team and your team selection. Liverpool gained more credit in defeat than Leicester did in victory.'

Mr Gill went on to do something that would be unthinkable today, as he wrote that fans hoped Leicester would be beaten by Manchester United in the FA Cup final: 'We plump for Manchester United, we would rather see a footballing side gain the honour than a team of Leicester's style.' Finishing off he looked forward to the following season and claimed that the Reds could do the double as 'nothing is impossible under your leadership.'

On 17th May, the day before the last game of the season at Aston Villa, Leslie Edwards, the *Liverpool Echo*'s main football correspondent wrote that the outlook for Liverpool was 'very settled', pointing to Gerry Byrne, Jimmy Melia and Gordon Milne all earning their first England caps during the season, at a time when caps were not handed out like confetti as they are today. There was also optimism due to the young players at the club as three teenagers – Chris Lawler, Tommy Smith and Gordon Wallace - had made their debuts during the season and two of these would become pivotal figures in the glory years ahead. The club had also reached the FA Youth Cup final for the first time, but a side captained by Smith were beaten 6-5 on aggregate in the final by West Ham, who had Harry Redknapp playing on the right wing. The Reds won the first leg 3-1 at Anfield in front of 14,930 fans but went down 5-2 at Upton Park in the second leg, played on the same day as the FA Cup final, which saw Mr Gill's wish come true as Manchester United beat Leicester 3-1.

On Monday 20th May, a special function was held at the Supporters' Club on Lower Breck Road where comedian Ken Dodd provided the main entertainment. All the players attended and Bill Shankly was presented with a silver tea set as a token of his efforts during the season. Captain Ron Yeats wrote in his weekly *Liverpool Echo* column the following Saturday that all the players were 'more than delighted to be present' and that Shankly was 'most impressed' with his gift.

The players were rewarded for their efforts with a week's holiday in the sun at the Italian resort of San Remo, flying from Manchester to Nice on 28th May. However Melia, Milne and Roger Hunt had to miss out as they were called up by England for friendlies in Czechoslovakia, East Germany and Switzerland.

There was better luck for Tommy Lawrence and Ian St John, who were allowed to go on the first few days of the holiday before joining the Scotland squad for a friendly in Norway on 4th June followed by other games against the Republic of Ireland and Spain. For the two previous years Liverpool's end of season breaks to Czechoslovakia and Ireland had involved playing games, but this time there would be relaxation and nothing else.

Shankly said, 'We shan't ask the lads to kick a ball when they are away. I think it more than ever necessary, after this prolonged season, for players to get all the rest they can.'[1] The Reds party returned on 5th June but there was more socialising to be done by Yeats before he took a golfing holiday in Scotland with his family. First he had to attend the Grafton Rooms in West Derby Road on 6th June for a dance organised by the Liverpool & District Sunday Football Association where he presented the trophies.

As the players soaked up the sun, there was some concern for fans over Shankly's future. The Reds' boss had never signed a contract with the club so was free to walk away at any time and Leslie Edwards had written in the *Liverpool Echo* three days before they set off to Italy, 'There are some plum managerial jobs coming up within the next few weeks and if some club does not try to tempt Mr Shankly to their aid I shall be surprised.' Most worryingly, Shankly had stalled on signing a three-year contract that had been on the table since March saying, 'I considered the contract totally unsuitable. That's why I have not signed it. I am not tied to Liverpool of course.' Chairman T.V. Williams moved to re-assure supporters though, claiming there was no disagreement between them and if Shankly didn't want to formalise things that was fine.

> 'He had never wanted a contract before and when it came to signing he decided he still did not like the idea. We have left it to him, it is still open to him to sign it if he wishes to do so, but of course we will not press him. If he is happier that way, so well and good. I would like to add that there is absolutely no ill feeling between club and manager and it would be entirely wrong to assume that the manager's attitude in regard to his contract marks any deterioration in our relations.'

It was understandable that fans had some concern though, considering Shankly had come close to walking away a year earlier when the board sold Johnny Morrissey to Everton for £10,000 without his knowledge.

There was also some uneasiness throughout the summer on the playing front, with fans facing an anxious wait for players to re-sign. At that time, contracts worked on a retain and transfer system with players being signed for one year at a time then either offered new terms or let go. This meant they were free to join another club although a transfer fee could still be demanded for the registration to be released. Liverpool's board naturally wanted to keep hold of the crowd favourites, but there was still the possibility they would refuse to accept the terms offered although to do so would be a risk, given that the club could refuse to release the registration at any price leaving the player redundant.

It turned out that 1963 would be the last summer of the retain and transfer system, as it was declared illegal in the High Court on 4th July when Arsenal forward George Eastham, backed by the Professional Footballers' Association, successfully sued his former club Newcastle over their refusal to transfer him for several months in 1960. Delivering judgement, Justice Wilberforce said the system was 'inhuman and incongruous' and it threw into chaos something that had been in place since the 1890s. Writing in the *Liverpool Echo* the following evening, Michael Charters described the ruling as having 'turned the world of professional football upside down'. However there would be no immediate solution as clubs and the football authorities needed to digest the ruling and an appeal hadn't been ruled out so it was a case of business as usual. It was not until the following summer when the system was modified, with the retain element being done away with and an agreement reached whereby fees for out of contract players would be fixed by an independent tribunal.

The retained list had been released on 24th May and there were no surprises, with reserve full back Allan Jones being the only player with first team experience of the six whose contracts would not be renewed. The club required a fee for him along with Scottish youth international Hamish Mackenzie (who would later join Dunfermline), but Monty Maclaren, Benny Hill, Robby Reason and David Corkhill were all granted free transfers. The club had also agreed to cancel the contract of winger Johnny Wheeler at the player's request so he could become manager of New Brighton. He had made just one first team appearance in two seasons, but in the end he didn't take up that position, instead becoming an assistant trainer at Bury.

When it came to securing the services of those players who were being retained, it wasn't until seven weeks after the list was issued that the last of those actually signed when St John put pen to paper on 17th July. There were reasons for fans to be concerned as there was much gossip in the city that some players were holding out for more money and when the *Liverpool Echo* had tried to seek confirmation of this on 25th June, they were unable to get any answers as Shankly was away on holiday in Scotland. However the following week, chairman T.V. Williams said that fans needn't worry about any delays which were purely down to players being on holiday. On 1st July, the day Yeats signed, he told the *Liverpool Echo*:

> 'Ron Yeats visited Anfield today and in the absence of manager Bill Shankly I told him the terms offered. He signed straight away without hesitation. Our players know we shall make proper allowance under the crowd bonus scheme. We don't anticipate any trouble in securing the signatures of the others. Our players are on very big money and they know it.'

After Yeats had signed, a routine board meeting took place at which it was decided not to enter the League Cup for the coming season. The Reds had entered the inaugural competition in 1960-61, going out to Southampton in the third round but had declined to take part in the following two seasons. One of the reasons behind the decision was probably the fact that Liverpool were one of four teams who were on standby to compete in the Inter Cities Fairs Cup, a forerunner of the UEFA Cup.

Tensions remained high between East and West following the Cuban missile crisis and at the time Britain was gripped by the Lord Denning-led enquiry into the Profumo Affair, which was looking into the relationship between Secretary of State for War John Profumo and Christine Keeler, a call girl who was also seeing a Soviet naval attaché. As such there was every possibility that teams from Warsaw Pact countries may decline to take part, opening the door for the Reds.

During the summer the club was shocked and saddened to hear of the death of a man who had done much to bring some of their key players to the Reds. On 13th June Tom Moore, described by the *Liverpool Echo* as 'one of their most valuable unpaid servants' died suddenly at his home in Litherland at the age of 57. A master at Our Lady of Mount Carmel School in Prince's Park, he was a former manager of the Liverpool schoolboys' team and secretary of the Liverpool Schools FA and he helped unearth Gerry Byrne, Ian Callaghan and Jimmy Melia for the Reds.

Former player Tom Bush, who worked closely with the reserves and junior teams at Anfield in a coaching and administrative role, said it was a sad loss. 'He was a character. Nothing was too much trouble to him. He did his work here just for the joy of being part of the Liverpool FC setup. He was tireless in his efforts for schoolboy football and Liverpool FC. He will not easily be replaced.'[2] Twelve years later, in *The Ian Callaghan Story*, co-written with John Keith and published by Quartet Books, Callaghan recalled of Moore, 'Mr Moore was a great character who knew his football and was partial to an occasional glass of whisky.'

Around the time the players' contracts were being finalised, speculation also began to intensify over Shankly's situation, as it was reported nationally that he was the number one candidate on Nottingham Forest's list. They were seeking a successor to Andy Beattie who had resigned despite having finished a place below Liverpool in ninth, their best position for over fifty years. Forest had enjoyed some recent success, having won the FA Cup in 1959 and Shankly refused to completely distance himself from the job when quizzed on it by Horace Yates of the *Daily Post*. He told him that he knew nothing about any interest from Forest but also that he would prefer to say nothing. When asked directly if he had applied, Shankly responded 'You don't apply for these jobs. It is mainly cut and dried and it is the clubs who do the seeking.'[3]

Although this may not have been the answer that fans were hoping to hear, there seemed no doubt about Shankly's commitment in preparing the Reds' squad prior to the start of the new season. It was clear that a new left winger was needed as Alan A'Court's best days were behind him and Kevin Lewis was not good enough for the First Division. Shankly may have had his previous battles with the board over securing money for players but given the rapid progress made, they were willing to sanction further spending on an area of the team where there was a clear weakness. In the *Daily Post* on 17th June, Horace Yates wrote that Huddersfield Town's Michael O'Grady was a Reds' target and they had been invited to make an offer as he had refused to sign a contract with Huddersfield. O'Grady had expressed his desire to play First Division football having already appeared for England despite Huddersfield's lower league status.

O'Grady was a player well known to Shankly as the Reds boss had signed him from Leeds when he was in charge of Huddersfield. On 18th June, Leslie Edwards wrote in the *Liverpool Echo* that Huddersfield wanted £40,000 for him and that Shankly's reaction was, 'If O'Grady's for sale, we're interested. When I signed the boy from Leeds it didn't even cost a packet of fags.' Edwards added that £40,000 was a cheap price to pay for such a talent. As things rumbled on though, the first new arrival of the summer slipped in virtually unnoticed, the *Liverpool Echo* dedicating just four lines on 26th June to the signing of Welsh amateur international goalkeeper Trevor Roberts. The main question mark now hinged over the future of Jim Furnell, who was attracting interest from other clubs and the paper stated that the arrival of Roberts may lead to the club considering his sale.

It wasn't until Shankly's return from holiday on 8th July that the race for O'Grady intensified. That morning Shankly rang his old club but was unable to make any progress as their chairman had only just returned from his own break. He told Leslie Edwards at the *Liverpool Echo*, 'You can say that we are interested, we have already had discussions with Huddersfield.' Shankly would not say what fee the Reds were willing to pay but Edwards speculated that the price could go as high as £50,000. Ten days later though the deal was well and truly off as the player opted to re-sign for Huddersfield, a decision that surprised many as it appeared unlikely his desire to play in the First Division would be fulfilled with the West Yorkshire club. Shankly expressed his disappointment at the failure of the transfer to go through but made it plain the club were looking for a new left winger and even named the new target, telling Edwards on 18th July,

> 'We have been in touch with Huddersfield about O'Grady since the back-end of last season. I think he would have made a great success at Anfield. We are still in the field for a top class left winger, Peter Thompson of Preston. He played against us twice in the FA Cup two seasons ago. Like O'Grady he is still just about 21 years old. He too is on monthly terms. We've been interested in him all along and been in touch with Preston several times.'

It wasn't just off the pitch that the club was willing to splash the cash that summer, as £120,000 was spent on a new stand along the Kemlyn Road side of the ground. Disruption to supporters was kept to a bare minimum with the old stand being demolished prior to the final home game of the 1962-63 season with the aim of completing the new one in less than four months. Progress was so fast that by 7th June the whole of the steelwork was completed and half of the concrete in place. A fortnight later Leslie Edwards wrote in the Echo that he was marvelled 'that so much steel and concrete could go up in such a short space of time.'[4]

There were also improvements being made to the Main Stand with better facilities for the match officials and visitors, meaning the players' tunnel had to be relocated away from the halfway line. The funds for the ground improvements had been raised thanks to the increased revenue from First Division fixtures, and it wasn't forgotten that more success on the pitch was needed and the conditions had to be just right for the players to produce that. Edwards wrote on 20th June that the pitch, which had been 'braziered iron hard and bare' by the wintry conditions of the previous season, was now 'a carpet of grass.'

Although the stand provided 7,000 seats, it would mean an overall reduction in capacity to around 54,000 with Anfield's total number of 11,000 seats still far less than Everton's 18,000, the highest in the league. It did however mean some improved catering facilities which were needed according to a report presented to the Liverpool Corporation Health Committee on 21st June. Poor catering was one of a number of issues highlighted at Anfield and Goodison Park by Professor Andrew Semple, the city's Medical Officer for Health who told the committee, 'The unsatisfactory conditions at the grounds observed include inadequacy of public conveniences, unsatisfactory provision for food, inadequate artificial lighting of passages and approaches to the conveniences during evening matches and lack of adequate cleansing.'

Liverpool director Harold Cartwright made it clear there would be no such problems in the new stand, telling the *Liverpool Echo* the following day, 'There will be adequate provision for toilets and four or five modern, hygienic, cafes.' He expressed surprise at the poor lighting however, saying that the club was not to blame when he responded, 'Light fittings and bulbs that are provided are the target for a minority of hooligans.' When the stand did come to open at the start of the season though, things didn't quite go as planned as will be seen later.

4

Back To Training and the Arrival Of Peter Thompson

Liverpool's pre-season programme prior to 1963-64 was far different from today with no foreign training camps or friendlies being played. There was also very little transfer speculation, with the arrival of a much sought after left winger being the only addition to the squad while Bill Shankly's future at the club was formalised.

Although Shankly had still not signed a contract, speculation regarding him joining other clubs reduced during July, with Johnny Carey having been appointed at Nottingham Forest at the beginning of the month. Shankly was certainly not talking like a manager who considered his future elsewhere, believing he could fulfil all his ambitions with Liverpool. On 21st July, three days before the Reds were due to return to training the *Daily Post* reported that he had said, 'I am looking forward to the day when Liverpool will be the game's undisputed top team. We have made a lot of progress in that direction already.'

The terrible winter of 1962-63 which saw snow remain on the ground from the end of December until the beginning of March, played havoc with the fixtures and led to the season lasting well into May. It meant a shorter summer break than usual, with Liverpool's players returning to be kitted out on 23rd July in readiness for the first training session the following day. With chairman T.V. Williams on holiday, vice chairman Sidney Reakes welcomed the players back, telling them, 'I am looking forward to a good season. I wish you well in your efforts to make further headway than last year. Under the guidance of the staff and coaches I think we shall do that.'[5]

Shankly advised the press that Liverpool were equal to, or better than, any other team and the aim was to get the players as fit as possible for the new season with various drills set up at Melwood. One of the routines was for players to work in pairs on small pitches marked out between boards. The balls would constantly rebound off these boards and they would look to fire as many 'goals' as possible.

Shankly maintained that much of Roger Hunt's sharpness in previous seasons was down to the reflexes developed in these routines.[6] On the whole, Shankly wanted training to be well thought out and varied so that the players could approach it with dedication and the rewards would then come on matchdays. The exercises he had the players undergo would involve having a ball and he did not see the value in players lifting weights or running laps of a field.

Writing in the *Liverpool Echo* on 24th July, exactly one month before the opening game of the season at Blackburn, Leslie Edwards expressed his belief that the Reds could finish higher than last time due to 'their manager's infectious enthusiasm, plus the crowd's support are always worth a goal start to them.' He felt there was just one change needed, on the left flank, adding that a new signing in this position would be 'the player who might well make all the difference.'

When it came to ground developments, progress on the new Kemlyn Road stand remained phenomenal, with all the seats being installed by the time the players returned to training.

With Michael O'Grady's transfer falling through, the Reds immediately increased their efforts to sign Peter Thompson, having kept an eye on his contract situation at Preston all through the summer. He was on monthly terms there having refused to sign for the season and on 25th July, Preston agreed to his request to be transferred, although he would not be made available on the cheap with a fee of £40-50,000 being mentioned.

Liverpool too, were keeping all options open and although Shankly was quoted in the following evening's *Liverpool Echo* as saying 'now he has been given permission to go our interest heightens', the paper also reported that 'at least two others – one in Scotland – have been watched for some time.' On 30th July, the Reds tabled a firm bid although the figure was not disclosed, but the *Echo* reported the following evening that as some of Preston's directors were away it would be a week before any full board meeting was held and a response given.

The imminent arrival of a new left winger placed great uncertainty on the future of Alan A'Court who, along with Ronnie Moran, was the only player to have played for the Reds in the First Division both before and after relegation. The fact that he had been at the club eleven years implied he was a veteran yet he was still only 28 and still felt he had a lot to offer, meaning he was not willing to join Preston in a part exchange deal for Thompson, which the Deepdale club were happy to consider.

With a week of pre season training gone, Shankly confirmed to Leslie Edwards of the *Echo* that there would be no friendly games prior to the start of the season, which were then referred to as 'public practice matches.' He said, 'We have no need of pipe openers, our training is designed to give our players plenty of those and besides, the only day we could stage a game for the public at Anfield would clash with Everton's Charity Shield match.[7]

Liverpool's preparations were in stark contrast to those of West Ham who spent the whole of June in North America playing in the International Soccer League topping a group of seven teams. At the end of July they crossed the Atlantic again, trained in temperatures of over ninety degrees in Central Park before playing two games against Polish side Gornik Zabrze to decide the soccer league champions, then another two against Dukla Prague for the American Challenge Cup.

On 6th August Liverpool still hadn't received a response from Preston regarding the Thompson bid and although no figure had been disclosed, Shankly described it as 'a very substantial one'.[8] A board meeting at Anfield that day revealed that 1962-63 had seen record gate receipts of £216,613 and that players wages were also the highest they had ever been, increasing by £7,000 to £43,556. Profits had dropped to £12,755 but the club had no overdraft and had also splashed the cash on the new stand. Chairman T.V. Williams said though that a new stand at the Anfield Road end was on hold for now and would not be built for another four or five years.

Liverpool's cash was safely in the bank but that could not be said about some of the Royal Mail's as on 8th August, the Great Train Robbery took place in Buckinghamshire. In what the *Liverpool Echo* described as a 'Jessie James style ambush' a gang of 22 men (the exact total at that time was not known, the paper saying it was between twenty and thirty) held up the Glasgow-Euston mail train shortly after 3am. The Echo reported that £1.1 million was stolen, although the exact figure was later revealed to be £2.6 million, equivalent to over £40 million today. The Postmaster General at the time was Reginald Bevins, who was also the Conservative MP for Toxteth, and he flew from Liverpool to London that day, making it known to reporters that he was interrupting his holiday to do so.

As Preston continued to stall on responding to the Thompson bid, Shankly headed north on Saturday 10th August, the opening day of the Scottish league season. His destination was St Mirren's Love Street, where he watched St Mirren against Hibernian in a League Cup tie, with his interest focusing on the visitors' Eric Stevenson. Liverpool's constant pursuit of a left winger meant that Kevin Lewis decided his time was up and he handed in a transfer request, with Leslie Edwards writing in the *Liverpool Echo* on 12th August that he was a good player to have around in emergencies, but that if the Reds were to overhaul Everton, better quality was needed. One fan wasn't impressed at the fact that the Reds were rumoured to have offered just £30,000 for Thompson. On 12th August the Echo printed a letter from John C. Burns of which said:

> 'Here we have a young left winger of really great potential who wants to play for a Lancashire First Division club – just the man, one would have thought, to make this really good forward line great. Liverpool obviously do not see it this way and insult Thompson, Preston and their own supporters with this niggardly offer. It almost goes without saying that our worthy manager once again subjects the peasants with another gem of verbal overstatement by describing the offer as substantial. All credit

> to Mr Shankly and the board for getting the team together at a very advantageous price, but surely only a chump could expect this kind of thing to go on for ever. Left wingers are hard to find as our neighbours at Goodison Park will testify. Come on Liverpool. Let's have a realistic price offer for Thompson before this becomes a joke to all the footballing fraternity.'

Shankly's Scottish trip, where he was also impressed by St Mirren's nineteen-year-old right back Cameron Murray, may just have been what was needed to make the Preston board respond to the Liverpool offer and on the night of 13th August negotiations began. Shankly, T.V Williams and director Harry Latham went to watch Thompson appear for Preston against Blackburn in a practice game, then conducted two hours of negotiations with the Preston directors. Eventually it was announced at midnight that a fee had been agreed. The news made the front page of the following day's *Daily Post*, which reported that Thompson would be coming to Anfield for a medical and to discuss personal terms, with the fee believed to have been around £40,000 (it would later be confirmed as £37,500).

Thompson was driven to Anfield on the morning of 14th August by a business associate with whom he ran caravan sites along the Fylde coast. After stopping to sign several autographs Thompson finalised terms and signed, telling reporters that he had not known about the fee being agreed until that morning. He then went to Melwood to meet the other players and undergo some light training on his own. Shankly said that he had first become aware of Thompson when he was Huddersfield manager, being tipped off about a promising fifteen-year-old playing for Cumberland schoolboys. T.V. Williams said that the deal was finalised after they decided to take a chance and turn up unannounced at the Preston game. The *Liverpool Echo* reported him as saying:

> 'Yesterday at midday we had no intention of seeing Preston about Thompson. We had told them that we would not do business until they named a fee. In mid afternoon we learned that Preston were playing Blackburn. We thought we would take a chance and go to Deepdale and see what they had to say. After the game we conferred for two hours. Preston gave us a figure and we worked from there. He should suit us very well. He was, you remember, the player whose goal put us out of the FA Cup two seasons ago.'

The arrival of Thompson was the final piece in the team jigsaw and the new stand was nearing completion too. It was confirmed that it would simply be named the Kemlyn Road stand after the road on which it was situated, despite calls from some fans to name it after Billy Liddell. The Echo reported on 15th August that the seats still hadn't been numbered and there was still work to be done underneath. T.V. Williams said that there was a lot of administration work to be done with respect to ticket sales and extra staff had to be recruited. There were some rumours too that the seats didn't allow much leg-room (something that any fans who ever sat in there would not disagree with) but Williams claimed that this had been overcome by hollowing out the backs of the seats and slanting them backwards. The construction of the new stand meant that the tradition of being able to swap ends at half time was now gone, as there was no longer terracing all the way around the ground. Seats in the new stand would cost nine shillings per game.

Thompson's first appearance for his new club was on 15th August in a behind closed doors practice match that saw the Reds beat Chester 6-0. He got off to a perfect start, scoring one and also having another shot that hit the post and rebounded to Ian Callaghan who scored. Ron Yeats said that Thompson's arrival had been a good boost for the club, writing in his Echo column two days later, 'It is a pleasure to welcome him and wish him all the luck in the world to back up his great ability.'

There was now just a week to go until the start of the season and Liverpool's spending looked to be over, with Shankly not going on any scouting mission on 17th August. There was the possibility of a junior signing though, with Roy Rudham, a sixteen-year-old inside forward who was the son of former Liverpool keeper Doug, arriving from South Africa on 19th August for a month long trial. Around the same time, Shankly's favourite player Tom Finney announced he was coming out of retirement. The 41-year old was now master plumber at a building works in Preston but had agreed to play for Irish League champions Distillery, who had been drawn against Benfica in the European Cup.

In the week leading up to the opening game at Blackburn the excitement continued to build, with Thompson's arrival having increased the optimism that the Reds could do something during the season. Ian St John wrote in the *Daily Post* on Tuesday 20th August that he had not looked forward to the start of the season so much for a long time and that the players believed they could start the season much better than the previous one. 'The opening of last season was a nightmare to us with only two wins from seven games and November was with us before Liverpool finally settled down to the First Division. Now we are acclimatised and ready to go.'

With just two days to go until the opening, Shankly finally confirmed that he had signed a contract with the club. He told Horace Yates of the *Daily Post*, 'I suppose it is the modern trend to have agreements such as this and I have just fallen into line. There were several little points to clear up and now that everything is settled I don't mind everybody knowing I intend staying in Liverpool which has become my second home.' He also gave an indication of where he wanted the club to be, sending out an ominous warning of what his ambitions were:

> 'I believe that my job with Liverpool FC has only just started. A lot of work has been done, the spadework. But a lot more work remains to be done. We have to build on the now very substantial foundation. I can not think of any club with which I could be happier than Liverpool. I am convinced that they will be one of the truly great clubs of our time. I will never be truly content until Liverpool are the undisputed champions of the land, a position I will strive to bring about in the shortest possible time. We are making giant strides in that direction and I am not at all unhappy with the prospects which now confront me.'

All the preparations and talking was now complete, it was time for Liverpool to begin their quest to overhaul Everton, who had demonstrated their power by beating Manchester United 4-0 in the Charity Shield. Captain Yeats identified them as the favourites for the title, along with Spurs and possibly Leicester. He also believed Manchester united could be a threat if they transferred their FA Cup form to the league.[9] The competition meant that the Reds had to get off to the best possible start on 24th August, away to Blackburn at Ewood Park.

5

Chaotic Beginnings

Liverpool's start to the season ended up making as many headlines off the pitch as on it, as crowd problems marred the season's opener away to Blackburn and then the opening home game saw thousands locked out due to complications to do with the new Kemlyn Road stand.

24th August 1963: Blackburn Rovers 1 Liverpool 2, Football League Division One

Unlike today, there was no major build up and analysis into the opening game of the season. The full list of fixtures was only published a fortnight before, although it had been known for some time that the Reds would be starting off their campaign away to Blackburn. In the week leading up to it, neither the *Daily Post* nor *Liverpool Echo* carried any stories concerned with Liverpool FC on the Wednesday and Thursday beforehand. It was not until Friday's Echo and Saturday's Post that the game was covered and even then it was eight and six paragraphs respectively in each paper.

With the Post concentrating on the news of Shankly's contract on the Friday morning, it was left to that evening's Echo to start the previews of the Blackburn game. There was no need for speculation regarding the team, which effectively picked itself with ten of the preferred eleven at the end of 1962-63 retaining their places and Peter Thompson coming in for Alan A'Court. It was predicted that there would be 'a fair sized contingent' of Liverpool supporters at the game and that the Reds attack was now one with 'youthfulness, skill and experience.' The main threat for Blackburn was identified as right winger Brian Douglas, who had played in all England's matches during the 1958 and 1962 World Cups. The following morning the Post predicted that the Reds should at least secure a draw and that a win would see optimism raised to a 'high level.'

The demand to see Liverpool's start to the season was so great that staff at Exchange Station were totally overwhelmed by the sheer numbers of supporters attempting to travel. Three special trains were laid on, departing at 12.12pm, 12.35pm and 12.50pm, and each able to carry about 800 fans. Shortly after the first service had left an announcement was made stating that no more tickets were available for the remaining two trains, leading to a surge to the barriers and a gate torn from its hinges as fans rushed to the platforms. Station staff were helpless and although there was an announcement that ticketless fans would be removed from trains and a police squad car arrived, there was little they could do as the carriages were so packed that it was impossible to move through them and check tickets.

Many fans then arrived with tickets that they had bought in the preceding days and were unable to board, being instead directed to a 12.27pm stopping service to Preston. This only had three cars though leaving hundreds milling around. An announcement over the tannoy said: 'We regret there are no more trains to Blackburn. We regret we have neither the stock nor crews to operate any more trains. There is no use waiting or hoping, you are advised to disperse.' A guard then left a gate unattended leading to some making a dash for it and climbing through the windows of the 12.50pm service which was still on the platform. Those who had tickets and couldn't get on board were naturally furious, with John Rickerts from Kirkby telling the *Liverpool Echo*, 'I've never known anything like it. After a frustrating experience like this how do British Railways expect anyone to place any reliance on them in future.' Some fans took a chance and took the 1.10pm service to Preston, hoping to connect to Blackburn there, while others desperately tried to get on one of the coaches that were departing from various points around the city centre. Some did what would be unthinkable today and headed towards Goodison Park to watch Everton instead.

Those fans that did make it to Ewood Park were given a 'hearty welcome' by Blackburn's manager Jack Marshall in the match programme and had a day to remember as they saw the Reds come from behind to win the game 2-1. When Liverpool's players took to the field they were applauded from all corners of the ground with their fans seemingly in the majority despite it being an away fixture. Thompson, who was being watched by both parents, was involved in the action early on when he linked well with Willie Stevenson before playing the ball to Ian St John, but John Bray was on hand to clear before he could set up Roger Hunt. Bray was being given a hard time by Thompson and was forced to give away a free kick on one occasion while on another, the Reds' winger crossed dangerously but Ian Callaghan was unable to reach the ball. The Reds were piling on the pressure and Blackburn were forced to keep all their players except centre forward Fred Pickering back in defence, although on one occasion they did break clear only for Pickering to head a cross wide of Tommy Lawrence's goal.

Thompson was linking up brilliantly in the first half with Stevenson and in the 34th minute the Reds came closest to opening the scoring. Thompson robbed the ball off Bray and played Stevenson through on goal, but Fred Else managed to get his body in the way to deflect the shot to safety. Liverpool then began to really turn the screw, forcing two corners in rapid succession with Stevenson instrumental in stopping Blackburn even getting the ball out of defence and restarting attacks for the Reds. However despite the Reds' dominance they couldn't find the opening goal and two minutes before half time the home side took an undeserved lead, Mike Harrison firing the ball through a crowd of players into the net after they had forced a rare corner.

A minute into the second half Hunt thought he had equalised for Liverpool but the referee adjudged that he had fouled Keith Newton. The Reds didn't get disheartened and continued to dominate the game, eventually getting their reward in the 65th minute. The ball was played to Hunt in the area and as he tried to turn he was brought down and the referee had no hesitation in awarding a penalty. From the kick though it immediately looked like it wasn't going to be Liverpool's day as Else saved Ronnie Moran's shot, but the full back was able to score from the rebound.

With Blackburn's resistance finally broken the Reds sensed the game was there to be won and continued to pressurise the home side. Such was the ferocity of some of the challenges that the referee called both captains together to advise them over the conduct of both sets of players. They didn't take heed however and a few moments later Pickering was lectured for a foul on Stevenson. With fifteen minutes remaining Liverpool took a deserved lead, which came about after a refusal to give up the ball after it was lost. St John intercepted Mike England's poor clearance and played in Hunt, who drove the ball past Else. It confirmed a deserved victory for Liverpool, one that St John believed was down to Shankly's training methods having made the players fitter than they had ever been before at the start of a season. He said of the second half,

> 'Ask any of the players and I shall be surprised if he doesn't tell you that he has never been fitter at the opening of a season. We played Blackburn into the ground. The longer the game went the stronger we became and already I have the sort of fitness feeling which generally only comes after the season has been going three or four weeks.' [10]

Hunt's winning goal led to him being mobbed during a pitch invasion by hundreds of younger fans who were sat around the pitch, having been allowed to go there by Blackburn officials due to the terracing being packed to capacity. This led to the referee telling some of them that the game would be abandoned if they didn't leave the playing area and order was soon restored. The following week, the Chief Constable of Blackburn announced that for all future matches youngsters would not be allowed around the side of the pitch. Such crowd encroachment had never been seen at Anfield, which the Echo reported on 27th August was down to a higher visible police presence deterring it.

Liverpool fans were naturally delighted with the victory, although there were some unsavoury scenes in Preston that night where a coach taking fans home from the game had stopped. During a disturbance outside the Black Bull pub in Friargate a policeman was knocked unconscious and one Reds fan along with two Preston men were charged with grievous bodily harm and appeared in court the following Monday.

On the whole,Liverpool's army of travelling fans had been well behaved and even the scenes at Exchange Station beforehand were put down to a 'handful of hooligans' by British Railways.[11] They also announced that any fans who had purchased tickets and were unable to take trains would be refunded. A subsequent comment by the Chief Constable that Liverpool's fans travelled with the intention of causing trouble didn't go down too well and led to a surge of letters to the Echo, pointing out that only a dozen arrests were made out of an estimated 15,000 Reds fans who went to the game.

Putting aside any negative headlines regarding crowd behaviour, the critics were certainly impressed with Liverpool's attack. Horace Yates wrote in the *Liverpool Echo* on 26th August that it had been 'revolutionised' by Thompson who had been 'sensational' and that if they could improve their finishing it would be 'a memorable season ahead.' He also highlighted the improvements in the game of Callaghan, Jimmy Melia and Gordon Milne and described the whole team display as 'top class.' Yates's *Daily Post* column that morning had been even more optimistic, as he opened his analysis with the words 'Look out Everton' and suggested that the Reds would be the most likely challengers to their quest to retain the league title.

Yates had suggested that if Thompson's debut had been at Anfield such a performance would have had the crowd in raptures. St John said that the players had expected good things from the new signing but that his display was 'greater than anything any of us could have forecast.'[12] There were now two home games coming up for Liverpool's fans to get down to Anfield and see just how exciting their new signing was.

Liverpool: Lawrence, Byrne, Moran, Milne, Yeats, Stevenson, Callaghan, Hunt, St John, Melia, Thompson.

Blackburn: Else, Bray, Newton, Clayton, England, McGrath, Douglas, Ferguson, Pickering, Byrom, Harrison.

Referee: Mr K. Walker (Blackpool).

Attendance: 34,390.

28th August 1963: Liverpool 1 Nottingham Forest 2, Football League Division One

Following on from Liverpool's victory in the opening game of the season the local press highlighted how lucrative victories could be for the Reds players. On Monday 26th August the main headline on the front page of the *Daily*

Post was SUPERTAX SOCCER CITY, followed by an article by Horace Yates explaining that Liverpool's players were on a crowd bonus of £2 for every 1,000 fans above 28,000. With the capacity of Anfield now 53,000, it meant that if they could play the sort of football that could fill the ground every game they stood to make £50 on top of their minimum £35 a week wage. Everton's stars had the potential to be even richer given that Goodison Park's capacity was 73,000, although their bonus scheme didn't come into effect until a 35,000 gate was reached.

Liverpool's opening day victory at Blackburn and the reports of it certainly raised the expectation level amongst Reds fans, although they would be faced with the prospect of fewer places available at Anfield due to the new Kemlyn Road stand. This had also alarmed the players as the previous season the crowd had surpassed 53,000 on five occasions, and as such the basic wage was raised to make up for this. In his *Liverpool Echo* column the Saturday before this game Ron Yeats wrote of how much he admired the new stand, describing it as a 'truly magnificent structure' but he also joked that fans sitting in the first few rows would need to take out adequate insurance as they were in the line of where his clearances would be going.

The day before the Forest game Kevin Lewis, who had fallen further down the pecking order for a left wing slot due to Thompson's arrival left Anfield, signed for Second Division Huddersfield for a fee of £20,000, quite a sum for a player who was now third choice. Lewis was with the Yorkshire club little more than a season before going on to play in South Africa.

Capacity crowds were predicted for both home games in the coming week, with Blackpool due at Anfield on the Saturday after the Nottingham Forest game. Fans with Kemlyn Road tickets though were advised that due to a strike among building workers it hadn't quite been completed, meaning that not all refreshment or toilet facilities would be available.

There was no need for any team speculation, with Bill Shankly confirming the day before the Forest match that Peter Thompson had recovered from a slight knock and would be making his Anfield debut. The previous season Forest had beaten Liverpool twice and Ian St John wrote in the Post on 27th August that extra wing capability for the Reds could be a key in unlocking tight defences this time around. On the morning of the game Horace Yates's preview in the *Daily Post* predicted that the Kop would raise the roof if Thompson played as well as he had at Ewood Park, and that the day before the player had told him he couldn't wait to play at Anfield with the crowd on his side instead of against him.

Forest were now managed by Johnny Carey, who had preceded Harry Catterick at Everton and was infamously sacked in the back of a taxi by director John Moores after they had attended a meeting with the FA in London. It's a sign of how different things were that he was warmly received by the home crowd as he emerged from the tunnel. Despite the two clubs finishing with an almost identical record in 1962-63, Liverpool's bright start at Blackburn made them favourites for this match but it didn't quite go that way. Forest left Anfield with both points and the *Liverpool Echo* described the Reds as 'predictable in their unpredictability.'

Liverpool let themselves down by some poor finishing, trying too hard to get the ball forward in contrast to Forest's slower composed football, while Jimmy Melia was singled out by the crowd as he had a particularly poor display, giving the ball away virtually every time he was in possession of it. Yeats was given a particularly tough time by Frank Wignall, with Leslie Edwards claiming in the following evening's Echo that it was the 'most testing time in the air' that he had endured since arriving at Anfield two years earlier. When the Reds did manage to create some chances, Forest keeper Peter Grummitt was in fine form but Thompson himself enjoyed a sound debut, crossing well and having a few powerful shots himself.

Forest took the lead in the 26th minute, Wignall beating Tommy Lawrence to flick on a corner to Johnny Quigley whose overhead kick stunned everybody in the ground as it flew past the keeper into the net. Eight minutes into the second half the Reds were level in comical fashion much to the delight of the Kop when Bob McKinlay, who had been commanding at the back so far, completely misplaced a backpass to Grummitt who had no chance of stopping it.

Whereas Liverpool's equaliser at Blackburn had led to them stepping up another gear to finish the game off, this time there was no dominance and Forest responded well to their misfortune. In the 67th minute Dick Le Flem crossed from the left and Wignall glanced a header past Lawrence from the edge of the six yard box. The Reds huffed and puffed for the rest of the game but couldn't get past Forest's well organised defence, with Leslie Edwards summing up in the Echo that they had been too similar to the side that had struggled at the start of the previous season. He described them as having 'plenty to like about them' but also being 'too hasty' and 'too excitable.' Captain Yeats admitted, 'We certainly did not deserve to win. I cannot remember an occasion when so many of us had poor games. Poor Jimmy Melia had one of those nights that happen to all players at one time or another when nothing went right.'[13]

Towards the end of the game the crowd started to slow handclap and in what would become a standing joke in future seasons, many of the fans in the Kemlyn Road stand got up and left early. Edwards described how the new stand seemed to take some time to empty at the end and that it was inevitable there would be teething problems. But it was blamed by many for chaotic scenes before the game when 10,000 were locked out of the ground. The attendance of 49,829 was short of capacity, but the delay in completing the stand due to the building strike meant that the site office was still in Anfield Road, meaning half of that terrace was closed.

The gates were closed half an hour before kick off and mounted police moved in to control the crowd who surged forward chanting 'we want in' and they also started to form queues in the hope of getting to see the closing stages when the gates were opened at 'three quarter time.' Even if the stand had been completely finished, the capacity of Anfield was now smaller than the previous year anyway and those outside directed angry words towards the club, with the *Daily Post* reporting that seed grower Leslie Ball from Orkskirk had told them, 'They should pull this stand down straight away and have some consideration for loyal supporters.'

Those locked out had to be content with staying outside and gauging how the game was going by the roar of the crowd, or listen for updates on the radio at home. Those that went home would also have heard news of Martin Luther King's 'I Have a Dream' speech that was delivered in Washington DC whilst this match was going on. To compound their disappointment when it came to the result, they would then learn that Ian St John could be a doubt for the game against Blackpool. He had received a gash to the head in the second half that had led to him having three stitches afterwards.

Liverpool: Lawrence, Byrne, Moran, Milne, Yeats, Stevenson, Callaghan, Hunt, St John, Melia, Callaghan.

Forest: Grummitt, Wilson, Mochan, Whitefoot, McKinlay, Winfield, Hockey, Addison, Wignall, Quigley, Le Flem.

Referee: Mr W. G. Handley (Staffordshire).

Attendance: 48,829

31st August 1963: Liverpool 1 Blackpool 2, Football League Division One

Bill Shankly was quick to reassure fans over Ian St John's head injury, confirming to the *Daily Post* the day after the Forest game that he would be fit to face Blackpool. The Seasiders had drawn 2-2 against Sheffield United on the opening day of the season and then lost 3-1 at West Ham the following Monday night. The previous August they had been Liverpool's first top flight opponents at Anfield since 1954 and beat the Reds 2-1 so fans were hoping there would be no repeat this time.

Writing in the *Liverpool Echo* on 30th August, Leslie Edwards described Blackpool without Stanley Matthews as like 'strawberries without cream.' The 'Wizard of the Dribble' had left Bloomfield Road in 1961 after fourteen years at the club to re-join Stoke City at the age of 46, but Blackpool were coming to terms with life without him. Edwards compared the situation to how Liverpool took a few years to get over the retirement of Billy Liddell, with the 'general competence of the team' eventually overcoming the absence of the star man. In the *Daily Post*, Horace Yates wrote that if Jimmy Melia, Gordon Milne and Willie Stevenson could regain their composure and confidence of the Blackburn game then victory should be on the cards.

The main issue for Liverpool's fans that week wasn't whether or not they could get their first win of the season at Anfield, but whether they could even get in to see their team in action. There remained anger that the Kemlyn Road stand had reduced the overall capacity and it led to a further problem in the Kop, with some parts of the terracing now having the view of the pitch obstructed by the stand roof. The whole issue led to director Harold Cartwright giving a statement to the *Daily Post* that was printed on 30th August.

'If football is to succeed we must make our spectators comfortable and we are doing everything we can to ensure that end. At the present time a review is under way to discover what further steps that can take. The complaints about Anfield not being big enough only apply to a handful of games over the season. Last season our average attendance was 42,462, a figure well below capacity. I think it is true to say that no matter how big a ground is, there will always be occasions when it will not be big enough.'

The complaints from fans didn't deter Liverpool's directors from pressing ahead with further plans to redevelop Anfield, with Cartwright telling the Annual General Meeting that night that work would begin in a few years on a 5,000 seat double decker stand at the Anfield Road end, although this would not reduce the overall capacity. This spending would not be to the detriment of the team however, with chairman T.V. Williams telling shareholders that the aim of the board was to 'provide a team worthy of the city of Liverpool' and to 'go into the market for players of proven ability should the occasion arise.' It meant that for now the Anfield Road end remained terracing and the removal of the site office meant that for this game it would all be open for the Blackpool game, making 2,500 extra spaces available. Those that had Kemlyn Road stand tickets were glad to know that all refreshment bars were now ready, as were the ladies toilets.

The facilities were better than for the previous game, as was the football on offer by the Reds, but once again they were defeated as they rued their inability to take their chances. They were in good form in the first half, twice hitting the bar and forcing good saves from the visiting keeper. However these efforts came after John McPhee had given Blackpool a ninth minute lead, stroking the ball past Tommy Lawrence after being played in by Pat Quinn. Tony Waiters, later to become a youth coach at Liverpool, was in top form for the rest of the half and when he was beaten by shots from Melia and St John, the ball flashed just wide of the post. Blackpool then gave a further lesson in finishing two minutes before half time when Quinn passed to Ray Charnley who hit a fine left foot strike past Lawrence to leave the Reds with a mountain to climb in the second half.

In the 63rd minute Liverpool were given a lifeline when Jimmy Armfield handled the ball in the area, but from Ronnie Moran's resulting penalty kick Waiters guessed right to save. From then on the players seemed to sense it was not going to be their day and became more jittery, relying on long balls and rarely stringing more than three passes together. Peter Thompson was the best player, regularly having the beating of Armfield, but on the right Ian Callaghan didn't get forward enough and behind the two wingers, both Milne and Stevenson were below par. A consolation goal eventually came in the 83rd minute when Stevenson's shot came back off the post to allow Melia a tap-in with Waiters prostrate on the ground.

It was a disappointing afternoon for the crowd of 42,767 which was way below capacity. This may well have been due to the problems that had been encountered against Forest, with many choosing to stay away fearing they would not gain admission. Opposition fans couldn't wait to rub it in, with Liverpool supporters working at the Atomic Energy plant in Risley, near Warrington, being presented with a stick of rock with Quinn etched into it by Blackpool supporting colleagues.

However writing in the *Daily Post* the following Monday, Horace Yates claimed that the pre-season optimism of the fans was still justifiable, as it was only failure to take chances that cost them this game. He concluded: 'I see no reason why Liverpool cannot become a formidable combination.'

There were no statistics in those days about who had the most shots, possession and so on to back up his claims, but Ian St John wrote in his Post column on 2nd September that he believed Liverpool had been far more dominant than their results suggested.

> 'It is curious that nearly every goalkeeper that comes to Anfield these days plays like a world beater even though his reputation hardly puts him in that class. It could be that they are all inspired by the Anfield roar against them, but delving a bit deeper I think we must be held guilty of contributing to some of the reputations some of these fellows make against us. I would not be surprised if a check were made to find that Liverpool this season had hit the posts or bar more than any other side. Bad finishing, you might say, but it is hardly that when we get as near as the framework. Sooner, rather than later, I think we are entitled to expect some of those to go in instead of out.'

It was to be nearly a fortnight before the Reds could return to Anfield to put things right and between now and then they had three away games to worry about as they sought to prove to their fans that they could be genuine title challengers.

We Love You Yeah, Yeah, Yeah!

Liverpool: Lawrence, Byrne, Moran, Milne, Yeats, Stevenson, Callaghan, Hunt, St John, Melia, Thompson.

Blackpool: Waiters, Armfield, Martin, McPhee, Gratrix, Durie, Lea, Quinn, Charnley, Parry, Horne.

Referee: Mr G. McCabe (Sheffield).

Attendance: 42,767

Top of Table

		Pl	W	D	L	F	A	GA	Pt
1	Leicester City	3	2	1	1	11	3	3.67	5
2	Manchester United	3	2	1	0	10	4	2.50	5
3	Tottenham	3	2	0	1	9	4	2.25	4
14	Liverpool	3	1	0	2	4	5	0.80	2

6

Consistently Inconsistent

After the disappointment of losing two successive home games Liverpool faced three away games in early September as they sought to restore the form from the opening day of the season. They managed to cope with this quite well but only to find home form continued to let them down. When they finally got going at Anfield, they encountered problems on the road as they struggled to get any form of consistency going.

3rd September 1963: Nottingham Forest 0 Liverpool 0, Football League Division One

In just their fourth game, Liverpool met Nottingham Forest for the second time of the season as they travelled to the East Midlands for a midweek fixture. Although a coach journey that could be expected to take three to four hours was involved, the Reds didn't stay overnight, instead remaining in Liverpool so that Bill Shankly could conduct as much training and discussions as necessary to iron out the faults that had led to two home defeats. The day before the game the *Liverpool Echo* reported that there were doubts over the fitness of Willie Stevenson who had been struggling with a groin injury since the start of the season. When he failed to convince Shankly that he was able to play on the Wednesday morning, Phil Ferns boarded the coach instead with the Reds' boss predicting that Stevenson would be fit again by the weekend.

In between the meetings with the Reds, Forest had lost 4-1 against Tottenham Hotspur at White Hart Lane although their programme notes for this fixture believed that was not a fair reflection of the game. They reported that the game had been evenly matched and that, 'We were very much the superior side in the second half but, alas we had not a Jimmy Greaves.'

The game against Liverpool was described as an attractive fixture and it was anticipated there would be plenty of good football and goals to come, but it didn't turn out to be the case as the sides had to settle for a 0-0 draw.

It was a game in which both defences ruled, and when they were breached the finishing of the forwards left a lot to be desired. 25-year-old reserve captain Ferns, who had just five first team appearances to his name, put in a solid performance breaking up Forest attacks but also spraying some nice passes around.

Liverpool had a great chance early in the game when Roger Hunt was put clean through on goal by Jimmy Melia, but he went for precision rather than power and dragged his shot wide. Forest were the better team in the first half but Liverpool were defensively sound, with Gordon Milne complementing Ferns well on the other side of the pitch, and Ron Yeats being equal in the middle to anything that was thrown at him in the air. Right back Gerry Byrne also put in one of his best performances to date, rarely allowing Dick Le Flem to get past him although on the left flank, Ronnie Moran was given a much harder time by Trevor Hockey, who didn't get put off by two blows he received to the head.

After the break, Liverpool got themselves into the game and were far more composed than they had been against Forest at Anfield a week earlier and also in the Blackpool game. Peter Thompson and Ian Callaghan were both dangerous on the wings but Hunt was well marked by Bob McKinlay and didn't get much sight of the ball. Melia was again not at his best, although on one occasion he played a perfect pass to Ferns whose shot went wide. Ian St John also had a golden chance when set up by Thompson but his shot was weak and easily held by Peter Grummitt. Summing up though, Horace Yates concluded in his *Daily Post* report, 'It was hard to be critical of Liverpool in any respect after such a full-blooded effort to rehabilitate themselves.'

Leslie Edwards was complimentary in the Echo too, writing, 'Liverpool snapped out of their unexpected spell of failure and pleased their manager and their following by their industry, their incisive tackling and their general cover of each other.' Edwards predicted that the result bode well for the next two games and they could expect at least a point from each.

Liverpool: Lawrence, Byrne, Moran, Milne, Yeats, Ferns, Callaghan, Hunt, St John, Melia, Thompson.

Forest: Grummitt, Wilson, Mochan, Whitefoot, McKinlay, Winfield, Hockey, Addison, Wignall, Quigley, Le Flem.

Referee: Mr A. Sparling (Grimsby).

Attendance: 21,788

7th September 1963: Chelsea 1 Liverpool 3, Football League Division One

The run of three away games for Liverpool meant there was some respite for the residents of Anfield who were getting more and more annoyed by parking problems around the ground on match days. On 30th August the *Liverpool Echo* had reported that Liverpool City Council's Education Committee were considering allowing local school playgrounds to be used as car parks on match days, something which drew an angry response from a Stanley Kinder of Haggerston Road in Walton. On 4th September the Echo published his letter which said,

'I hope the Education committee will resist any proposal to use school playgrounds as car parks. The word playground means what it says, it is a ground to play on not park cars on. Why should municipal transport be allowed to decay whilst football commuters go on their merry way. This is as much a problem for the clubs as it is for the public and they should be thinking and doing something about it.'

Other readers had written to the paper both for and against an idea that Stanley Park was a suitable venue for car parking, but there was general consensus that the club had to do something about the issue, as did Everton when it came to the situation around Goodison Park. On 5th September at a full meeting of the council, C.P. Wall, who represented County ward where Goodison is situated, tabled a motion that the problems be monitored. This was seconded by Eric Heffer (who was elected MP the following year for the constituency of Walton, where the two grounds are situated), and he called for representatives of the clubs to meet councillors to come up with a long term plan.

The parking was not Bill Shankly's concern though and he was thinking of nothing except securing two points at Stamford Bridge. Shankly told Horace Yates of the *Daily Post* that he didn't think Liverpool had deserved to lose two successive home games and that the players were determined to put things right and he was sure they could,

'They are desperate to atone as those unexpected defeats have cost them a lot, not just in prestige but actual cash. Instead of being in a position of challenging Manchester United at the top of the table we are now having to prove ourselves. I am confident we can do it. I am sure our training system can pay dividends soon. I hope that tomorrow will be the beginning of a scoring burst by the attack, for once they capture a goal fever I think a lot of teams will feel the full weight of their assault.'

On 6th September the day the Reds travelled south, the main story in London concerned Christine Keeler, who was appearing at Marlborough Street Magistrates Court charged with conspiracy to obstruct the course of justice and perjury, having been arrested the night before. The charges related to her having allegedly lied in court in June at the trial of her former lover, Aloysius Gordon, who was convicted of assaulting her. The Profumo Affair had made Keeler into something of a celebrity, especially in light of the semi-nude photographs of her sat astride a chair that had been published in the *Sunday Mirror.*

Chelsea were managed by Shankly's fellow Scot Tommy Docherty, who was keen to put one over his compatriot as Shankly had suggested towards the end of 1962-63 that the London club were not quite good enough for promotion. The main injury worry for Liverpool was whether Willie Stevenson would recover from injury in time but if he didn't, Phil Ferns had proved a more than able deputy at Forest. Stevenson took part in training on the Friday morning then both he and Ferns travelled to London with Shankly telling reporters that he would make a decision on the morning of the game.

Shankly's injury worries weren't as bad as those of Everton boss Harry Catterick though. Both his first choice and reserve left backs were injured and that morning a player who would later go down in folklore amongst Reds fans was signed to plug the gap. Sandy Brown, who would score a classic diving header into the wrong net when Liverpool beat Everton 3-0 at Goodison in 1969-70, signed from Partick Thistle for £25,000.

At Stamford Bridge it was decided not to risk Stevenson's fitness given no substitutes were allowed, and Ferns retained his place at left half. It was a game that saw the Reds come out on top through sheer determination to win as the superior stamina that Shankly's training methods were designed to bring out paid dividends.

Chelsea started the better team with Bobby Tambling a real handful for Ron Yeats while Jimmy Mulholland tested Tommy Lawrence early on. Eddie McCreadie then forced a fine save from Lawrence and the Reds' keeper also did well to hold on to a drive from John Mortimore. Against the run of play though, Liverpool took the lead in the ninth minute when they were awarded a free kick after McCreadie fouled Ian St John. Ian Callaghan floated the ball into the penalty area and it was cleared for a corner, from which St John headed the ball past Peter Bonetti. However the Reds were in front for just eight minutes after some slack defending on the right allowed Tambling to get through on goal, and although Lawrence managed to beat away his shot, Mulholland was on hand to turn it into an unguarded net.

Liverpool continued to play a passing game but sometimes they weren't finding each other, while Chelsea were much more direct with their approach but Yeats handled things quite well. The Reds did have a lucky escape when Gordon Milne passed back to Lawrence who had come off his line. Although the ball went over the keeper, Ferns got back to clear off the line and required treatment after he was entangled in the net.

Ferns was doing a creditable job as cover for Stevenson, on one occasion closing down McCreadie to concede a corner when Chelsea attackers were lined up in the box ready to receive his cross. The Reds had some good first half chances, Callaghan hitting a drive just over the bar and Jimmy Melia dallying for too long allowing defenders to get back into position when he was in a good position to try a shot. The Reds were then denied a clear penalty when Roger Hunt had his shirt pulled inside the area by Mortimore when he was clean through on goal.

From the kick-off for the second half the Reds had a lucky escape when McCreadie's punt upfield was misjudged by Yeats and he handled the ball just outside the penalty area, but Chelsea wasted the resultant free kick.

Liverpool were enjoying plenty of possession but they were playing too narrow and not utilising their wingers, with Callaghan and Peter Thompson coming inside to get the ball too often. The game was also developing into a physical affair with both McCreadie and Gerry Byrne putting in two-footed tackles but neither were spoken to by the referee, while Callaghan and McCreadie were on the ground for several minutes after a clash of heads.

Liverpool began to take control with Melia and Thompson beginning to link well on the left, the winger hitting a shot just wide and Hunt being sent through on goal by a fine pass only for Bonetti to race out of his area to clear. They still had to be ready for Chelsea's fast counter-attacks but eventually the Reds' persistence paid off when Hunt scored in the 72nd minute. He tapped in at the near post after Milne had played the ball into the area from the right hand side.

Chelsea hit back and Lawrence's handling had to be at its best as they pumped high balls into the area, while Yeats remained commanding and also made some crucial tackles. On the one occasion Lawrence misjudged a cross, Milne was on hand to clear Tambling's header off the line. Then, after absorbing all the pressure, Liverpool got a third with the last kick of the game. Ronnie Moran hit a long clearance down the left for Hunt to chase and as he took the ball towards the area Bonetti was drawn from his goal, allowing the Reds striker to square to St John who rolled the ball into an empty net.

Paying tribute to Liverpool's players in the *Liverpool Echo* the following Monday, Horace Yates wrote that they 'had to fight like tigers, defend like heroes and strike with deadly efficiency when chances were created.' Chelsea were described as 'fast, speedy and dangerous opponents who might easily have run riot against a less determined defence.' Scotland manager Ian McColl was watching from the stands and must have been impressed by the performances of Liverpool's Scottish trio, with Yates describing Lawrence as in 'eye catching form', St John as having 'rarely worked harder' and Yeats as 'supreme' in the air.

Liverpool: Lawrence, Byrne, Moran, Milne, Yeats, Ferns, Callaghan, Hunt, St John, Melia, Thompson.

Chelsea: Bonetti, Shellito, McCreadie, Venables, Mortimore, Harris, Murray, Tambling, Mulholland, Moore, Blunstone.

Referee: Mr H.G. New (Havant).

Attendance: 38,202

9th September 1963: Wolverhampton Wanderers 1 Liverpool 3, Football League Division One

The Reds were clocking up the miles thick and fast as they faced a third away match in six days, this time away to Wolves at Molineux. They travelled on the day of the game with Bill Shankly again refusing to give any indication as to whether or not Willie Stevenson would return to the side, saying that he would make a decision shortly before the 7.15pm kick off.

The controversy over parking around the two grounds on match days continued to rumble on. On the evening of the match the *Liverpool Echo* reported that Councillor Reg Flude, who like C.P. Wall was an elected member for County, had put forward proposals for a 3,500 capacity car park in Stanley Park. He denied that it would be to the detriment of play space as most of the land he was suggesting be used was covered in shrubs. He also claimed up to £20,000 per season could be raised for the council and that on non-match days it could even be used as a park and ride to ease city centre congestion.

Wolves had made a topsy-turvy start to the season, with an impressive 3-1 win at Arsenal on the opening day being followed by a 4-1 loss at home to Tottenham. They then beat Stoke 2-1 at home, before losing 4-3 at Tottenham, although they did battle well after trailing 3-0 at one stage. Two days before the game with the Reds, they had been beaten 3-0 by Nottingham Forest at the City Ground, leading to Stan Cullis announcing to the press that changes were being made for Liverpool's visit. John Kirkham was dropped from wing half and inside forward Peter Broadbent moved into his position with Barry Stobart coming in for his first start of the season. These changes could do nothing to prevent his side being torn apart by a Liverpool team that put in a virtually faultless performance, winning far more comfortably than the 3-1 scoreline suggests.

It took the Reds just thirty seconds to score the opening goal. Peter Thompson collected a throw-in from Jimmy Melia before turning a defender and crossing from the left to the far corner of the six yard box where Roger Hunt controlled the ball well before firing past the keeper. Wolves though could never be written off at Molineux and that proved correct, with Tommy Lawrence having to be at his best moments later to make a point blank save from Terry Wharton after he had been played in. He could do nothing in the seventeenth minute to prevent Ron Flowers from scoring when his deflected shot gave him no chance, with the ball going one way as he dived another. Liverpool soon regained control of the game, passing the ball well and moving quickly for each other, but at half time there was no further scoring although the Reds fans that made the trip had reason to be satisfied with the performance.

Ten minutes into the second half the Reds got the lead they deserved. Melia swapped passes with Hunt only to see his shot cleared off the line by George Showell. St John then sent it back goalwards where Melia was able to stab it home. This time there was no getting back into the game for Wolves thanks partly to a solid display by Phil Ferns, who retained his place at left half despite Stevenson having returned to full fitness. In the 69th minute the Reds extended their lead when St John's shot was only parried by Fred Davies and Hunt was left with the simple task of tapping the ball into the net.

There was no way back for Wolves and their fans knew it, thousands of them leaving the ground long before the final whistle. Every Liverpool player played his part in a performance that saw them all work well for each other. Ian Callaghan and Thompson were dangerous on the flanks, Melia had rediscovered the form that was so lacking in earlier games, and St John was a constant threat. Gordon Milne also had once of his finest performances in a red shirt in front of watching England manager Alf Ramsey who told chairman T.V. Williams afterwards, 'That was the way England played it on the Continent – sharp, accurate passing, progressive and the way football should be played.'[14]

The Reds coach arrived back at Anfield around midnight, with the following evening's Echo reporting that Stevenson had jokingly told Ferns not to play so well next time. The forced introduction to the side of the reserves captain had coincided with five points gained from a possible six, and Shankly was now able to think of the championship again. All the Reds needed to do was beat West Ham United at home the following Saturday.

Liverpool: Lawrence, Byrne, Moran, Milne, Yeats, Ferns, Callaghan, Hunt, St John, Melia, Callaghan.

Wolves: Davies, Showell, Thompson, Broadbent, Woodfield, Flowers, Wharton, Stobart, Murray, Crowe, Hinton.

Referee: Mr K. Stokes (Newark).

Attendance: 25,000.

14th September 1963: Liverpool 1 West Ham United 2, Football League Division One

After picking up five points from a possible six away from home, hopes were high as Liverpool prepared to face West Ham at Anfield on Saturday 14th September. For the first time that season, the Reds were being mentioned in the press as possible champions, with Leslie Edwards writing in the *Liverpool Echo* the evening after the win at Wolves,

> 'No wonder manager Bill Shankly is thinking in terms of a championship win this season. No wonder the players are looking confidently ahead to their match against West Ham on Saturday. They have snapped out of their early season anxiety quicker than a season ago. They played last night like champions, with quick-silver passing, a half back line well integrated with the attack, and a defence as effective as it ever has been.'

During the week the Reds signed seventeen-year-old forward John Sealey on amateur terms from Mid-Cheshire League side Warrington Town, the same club that Roger Hunt had signed from in 1958, when they were known as Stockton Heath. Sealey though would not have the same success as his predecessor, playing just one game for Liverpool at Wolves in the final league game of 1964-65, when Bill Shankly made eight changes to the line-up as he rested others ahead of the FA Cup final.

Liverpool's hopes of securing their first Anfield points of the 1963-64 season were boosted by injury worries at West Ham, with centre half Ken Brown being ruled out and debutant Dave Bickles being lined up to take his place. The *Daily Post* reported on 13th September that the Reds had one or two minor knocks but they weren't expected to rule anybody out of the game. Willie Stevenson was fit again, but that didn't mean he would be playing for the first team at Anfield. The form of Phil Ferns during his absence meant that it was quite possible that he may have to make do with appearing for the reserves at Barnsley instead. It was then confirmed by Leslie Edwards in that evening's Echo that Oakwell would be Stevenson's destination the next day with Ferns retaining his place.

A win could lift the Reds into second place and in his Echo preview, Edwards saw no reason why they couldn't get that first home win of the season. He described West Ham as 'a goodish side with several outstanding players' but also that Liverpool were now playing football that the Kop 'had rarely seen before, even in past championship seasons.' They were now playing with confidence and Shankly's decision to stay at home for as long as possible before the Nottingham Forest game, when he had a day long discussion with players as to where they were going wrong, was now paying dividends.

In the *Daily Post* on the morning of the game, Horace Yates speculated that the reason the Reds had struggled at Anfield was because they were trying too hard but they had now put that behind them. He wrote,

> 'They are much more composed away from home. The adulation of their supporters which should be an encouragement has become a trial. Instead of taking games in their stride they become too hurried and lose their poise and punch, with a resultant frustrating failure. I think they will by now have learned their lesson and there should be a far more formidable show from them today.'

Once again though, Liverpool went down 2-1 at home for the third game in succession, with Ronnie Moran again having a penalty saved as the Reds failed to break down a West Ham side who were solid in defence and lethal on the counter attack. It was a tactic that frustrated Liverpool's fans, but as Jack Rowe wrote in his report for the *Daily Post* the following Monday, it was 'perfectly legitimate' and 'it was up to the players to use their skill to conquer it.'

Liverpool suffered a pre match blow when Tommy Lawrence was ruled out with a thigh injury, meaning Jim Furnell came into the side for the first time in eleven months. The absence of the first choice keeper had no bearing on the result however, as Furnell was a spectator for most of the game.

West Ham's players did not adopt particular positions, they simply all got back into defence and all attacked when the chance arose, a tactic that the Reds had no idea how to handle in the first half. All three West Ham players who would go on to appear for England in the 1966 World Cup final played a part in their team's victory, with Martin Peters and Geoff Hurst scoring the goals and Bobby Moore having a tremendous game. He was described by Michael Charters in the *Liverpool Echo* as a 'brilliant world class player who showed outstanding ability in everything he did.' In the first half he seemed to cut out every ball the Reds played, but was also potent on the wings when he got forward, leading Charters to conclude that 'there are few players of Moore's skill in this country.'

The Reds started off too narrow and Gordon Milne and Jimmy Melia, so often the catalysts for attacks, found themselves running into too many blind alleys or allowing forwards to be picked up by defenders before they could play the decisive pass. West Ham on the other hand were fast and fluid with their attacks, getting the ball from one end of the pitch extremely quickly and causing significant problems for Ronnie Moran, Ron Yeats and Gerry Byrne as the half backs weren't getting back quickly enough. They opened the scoring after eleven minutes through a cleverly worked move from a corner. The ball was played in from the left but then knocked back out of the area by centre forward John Byrne to full back John Burkett. He then played the ball back forward to Peters who side footed it with precision into the top corner of the goal, an astonished Furnell remaining rooted to the spot.

Liverpool laboured on for 22 minutes with the only chance of any note coming when Ian Callaghan forced a good save from Jim Standen, otherwise Moore mopped up everything before the Reds forwards were able to pose a danger. Then in the 33rd minute West Ham were 2-0 up with just three players touching the ball as it went from their penalty area into the back of the Reds net. Standen threw it long towards the halfway line, where Ronnie Boyce helped it downfield with a punt towards the area. Hurst controlled it beautifully, swivelled around Yeats and placed it past Furnell who perhaps should have stayed on his line.

At half time nobody would have expected the Reds to come back, such was their lack of ideas in the first period, but kicking into the Kop after the break they found a new impetus and got the ball into the box more often. Just after the hour mark Liverpool got the break they were looking for when Moore made his first mistake of the game by handling a Callaghan cross. A penalty was awarded but for the third time of the season Moran saw his kick saved by the keeper with Standen diving to his right to turn away the powerfully struck kick. The Reds refused to allow themselves to get deflated though and began to play more composed football, passing the ball about rather than just hoofing it into the box. In the 65th minute they got one back when Hunt picked his way through some tackles before unleashing a fierce shot that gave Standen no chance.

The rest of the game was played in the West Ham half, with Charters estimating in the Echo that the Reds enjoyed 95% possession. When Moore couldn't stop the attacks, Standen showed magnificent handling ability, saving well from Hunt, Peter Thompson and Ferns and in one crazy goalmouth scramble he managed to deny both Hunt and Ian St John at point blank range after parrying Melia's shot. When Standen was beaten he was saved by the post on one occasion after Callaghan's lob had deceived him, and then by the linesman's flag after Hunt's header from Melia's cross was ruled out.

It was after this match that Shankly famously told the directors that the club would win a home game before the end of the season. It was obviously frustrating to lose a third successive home game, but the positive signs had been there in the second half. Charters correctly made the point that Liverpool struggled to break down teams that adopted defensive tactics, pointing to the game with Leicester in the preceding season's FA Cup semi final. However he also predicted that the next home game against Wolverhampton Wanderers was sure to be far more open.

Liverpool: Furnell, Byrne, Moran, Milne, Yeats, Ferns, Callaghan, Hunt, St John, Melia, Thompson.

West Ham: Standen, Kirkup, Burkett, Peters, Bickles, Moore, Bradbrook, Boyce, Byrne, Hurst, Dear.

Referee: Mr V. James.

Attendance: 45,497.

16th September 1963: Liverpool 6 Wolverhampton Wanderers 0, Football League Division One

Just two days after the West Ham defeat, Liverpool were back at Anfield with a chance to put things right against Wolves in a game that was played early in the week due to Everton's participation in the European Cup.

Everton's European Cup first round game against Inter Milan which was scheduled for the Wednesday that week meant this game was brought forward to the Monday. It was also suggested by the local press that many Liverpool supporters would take the opportunity to see a competitive match involving top class Continental opposition, despite the fact Everton had raised prices for the game.

Wolves had lost their last four matches conceding seventeen goals in the process. It would have been thought that given this a new striker would have been the last signing on their minds, but on the day of the game they broke their club record when they paid Ipswich £55,000 for forward Ray Crawford. The Suffolk club's first England international, he had scored 143 goals in 197 games for them since joining in 1958 when they were in the Third Division and went straight into the Wolves side for this game.

Bill Shankly confirmed to the *Liverpool Echo* on the afternoon of the match that Willie Stevenson would return to the Reds side at the expense of Phil Ferns, while Tommy Lawrence's thigh strain would also be assessed shortly before kick off. Ian St John was a doubt too, having suffered a bruised ankle in the West Ham game and reserve forward Alf Arrowsmith, who had played only four games for the Reds so far, was on standby.

Both Lawrence and St John failed to shake off their injuries and the replacement centre forward took just a minute to score the opening goal which sent Liverpool on their way to a home victory at last. Arrowsmith's goal came with just his second touch of the ball, the first having been the kick-off, when he beat the keeper from ten yards after Ian Callaghan crossed to him in the box and he was unmarked. The goal meant Liverpool had the lead at Anfield for the first time that season and you could feel the tension ease around the ground. Arrowsmith followed his goal up with a header that went just wide, Stevenson's shot was well saved by Malcolm Finlayson and the Wolves' keeper also did well to come out of his goal and dive at Roger Hunt's feet after he found himself in a one on one situation. The game then went flat for a while but the crowd was ignited in the 33rd minute by Peter Thompson's first Liverpool goal. Gordon Milne crossed from the right and John Kirkham's attempted clearance went straight up in the air, eventually falling at Thompson's feet and his sweet volley beat Finlayson to make it 2-0.

Twelve minutes into the second half ICallaghan scored from near the corner flag, the ball sailing past a static keeper and defence, and then in the 67th minute Arrowsmith crossed from the left and Hunt scored from close range with Wolves in total disarray. Their manager, Stan Cullis, had made ten changes to the side that lost 5-1 at home to Blackburn two days earlier and it showed,as they were totally disjointed and never looked like getting anything from the match. Their hopeless situation was then made worse shortly after the fourth goal when Finlayson injured his hand making a save from Thompson and was forced to go off. Murray had endured a nightmare game at inside right and it didn't get any better for him in goal, as after only five minutes between the sticks he just stood on his line and admired as Milne's lob from the edge of the area went into the net. The Kop were chanting 'We want six' and with three minutes remaining Hunt complied, converting Thompson's cross from the left.

Wolves had been woeful, with Crawford hardly getting a touch as he was easily contained by Ron Yeats who said afterwards that 'the ball suddenly started to run for us instead of against us.'[15] Only Chris Crowe, who twice hit the post, came out of the game with any credit and in the *Daily Post* the following morning Horace Yates wrote that Wolves were 'as poor an outfit that has sported their colours in years.' That said though, the Reds could only beat what was in front of them and given their woeful finishing in other games, they still needed to take their chances and they certainly did on this occasion in what surely was the confidence boost they needed to get a winning run going.

Liverpool: Furnell, Byrne, Moran, Milne, Yeats, Stevenson, Callaghan, Hunt, Arrowsmith, Melia, Thompson.

Wolves: Finlayson, Thomson, Harris, Kirkham, Showell, Flowers, Crowe, Murray, Crawford, Broadbent, Wharton.

Referee: Mr E. Crawford (Doncaster).

Attendance: 44,050.

21st September 1963: Sheffield United 3 Liverpool 0, Football League Division One

As Liverpool's players and fans breathed a collective sigh of relief after finally winning a home game, Buckingham Palace announced the news that Queen Elizabeth II was expecting her fourth child in the New Year. The story was on the front page of the *Daily Post* on Tuesday 17th September, with the news being announced from Balmoral Castle were she was staying until October.

The local press was dominated that week by the first competitive European game on Merseyside as Everton played the first leg of their first round European Cup tie against Inter Milan. Many fans were angry at the raising of ticket prices, with the stands being priced at £2 and standing places at 25 shillings. Despite this a crowd of 62,408, including Reds captain Ron Yeats, were inside Goodison to watch a 0-0 draw, 14,000 more than had turned up for their previous home game against Bolton.

Four Liverpool players were recognised that week for their improving performances, as Ian Callaghan, Roger Hunt, Jimmy Melia and Gordon Milne were all called up by Alf Ramsey to a Football League XI that would meet the League of Ireland in Dublin on 2nd October. Looking to the immediate future though the Reds still had injury worries for the game at Bramall Lane, which was a three-sided ground due to the club sharing it with Yorkshire County Cricket Club. Keeper Tommy Lawrence had returned to full training by the Thursday but Ian St John remained a major doubt due to an ankle problem. However the performance of Alf Arrowsmith against Wolves meant there was a capable replacement. Horace Yates had written in the Post of his performance in that match, 'The youngster was a problem for Showell in all the aerial battles and his speed was more than troublesome. Moreover his willingness, nay his eagerness, to shoot on sight is a quality full of possibilities.'

The day before the match it was announced that Lawrence was able to return to the side but St John would have to stay at home and Arrowsmith would continue to deputise. Yates again reiterated in the Post on the morning of the game that 'Arrowsmith would not reduce the fire power of the line'. Unfortunately for the Reds though, he was unable to reproduce the form shown in the Wolves match as they lost on the road for the first time of the season, going down 3-0.

Sheffield United employed tactics that frustrated Liverpool, getting as many players in a defensive line as possible then successfully employing the offside trap at every opportunity. It may have been monotonous but it was up to the Reds to break them down and they failed to do so, passing the ball sideways and backwards but never finding the penetrative defence splitting pass.

Liverpool had started brightly, Hunt having an effort that failed to test the keeper and Peter Thompson twice cutting inside but having his shots blocked, but by midway through the half they had ran out of ideas. Then in the 41st minute the home side took the lead when they showed how to get the ball from one end of the pitch quickly and effectively. A Callaghan cross was collected by the keeper Alan Hodgkinson. His long throw found Derek Pace who laid the ball off for Keith Kettleborough and he kicked it down the middle of the field for Tony Wagstaff to chase. The United inside forward held off the challenge of Gerry Byrne to poke it past Lawrence and into the net off the post.

There were a number of Liverpool supporters spread around the ground and every offside decision had led to slow handclapping, which caused one or two scuffles and some fans were removed from the crowd by police and led away across the cricket pitch. The second half started much the same as the first with Liverpool frustrated by offside decisions, Hunt waving his hand at the linesman in disgust on one occasion. Their chances of getting back into the game were then made worse in the 51st minute with another quick fire United goal from a move that culminated in Pace diving in to head home Brian Richardson's cross. Had Ron Yeats had more luck a minute later the Reds may have made a game of it, but from a corner he was unlucky to see one header pushed away by the keeper and another cleared off the line after Callaghan had quickly played the ball back in.

For the rest of the game Liverpool continued to play the same game, having little or no idea how to break down the home side's solid defence. Thompson and Callaghan on the wings were devoid of ideas and Milne wasn't as penetrative as he could be. Hunt tried his best but was frustrated too often and Arrowsmith hardly got a kick. The only Reds player who had come out with any real credit was Yeats, who remained commanding in the middle, breaking up attacks but also getting forward to try and instigate a more direct approach and pose a danger at set pieces. Liverpool's misery was then complete two minutes from time from another breakaway goal, with Pace finishing off the move when he flicked on Ron Simpson's goal-bound shot into the net.

Liverpool's defeat meant that the only unbeaten away record in the First Division had gone and in the late edition of the *Liverpool Echo* that night Jack Rowe commented that they had 'scarcely deserved to retain it.' Rowe also wrote the analysis in the *Daily Post* the following Monday and he was just as scathing, saying that 'so few of them were at their best' and that St John was missed as Arrowsmith, 'trier though he was, lacked the skill and ability to beat a man like Joe Shaw.'

In his Echo column the following Saturday, Yeats described Sheffield United as 'a good, workmanlike team who took their opportunities well' but that 'the offside trap does nothing for the game as a spectacle.' It was up to the Reds to deal with what they were up against though and if they were serious about a title challenge they had to improve fast. The next game gave them the perfect opportunity to do this as it was against local rivals and champions Everton.

Liverpool: Lawrence, Byrne, Moran, Milne, Yeats, Stevenson, Callaghan, Hunt, Arrowsmith, Melia, Thompson.

Sheffield Utd: Hodgkinson, Coldwell, Shaw B, Richardson, Shaw J, Matthewson, Allchurch, Kettleborough, Pace, Wagstaff, Simpson.

Referee: Mr P. Brandwood (Walsall).

Attendance: 24,932.

Top of Table

		Pl	W	D	L	F	A	GA	Pt
1	Nottingham Forest	9	6	1	2	15	8	1.88	13
2	Manchester United	9	5	2	2	23	10	2.30	12
3	West Bromwich Albion	9	5	2	2	16	7	2.29	12
10	Liverpool	9	4	1	4	17	12	1.42	9

7

Fortress Anfield

After finally getting a home win only to follow it up by losing an away game for the first time of the season, Liverpool needed to develop some consistency if they were to realise their ambition of making a title challenge. The coming month gave them the perfect opportunity to do so as four of their next five scheduled games were at home and they didn't let themselves down.

28th September 1963: Liverpool 2 Everton 1, Football League Division One

The disappointment of losing their unbeaten away record would soon be forgotten if Liverpool could secure a first league win over Everton since September 1950. Everton had been relegated in 1950-51 and were then promoted back to the First Division as the Reds went down in 1954, so the return of league derbies had been eagerly anticipated. In September 1962, a last minute goal by Roger Hunt had secured a 2-2 draw for the Reds in front of 73,000 at Goodison Park then, when the teams met at Anfield the following April, the game ended in a 0-0 stalemate.

The crowd for the match was restricted to 52,000 with Liverpool secretary Jimmy McInnes announcing on the Wednesday that the game was completely sold out with the exception of a few hundred tickets that remained for the Boys Pen. Tickets had gone on sale at the ground the previous weekend on a strictly one per person basis, with prices ranging from three shillings in the Kop to nine shillings in the Kemlyn Road stand, 15p to 45p in today's money.

On the same day that fans found out they had no chance of obtaining a ticket, Master of the Rolls Lord Denning released his report into his inquiry into the Profumo Affair in which he concluded that there had been no breach of national security. Relations between East and West were slowly improving to such a degree that President John F. Kennedy suggested a joint mission to the moon. In a speech made to the United Nations General Assembly on 20th September he said that peaceful co-operation provided more security than the hydrogen bomb, and that research should be pooled to send a joint team to the moon to represent all humanity.

The build up to the first derby of 1963-64 was not as intense as might be expected, as Everton were playing the second leg of the European Cup tie with Inter Milan in Italy on Wednesday 25th September, three days before the Anfield showdown. They had some problems on the way out as a storm over Europe led to flight delays on the Monday evening and they eventually arrived in Milan at 4.30am on the Tuesday, causing serious disruption to their training plans. They went on lose 1-0 with Jair scoring the only goal for Inter in a bruising game that saw Alex Young suffer a cut knee making him a serious doubt for the derby, while several other players returned home with knocks.

Liverpool's main injury concern remained around Ian St John, who seemed to be losing his battle to recover from an injured ankle and wrote in his *Daily Post* column on the Tuesday:

> 'It doesn't look as though I have any great prospect of playing unless there is a sudden and unexpected improvement in the condition of my ankle. As I write this I can only report that there is still considerable pain. The thought of not being able to play could hardly be more depressing. It is bad enough to miss an ordinary game in the league programme but these derby games are something quite apart.'

As the week wore on Liverpool did all they could to get St John ready for the game and he saw a specialist on the Wednesday, but Bill Shankly admitted on the Thursday that he remained a major doubt. However on the Friday as Alex Young was confirmed as unavailable for Everton, St John was one of thirteen players named in the Liverpool party. Phil Ferns was also recalled as Shankly tried to address the problem of the Reds being prone to quick breakaway goals, and it was reported in both the *Liverpool Echo* and *Daily Post* that left back Ronnie Moran may make way for him.

One element of preparation that Shankly hadn't wanted to get out though was the use of a psychoanalyst who had been brought in to help ease pre-match tensions. When the Echo got hold of it on the Friday Shankly was furious and responded, 'We did not intend Mr Cotton's visit to be made known. We are not seeking publicity about the matter, it is no gimmick. We are giving it a trial because we feel if it gives our players some help in the slightest way it is worthwhile.'

Although the build up had been low key all week with Horace Yates writing in the Post on the morning of the game that the atmosphere 'had seldom been calmer' he predicted that once the fans were inside Anfield it would be different. He also suggested that the teams were as evenly matched as ever and that a key factor in the game would be the Liverpool defence's ability to cope with Everton's finesse in attack. The turnstiles would open at 12.15pm with spectators being urged to move into the middle of the terracing as quickly as possible, while it was also revealed that 200 Boys Pen tickets remained which would be on sale up until noon.

There was good news for fans arriving at the ground when they learned that St John had passed a fitness test on the morning of the match, meaning Arrowsmith was forced to drop out and instead play for the reserves in the mini derby at Goodison. Shankly also made the bold decision to drop Moran and play Ferns, who had done nothing wrong in his games at left half during Willie Stevenson's absence. The hero of the day though was Ian Callaghan who scored as many goals in this game as he had in the whole of 1962-63, to give Kopites a victory they would remember for a long time.

The teams came out of the tunnel side by side, as was tradition then in derby games but Everton won the toss and elected to change ends, meaning the Reds would be kicking into the Kop for the first half. They aimed to cause further frustration by playing Denis Stevens as an extra half back in a bid to stifle the Liverpool attack, a tactic that had worked so well for other teams at Anfield so far. However Everton almost gifted the Reds an early lead when Roy Vernon gave the ball away to Hunt but he shot straight at Gordon West after having a clear run on goal. The Reds were then forced to defend as both Derek Temple and Alex Scott caused problems down the flanks, and on one occasion Tommy Lawrence came out of his goal to catch a cross and then Ron Yeats hooked another dangerous centre to safety.

After a breakneck start the game turned into a dour defensive affair with the Reds being restricted to long range efforts. Stevenson saw his shot easily saved and Callaghan hit one along the ground that went well wide. At the other end Everton sorely missed Young's presence and Yeats easily dealt with any attacks that came his way. Their best opportunities came down the wings where Ferns was struggling to deal with Scott, while on the other side ex-Liverpool player Johnny Morrissey laid off nicely for Temple who let the ball run for an unmarked Vernon, but to the relief of the home crowd he was offside. Morrissey then got the better of Gerry Byrne and crossed for Vernon, and although his header beat Lawrence it was a weak one and Stevenson was able to clear off the line.

There were fears the Reds may go down to ten men when Gordon Milne pulled up after overstretching for a pass, but after some treatment from reserve trainer Joe Fagan who was standing in for the unwell Bob Paisley, he was able to continue. The game finally came to life three minutes before half time when a poor clearance fell to the feet of St John whose instinctive shot bounced down off the crossbar and spun back into the arms of Gordon West. There were appeals that it had crossed the line but the referee played safe and waved play on after his linesman, who was poorly positioned, failed to raise his flag. However, Horace Yates would write in the *Daily Post* the following Monday 'I fail to see, judging purely on the angle of descent, how the ball can fail to have crossed the line.'

The disappointment of St John's 'goal' not being allowed to stand was overcome less than two minutes later when Jimmy Melia passed to Callaghan and with no options available to him he simply let fly, the ball soaring into the top corner of the net giving West no chance. If this goal was a stunner, the same could not be said of his second, which came three minutes after half time. Collecting a Melia pass on the edge of the box, he hit a weak left foot shot that bounced along the ground but rather than gather the ball with his hands, West swung his boot at it and missed, meaning he could only watch in horror as it rolled slowly into the net.

Everton, already deflated after their European Cup exit, accepted the inevitable and the game descended into a training contest as they shut up shop at the back but Liverpool made no great determined effort to break them down. When Everton did try venturing forward the Reds defence dealt with things easily but with sixteen minutes remaining, failure to play to the whistle gave Everton a lifeline. Scott crossed and Temple headed down for Vernon to sweep the ball home as the Reds appealed for an offside flag that never came. This set up a frantic finale, which saw Lawrence save well from Temple and Vernon twice see shots go inches wide in a frantic last quarter of an hour. It wouldn't be a derby without some scuffles and Yeats and Kay tangled with each other after the Reds defender had carried the ball forward, but it didn't stop the handshakes at the end after the referee blew for full time to the delight and relief of Kopites.

It had been a deserved victory for the Reds who had shown great tenacity and worked well for each other. For Toxteth lad Callaghan, who was just 21 years old, it was a dream derby and he had now exceeded his goals tally for the whole of 1962-63. After the match, he said of his first goal, which came from a shot as powerful as any Billy Liddell had ever scored from, 'As I got the ball the defence suddenly fell away from me. They fanned out and to the surprise of my life gave me a clear sight of goal. The thought flashed through my mind – this is too good to last – and so I shot. You know the rest.'[16] Years later he would say it was the derby experience that stood out the most, writing in *The Ian Callaghan Story in 1975*, 'The one that stands out the most happened on 28th September 1963. It's a date that will always have a magical ring about it for me. I have never been a prolific scorer but that day I surprised myself and I suppose most other people by scoring both our goals in a 2-1 win.'

Not everybody in the ground had seen both Callaghan's goals though, with the new Kemlyn Road stand again coming in for criticism. One disgruntled fan, Mr Moon from Venice Street in Anfield, wrote a letter to the Echo that was published ten days later. Signing off as a 'disgusted season ticket holder' he wrote:

> 'Could not something be done about the constant parade of police in front of the new Kemlyn Road stand. Instead of seeing the back of a bulging net all I and many others saw was the bulging end of a cop. A dozen or more of us decided that we had no alternative but to stand when the parade started again in the second half. This we have decided to do in the future but it only causes abusive remarks from those behind. If they think we are going to rush on the field and riot like Continentals then

treat us that way. It would be more comfortable sitting behind barbed wire. I'm sure I speak for at least the first five rows '

While Mr Moon was unhappy with the view from his seat, somebody calling themselves only 'Red Fan' from Salisbury Road in Wavertree wasn't impressed with the fact the builders hadn't taken everything away with them. 'They build a brand new stand that looks fine but have you noticed the mess that has been left in the corner of the Kop where the old stand finished? Old buckets, old timber and sheets of metal left by the contractors.'[17]

The problems caused by the new stand aside, Liverpool's fans were happy. This win lifted them above Everton to eighth in the table and just three points behind leaders Manchester United with ten games played. As enjoyable as a derby win was though, you got the same two points for winning this game as any other and it was essential that the Reds kept the momentum going in the upcoming games.

Liverpool: Lawrence, Byrne, Ferns, Milne, Yeats, Stevenson, Callaghan, Hunt, St John, Melia, Thompson.

Everton: West, Parker, Brown, Kay, Labone, Harris, Scott, Stevens, Temple, Vernon, Morrissey.

Referee: Mr W. Clements (West Bromwich).

Attendance: 51,973.

5th October 1963: Liverpool 5 Aston Villa 2, Football League Division One

In the midweek after the derby there were seven First Division fixtures but Liverpool were one of the teams with a free week. However, this didn't give Bill Shankly an opportunity to have all his players together for a week's training as four were absent at the start of the week playing for the Football League against the League of Ireland in Dublin. They were Ian Callaghan, Roger Hunt, Gordon Milne and Jimmy Melia.

In front of 20,000 at Dalymount Park on Wednesday 2nd October, Liverpool's Milne and Hunt combined to set up West Ham's Johnny Byrne for the opening goal, but the League of Ireland sprung a surprise in the second half when they came from behind to win 2-1. The winning goal was scored by St Patrick's forward Ronnie Whelan senior, whose son Ronnie would go on to star for Liverpool in the 1980s.

The performance of Melia, Milne and Hunt was enough to convince Alf Ramsey to name them in the England side for the forthcoming international with Wales on 12th October. Ian St John, who had been watched by Scottish selectors in the derby, was also handed a call-up for his country's game against Northern Ireland in Belfast. This meant that Liverpool's scheduled trip to Birmingham City that day was postponed and the Reds were now in a run of four successive home games.

Once the dust had settled from the derby and the analysis completed in the local papers on the Monday, there was no other Liverpool-related news in the Post or Echo until the Thursday and even then it was to do with the opposition. The Echo reported that Villa manager Joe Mercer would be making some changes to the side. He was taking into account not only the fact that his side also had a game with Everton on the Monday, but recent poor form that had seen them lose four out of five home games. Amongst the changes was Scottish youth captain and future Arsenal manager George Graham getting a chance at inside left in place of Phil Woosnam, while another saw future Everton manager Gordon Lee move from defence to left half in place of Alan Deakin who was dropped.

On the day before the game Shankly confirmed that Phil Ferns would retain his place in the side at the expense of Ronnie Moran, leading to speculation over who would take the penalties. The Liverpool boss refused to divulge to the *Daily Post* who would be given the responsibility but did say the players would know what to do and that there were 'two or three possibilities.'

Following on from the news that Liverpool's players had seen a psychoanalyst prior to the Everton game, Shankly confirmed that he was still available to them if required. However there would be no more group sessions and it was up to them to arrange individual appointments if they felt they needed any help. He told the Echo's Leslie Edwards, 'It is now up to the players to consult Mr Cotton individually if they wish. He is a busy man and can only see them of an evening.'

As the Reds were making their final preparations for the match, fifteen people arrested in connection with the Great Train Robbery were making their first appearances at Aylesbury Crown Court. Driver Jack Mills told the court how he was clubbed from behind and made to drive the train to the point at where the mailbags were unloaded.

At Anfield on 5th October, Liverpool were nearly robbed themselves although it would have been due to their own carelessness. After cruising into a 2-0 lead they allowed Villa back into the game but eventually ran out 5-2 winners thanks to a fine second half performance.

Morning rain meant the surface was wet leading to the ball being slippery, something the Reds players tried to take advantage of early on but Villa keeper Nigel Sims held on well to Callaghan's cross. Peter Thompson then beat two men but his shot went high into the Kop, towards which the Reds were kicking after losing the toss for the second week running. St John also missed a good early opportunity, volleying wide after a poor clearance came towards him.

It didn't take long for the Reds to seize the initiative though as St John scored after ten minutes, poking the ball past Sims after Stevenson had played it into the area. Just a minute later, St John and Roger Hunt were at sixes-and-sevens when they both jumped for a corner, the ball rebounding off each of their heads before going over the bar. However in the fourteenth minute it was 2-0 when Melia exchanged passes with St John before crossing low for Callaghan to sweep the ball into the net from close range.

Villa were now demoralised and Ferns tried a cheeky lob from long range, but Sims held on to it easily, but he had no chance of saving a fierce Callaghan drive which just skimmed the bar. With three goals in two games, Callaghan was enjoying a new found confidence and a dangerous cross from him had to be turned away for a corner by John Sleeuwenhoek. Liverpool were coasting along but they let Villa back into the game in the 35th minute when Tony Hateley, who would join the Reds in 1967, pulled a goal back when there had looked no danger. The Kop was just finishing a rendition of *When the Reds go marching in* as Ron Wylie crossed the ball towards the box, but rather than attack it the defence stood still and the ball fell to Hateley who unleashed an unstoppable shot past Tommy Lawrence. Just after this Villa were almost level when Hateley played a perfect through ball towards Harry Burrows, but Ron Yeats got back just in time to make a crucial interception.

Liverpool were spurred into action and Hunt went on a good run but ran the ball out of play, then Sims collected crosses from both Callaghan and Thompson. With a minute to go until half time the crowd were stunned when Villa equalised thanks to Hateley's second goal. Yeats gave away an unnecessary corner that was taken by Wylie and the Villa striker scored with a tremendous header which Leslie Edwards couldn't speak highly enough of in his report for the *Liverpool Echo*. 'Not since the days of Dean have I seen a centre forward get up so high and make such a deliberate header. The ball fairly rocketed in to put Villa level.'

Hateley, a 22 year-old, had joined Villa from Third Division Notts County in the summer and it could be that his two goals here were remembered by Shankly when he broke the club's transfer record to take him to Anfield in 1967. If that was the case he certainly wasn't showing it as afterwards, Shankly said that Hateley could have shot twenty times in similar circumstances to the first goal and not scored.[18]

The second half saw Villa start off more brightly and the prospect of a fourth home defeat played on the minds of fans briefly, but just four minutes after the restart the Reds restored their lead after being handed a fortunate break. Melia played the ball to St John but he fell over, making it look like the opportunity had been lost, but Villa's defence only half cleared the ball to Thompson, who hit a shot that gave Sims no chance. This had the crowd going again but for all their possession the Reds couldn't create many more chances with Villa successfully employing the offside trap. There was a scare when George Graham was sent clear after the Reds defence had gone too far forward and Lawrence had to race out of his goal to make a sliding tackle.

Although the Reds were generally in control of the game, Villa's first half comeback meant the fans remained on edge and it wasn't until the 68th minute that their nerves were eased when Sims made his first error of the game. He handled the ball outside the area to concede a free kick which defenders managed to clear away for a corner. But from this the Villa keeper dropped the ball at the feet of Hunt who was happy to walk it into an empty net.

A few moments later the Reds almost had a fifth when Sleeuwenhoek intercepted a cross but almost ended up turning it into his own net, and Sims also dropped the ball over the goal line from a cross but to his relief the referee had signalled a foul. Alan Baker had a chance to reduce the arrears but his shot was tame and went wide then in the 77th minute Hunt got his second goal to put the game beyond doubt. Ferns played a brilliant cross-field pass to Melia whose ball into the box was nodded into the net by the Reds striker with Sims in no-man's land.

Villa were totally deflated following Liverpool's fifth goal and with Sims wavering, Callaghan tried his luck from thirty yards but the Villa keeper held on to his shot. Hunt then hit an effort across the face of goal but it went just wide. It had been a day when Liverpool's forward line had clicked perfectly and with a little more luck the Reds may well have had ten. In his *Daily Post* column the following Tuesday St John wrote that 'the moves we have practised so religiously came off' and that Ian Callaghan was 'tickled pink at his scoring burst.' However he did express concern at conceding two goals, writing, 'It put a nasty taste in the mouth to see two goals go in at the other end. That has happened too often at Anfield this season for comfort.'

The win meant that Liverpool were eighth in the table, four points behind leaders Manchester United but with a game in hand, and with the Anfield hoodoo well and truly quashed they were full of confidence looking ahead to the next two home games.

Liverpool: Lawrence, Byrne, Ferns, Milne, Yeats, Stevenson, Callaghan, Hunt, St John, Melia, Thompson.

Villa: Sims, Wright, Aitken, Crowe, Sleeuwenhoek, Lee, Wylie, Baker, Hateley, Graham, Burrows.

Referee: Mr J. Pickles (Southport).

Attendance: 39,106.

9th October 1963: Liverpool 3 Sheffield Wednesday 1, Football League Division One

As the Reds looked for a third straight win there was a word of caution from Leslie Edwards in his column in the *Liverpool Echo* on the Tuesday night (8th October). He wrote that complacency had allowed an extremely poor Villa side back into the game on the Saturday after the Reds had gone into an early 2-0 lead and that better quality teams could well have gone on to win the game.

Wednesday were thirteenth in the table and had lost four of their six away games so far, with their biggest threat coming from centre forward David 'Bronco' Layne. He was a player in the Hateley mould who would pose a physical test for Ron Yeats and who many journalists believed was deserving of an England call up. However Edwards wrote that the Reds should have enough to win the game, and it was on this day that he stated for the first time that season that they had a good chance of winning the title. He wrote on the evening of the match, 'Interest in Liverpool FC is getting white hot. It would not surprise me if towards the end of the season our two senior clubs are running neck and neck for the title.' That morning Horace Yates, who had been bold enough to predict it at the start of the season, had commented in the *Daily Post* that 'there could be nothing more absorbing than a Liverpool and Everton duel for the title. Is it too much to expect? Not at all.'

The win against Villa had certainly increased interest among fans, as 46,107 turned out, 7,000 up on that game. They would have to be patient but eventually they saw the persistence of the Reds pay off as the players put in an attractive display to take both points after going behind early on. Wednesday took the game to the Reds at the start, Alan Finney having a great dribble before shooting just wide. Then they took the lead in the eleventh minute when Edwin Holliday took a pass from John Quinn before hitting a shot that Tommy Lawrence couldn't hold. As the Reds keeper and Yeats got in each other's way trying to deal with the rebound, Holliday nipped in to score.

Wednesday almost doubled their lead when a neat backheel by Quinn gave Layne a great shooting opportunity but he hit tamely at Lawrence. Liverpool's defence and midfield were so open that Peter Swan was able to carry the ball sixty yards before shooting wide, but slowly the men in the middle of the park managed to assert their authority and take some control. Gordon Milne's passes started to find the right men and Roger Hunt had a good shot saved by Ron Springett, before a dipping Ian Callaghan volley went just past the post. Ian St John should have scored when Jimmy Melia passed back to him but he shot wide and Callaghan, Milne and Willie Stevenson all went close. The equaliser eventually came on the stroke of half time and was no more than the Reds deserved. Peter Thompson's corner was missed by Springett and landed at the feet of Callaghan who centred back across the goal for St John to head into an empty net.

Those who hadn't gone to the match and instead stayed at home had the opportunity to watch the BBC documentary *The Mersey Sound* which focused on Liverpool's music scene but didn't portray the city in too good a light, something many would see as a recurring theme in future years. It highlighted protection rackets, fights in clubs in which the police didn't intervene, and that clubs were being run by bouncers. This led to a denial by Deputy Chief Constable Herbert Balmer, who told the Echo that he did not believe there were any protection rackets in operation and that officers patrolled the streets to maintain order outside clubs, however they could not enter unless they had a warrant or were invited in. As such, bouncers generally ejected any troublemakers themselves and he saw no problem with this as the police would then deal with any aftermath outside.

It's been said by Liverpool people for many years that their city has been given a rough deal by Manchester-based media. When challenged by the Echo, the Manchester-based makers of the programme then backtracked regarding protection rackets saying, 'The reference to protection money was in the past. It was not suggested that anyone was being paid protection money nowadays.'

Liverpool began the second half as they had ended the first, dominating possession and creating all the chances. St John played a beautiful ball to Hunt but although he rounded Springett the ball ran out of play. Then they had a goal disallowed in contentious circumstances when St John scored, only for the referee to disallow it for a foul by Hunt. The linesman, whose raised flag had led to the goal being ruled out, found himself getting abuse by the crowd for the rest of the game as Liverpool continued to dominate with Milne and Stevenson winning every midfield battle to then launch attacks for the forwards. Springett though was in inspired form and made two brilliant saves from Thompson then another from Hunt.

The game was the most entertaining at Anfield to date that season but as Wednesday continued to defend desperately they resorted to some tough tackling, leading to some deriding comments from fans on the Kop. Finally in the 76th minute the Reds took the lead, the goal again coming from a Thompson corner as St John's header was beaten away by Springett only to fall at the feet of Melia who drove it into the net. Callaghan and Thompson forced saves from Springett as the Reds looked for a third but they had a let-off when a Layne goal was ruled out for offside. Seconds before full time Hunt hit the ball upfield to waste time, Swan missed his kick allowing St John to run on to the ball and fire it past the keeper to give the final score the margin the Reds' dominance had deserved.

Liverpool's captain Yeats said it had been a great game to play in and that the goal that was conceded early on was down to 'too many defenders spoiling the broth by being in the same place at the same time.' He believed that Wednesday had put too much effort into the first half that they couldn't keep the same pace for the rest of the game and of their danger man Layne he said, 'Bronco has a great reputation but he failed to live up to it for some reason or another and gave no trouble.'

One Wednesday player that stood out for Yeats was keeper Springett, who he described as 'magnificent' and although all of Liverpool's players had played very well he jokingly reserved praise for Melia, who scored the second goal, saying 'Jimmy is getting a bit uppish about the number of goals he is getting. Last year he scored five, this year he has now scored three. He is throwing out his chest and talking in terms of new records.'[19]

Around half an hour after the game finished, there was a tragedy in northern Italy when a landslide caused a dam to overflow, leading to a huge wave that engulfed the town of Longarone and killed more than 2,000 people. The Echo, which rarely led with national stories let alone international ones, had the story as its main headline on 10th October, describing how houses were 'crushed like matchwood.' Although the dam itself had been secure, the area in which it was developed was not and it was known for the instability which led to the level rising by 300 feet after the landslide. It was an example of how the drive for profits by the local electricity company led to a disregard of safety as the construction continued despite independent experts telling them of their concerns. Mario Pancini, the engineer of the dam project, killed himself prior to attending court to explain what he knew about the geology of the area prior to the construction.

Liverpool: Lawrence, Byrne, Ferns, Milne, Yeats, Stevenson, Callaghan, Hunt, St John, Melia, Thompson.

Wednesday: Springett, Hill, Megson, McAnearney, Swan, Young, Finney, Quinn, Layne, Pearson, Holliday.

Referee: Mr J.K. Taylor (Wolverhampton).

Attendance: 46,107.

19th October 1963: Liverpool 1 West Bromwich Albion 0, Football League Division One

The day after Liverpool beat Sheffield Wednesday, politics was thrown into turmoil with the announcement that Prime Minister Harold MacMillan was resigning. The 69-year-old had gone into hospital two days earlier and was operated on for a prostatic obstruction while other Tories were gathering in Blackpool for their party conference.

Foreign Secretary Lord Home made the announcement to the conference, reading out a letter from MacMillan who had told the British people in 1957 that 'they have never had it so good.' MacMillan stated that the physical burden of leading his party into the next General Election was too great and it now meant a power battle was under way with Deputy Prime Minister Rab Butler and Lord President Lord Hailsham the front runners. Politics the other side of the Atlantic was in the news too, as the House of Representatives vetoed President Kennedy's proposals for a joint mission to the Moon with the Soviet Union.

Saturday 12th October was a blank one for the Reds due to international call ups, the scheduled game at Birmingham being postponed. Given the number of postponements that had been endured due to the weather the previous season, having nowhere to go on a Saturday afternoon was not such a new experience for fans but some did use the opportunity to watch the reserves who were in action against Sheffield Wednesday at Anfield. Alf Arrowsmith gave a reminder of his scoring abilities when he hit four in a 5-2 win watched by crowd of 4,636, which was 1,000 more than the previous highest attendance in the Central League that season.

Bill Shankly took the opportunity of a free Saturday to go on a scouting mission, heading back to his native Scotland to take in St Mirren v Rangers at Love Street. It was believed that the player he was taking a look at was Cameron Murray who was also being tailed by Wolves and Second Division promotion hopefuls Chelsea. It wasn't just Shankly who was watching football as Jimmy Melia, Peter Thompson and Ron Yeats went to Deepdale to watch Preston versus Swindon. Others though had a more relaxing weekend with Phil Ferns spending it watching racing on the television, Willie Stevenson having a visit from his parents, and Ian Callaghan going camping.

In the international games, Gordon Milne put in a solid performance as England beat Wales 4-0 at Ninian Park, but Roger Hunt was not used in the game. Milne's performance was enough to earn him a call up for the forthcoming game against the Rest of the World on 23rd October. In Belfast, Ian St John was on the scoresheet for Scotland against Northern Ireland but they surprisingly went down 2-1. Writing in his column in the *Daily Post* the following Monday he said that the Irish players were 'fired with enthusiasm' and 'scarcely gave us a kick of the ball.' The referee for the match was coincidentally Mr Taylor who had been in charge of the Liverpool v Sheffield Wednesday game and St John took the opportunity to ask him about his disallowed goal. He was told that it was due to a foul by Hunt, but St John admitted he still couldn't see what the problem had been. His first thought was that the goal was disallowed as a penalty was being awarded because Hunt was being fouled, not the other way around.

Although the Reds were in a run of four successive home games, away fixtures weren't far from the mind and fans were relieved to hear that the 'football special' trains weren't going to be scrapped following some recent bouts of vandalism. The *Liverpool Echo* reported on 11th October that after a meeting of railway officials and police representatives it had been decided that the trains would continue, but there would no longer be any half fares for children. The reason for this was that the latest incidents that had occurred on a train carrying Everton supporters to Birmingham had been carried out by fans buying child tickets despite being the age at which full fares needed to be paid.

The issue of footballers' contracts was still being discussed in light of the Eastham case. On 16th October the *Daily Post* reported that contracts longer than the current maximum of two years were being proposed by the Football League, but that restrictions were also being sought on how much players could engage with the media. Another proposal, which would have a direct impact on Liverpool's players, was the payment of bonuses which the League envisaged as being paid on a quarterly rather than weekly basis. It was clear that more discussions were needed with Cliff Lloyd of the Professional Footballers Association saying that they would meet again in November and that it would be June before anything was finalised, at the League's Annual General Meeting. One player who wouldn't be offered a contract at Anfield though was trailist Roy Rudham, who was told after two months that he wasn't up to the required standard. Liverpool offered him a flight home at their expense but instead he opted to stay in England and seek trials with other clubs.

On Friday 18th October, the issue of who would be the next Prime Minister was settled at the recommendation of the outgoing MacMillan. Foreign Secretary Lord Home was asked to form the next administration by the Queen, but as he was a peer in the House of Lords it meant that he had to stand as MP in a safe seat to get him into the House of Commons. Conveniently, a vacancy had just arisen in Kinross and West Perthshire due to the recent death of Gilmour Leburn and all he had to do to stand was renounce his earldom.

On the same day when it was confirmed that Home was to be the new Prime Minister, Goodison Park was announced as one of the venues for the 1966 World Cup which was to be held in England. Anfield may have had improvements of late with the new Kemlyn Road stand but it was still a long way behind Goodison, which held 73,000 and was described by Horace Yates in the Post that day as 'probably the finest club ground in England.' It was announced that Goodison would stage three group games as well as a quarter-final and semi-final. Yates wrote that the stadium had been unfairly neglected for representative games but that it now had 'atonement with a vengeance.'

In the period since the Wednesday game, news directly relating to Liverpool FC had been very thin on the ground and it wasn't until the Leslie Edwards preview of the West Bromwich Albion game in the Echo on the Friday night that fans had something of interest to read about. He reported that Albion had some injury concerns, including right back Don Howe who had tonsillitis, and that a Liverpool win was probable although it wouldn't be easy. It was a prediction that wasn't too far out as on a windy day at Anfield the Reds notched up a narrow 1-0 win, their third successive victory, to lift them up into fifth place.

On a windy day Liverpool won the toss and Yeats unsurprisingly allowed Albion to kick into the Kop for the first half. It meant that the Reds had the wind with them for the first period but it was almost their undoing early on. Graham Williams hit a long ball upfield which swirled in the wind and was misjudged by Yeats, but thankfully the offside flag was also raised denying Albion forwards a clear run on goal. Shortly after this Melia almost scored from a corner when he let fly from Thompson's knock-down but his shot went just wide of the post. In difficult conditions both sides struggled to get any real rhythm going, but it was the Reds who had the more possession and even Gerry Byrne was joining the attacks, finding space for a shot that failed to trouble Ray Potter.

With Albion's side containing a number of inexperienced players, Liverpool remained in control and missed a good chance to go ahead when Willie Stevenson had a great run and passed to Hunt but rather than shoot, he laid off for St John who wasn't anticipating it and the ball ran beyond him. Despite having the wind on their side the Reds weren't testing the keeper often enough and they had an injury scare when St John collided with some photographers behind the goal and had to be treated by Bob Paisley for several minutes as the game carried on. He was able to resume although he was limping for a while, yet still managed to get in a dipping shot that only just went over the bar. On a rare foray into opposition territory Albion almost took an undeserved lead midway through the half when Ken Foggo had a shot that Yeats blocked. The deflection wrong-footed Tommy Lawrence but to the relief of nearly everyone in the ground the ball went wide.

In the 34th minute the Reds finally made the breakthrough, Milne playing a one-two with St John and beating Potter with a shot that gave him no chance. Before the break Milne almost got a second but Potter palmed away his fierce shot from the right side of the area. Liverpool then carried on where they left off in the second half, with Thompson testing Potter within seconds of the restart. There seemed to be plenty of niggling fouls going on in the game and the referee often held play up by insisting free kicks were taken from exactly the same spot where they were conceded. He also had reason to have words with Byrne after he brought down Clive Clark.

With the wind behind them, Albion searched for the equaliser and Lawrence faced some problems, only parrying a Clark shot but managing to then punch it out of play for a corner. The kick was taken and he misjudged it in the wind but defenders managed to clear. Conditions were made worse by the falling rain but Liverpool managed to reassert their authority with Melia going close with a shot and Thompson having an effort turned over the bar for a corner. Melia then set up Hunt but his shot was weak and went wide as the crowd started to turn restless at the inability of the Reds to increase their lead. They were almost handed a second goal on a plate though when Alex Jackson played a terrible back-pass to Potter. The keeper failed to hold on to the ball first time but, before any forwards could pounce he managed to grab it. Another pass back to the keeper also fell short but although Hunt capitalised on it, his shot was cleared off the line as was St John's effort from the rebound. Stan Jones was the defender in both cases.

Jackson almost atoned for his earlier errors when he shot just wide and it was only Albion's inability to get a grip of the wind and time their passes right that kept Lawrence from having much to do. When instead they tried to keep hold of the ball and run at the defence, Byrne and Ferns were solid with their tackles, the latter continuing to show why he was now being preferred to Ronnie Moran. In their anxiety the crowd chanted 'Thompson, Thompson, Thompson,' knowing that the Reds winger could run at defenders and create something out of nothing. They got their wish when he took the ball and had a run and shot, but it went inches wide.

In the dying seconds Albion almost got an equaliser when Tony Brown went on a twisting run through a static Reds defence, but Lawrence came out of his goal to dive at his feet and gather the ball. It would have been barely deserved, but the Reds failure to remain in total control for the whole of the ninety minutes was almost their undoing. As it was, results elsewhere were favourable and Liverpool were now fifth in the table, just two points behind leaders Manchester United after yielding maximum points from their four successive home games. It was extremely tight at the top though, with just two points separating ten teams, but the Reds had a great chance to keep their momentum going as they faced bottom of the table Ipswich in their next game.

Liverpool: Lawrence, Byrne, Ferns, Milne, Yeats, Stevenson, Callaghan, Hunt, St John, Melia, Thompson.

Albion: Potter, Drury, Williams, Fraser, Jones, Simpson, Foggo, Brown, Cram, Jackson, Clark.

Referee: Mr H. Wilson (Stockton-on-Tees).

Attendance: 43,099.

Top of Table

		Pl	W	D	L	F	A	GA	Pt
1	Manchester United	13	8	3	2	30	13	2.31	19
2	Tottenham	13	8	3	2	45	26	1.73	19
3	Sheffield United	14	7	5	2	29	18	1.61	19
5	Liverpool	13	8	1	4	28	16	1.75	17

8

The Leicester Bogey

As Liverpool approached the end of October, the season was almost a third over and they had every reason to be satisfied with their position in the league table after four straight wins. They were able to take this form into November as they continued to rise up the table, but once again they failed to beat a side against whom they had lost all three games the previous season.

26th October 1963: Ipswich Town 1 Liverpool 2, Football League Division One

Before Liverpool were back in league action with a long trip to Suffolk to take on Ipswich, three Liverpool players had to report to the FA training headquarters at Roehampton to prepare for a match against the Rest of the World on Wednesday 22nd October. However, despite training with the party, Peter Thompson and Roger Hunt weren't selected for the game leaving Gordon Milne as Liverpool's sole representative in the side for a match which was arranged to celebrate the centenary of the FA. Pele was arguably the best player in the world at the time but he couldn't be persuaded to appear in the game, although big names that did agree to take part included Eusebio and Ferenc Puskas.

The recent run of home games had given more opportunity for fans to have their say about the new Kemlyn Road stand. Following the Everton game Mr Moon from Anfield had expressed his disgust that a policeman had obstructed his view of one of Ian Callaghan's goals in the derby and now Mr Wren from Formby was just as frustrated. On 22nd October a letter from him was published in the *Liverpool Echo* which said, 'There is the unnecessary parade of policemen obstructing the view for ten minutes of every match. This is 11% of the ninety minutes.' What irked Mr Wren more than anything though was the fact that he was a season ticket holder getting wet when it rained, while those who bought one-off tickets were dry.

> 'A supporter who has paid for a season ticket after waiting a very long time for the opportunity should not have to sit almost on the pitch and get a soaking every time that it rains. The Aston Villa match gave an unpleasant foretaste of what we can expect when the weather gets really bad. The entire wing stands are at present set aside for ordinary weekly tickets. It would be more logical to have about the first ten rows for about the entire length of the stand for ordinary tickets with season tickets in the

rear. Surely season ticket holders should have the better seats and these are not in the exposed front rows, where one cannot see the pattern of the play properly.'

Liverpool's recent good form had meant that it wasn't just people connected with Anfield that saw them as title challengers, with Everton manager Harry Catterick tipping them to be there or thereabouts at the end of the season. Ian St John noted this in his *Daily Post* column on 22nd October, but he didn't believe Everton were the team the Reds had to finish above to be champions. Instead he pointed to Tottenham Hotspur, who had a top scorer in Jimmy Greaves in their ranks, as the most likely challengers.

St John's ankle was giving some fans concern as he had not looked at his best against West Bromwich after receiving treatment from Bob Paisley. But he re-assured fans that it was something that had troubled him for a year and he was receiving treatment on a daily basis from Paisley to ensure he could play in games.

Bill Shankly travelled to London to watch Milne in action for England as they beat the Rest of the World 2-1. Only the brilliant goalkeeping of Russian Lev Yashin kept the score down as the opposition, having reportedly been paid £1,000 each to appear, strolled through the game. The match programme had described Milne as the least known of the England team but he put in a performance that belied this, tackling and winning the ball, carrying it and distributing it perfectly. Shankly told Leslie Edwards, who covered the game for the Post and Echo, that he had done too much and left Bobby Moore with the simple task of solely defending.

Peter Thompson may have been unable to get into the side for the game but an Under-23 call-up beckoned, with the Post reporting on 24th October that both he and Callaghan looked set to face Wales in Bristol the following month. It is often the case today that managers discourage international call-ups, but Shankly was enthusiastic about the possibility, telling Edwards, 'Thompson should go into the international side, he is better than Charlton on present form. In fact I don't think you can find two wingers better anywhere than Thompson and Callaghan.'

It wasn't just England who were looking at the Reds side, with Scottish selectors enquiring as to the availability of Tommy Lawrence, Willie Stevenson, St John and Ron Yeats for their forthcoming British Championship game with Wales.

The journey to an Ipswich side managed by Newcastle legend Jackie Milburn was by far the most uncomfortable one that the Reds faced that season and they made the bulk of the trip by plane on the Friday, flying to RAF Horsham and spending the night in Norwich. Shankly was hoping to name an unchanged side with Phil Ferns now firmly established at left back and Edwards wrote in the *Daily Post* that, 'He has not done anything since his introduction to the side to undermine Mr Shankly's faith in him. He is a player not lacking confidence in himself who will thrive on encouragement.' As a precaution, Ronnie Moran accompanied the party due to Milne nursing a slight leg injury sustained at Wembley on the Wednesday night. If Milne was forced to drop out, it was anticipated that the versatile Ferns would play at right half with Moran slotting in at left back. Ipswich, who were bottom of the table with just one win from their opening fifteen games, had more problems to contend with as their regular keeper Roy Bailey was ruled out with a knee injury.

In contrast to the team's plane journey of about an hour, the two coachloads of Liverpool fans making the trip had to endure an overnight ride, setting off at 11.30pm. They arrived about ten hours later at the Ipswich Supporters club where a breakfast was laid on for them. Whereas the team were expected to arrive home by 8pm, the fans would not be back until the early hours of Sunday morning but it was just about a worthwhile journey as the Reds held on for victory.

Milne passed a late fitness test so the Reds remained unchanged, but Ipswich had a further blow when centre forward Ted Phillips was declared unfit shortly before the game and had to be replaced by Doug Moran. The game initially got off to a slow start but within ten minutes of kick off there were two goals, both coming after defensive mistakes. The first came when Jimmy Melia seized on a poor backpass by Robert Blackwood and rounded Bevis to score, but within a minute Ipswich were level. Joe Broadfoot crossed from the right and Yeats failed to clear it properly, instead just playing into the path of Danny Hegan who turned the ball into the net.

Ipswich's goal was a fillip for them and the Reds were on the backfoot for much of the first half with Melia having to drop back on occasions to help the defence. However, despite passing the ball around well, the home side were unable to find any way through a defence that remained solid and ready to put tackles in at the earliest opportunity. The closest they managed was when Broadfoot beat Ferns and put in a dangerous cross but Lawrence came off his line to keep hold of it. At the other end a rare opportunity came for the Reds when St John played a long ball out to Callaghan on the wing, allowing him a run on goal and shot, but it went inches over the bar.

After half an hour Ipswich began to lose some heart and Liverpool took control of the game with Melia and St John playing some wonderful touches and Callaghan posing a danger on the wing whenever he got the ball. A minute before half time Melia crossed from the right and St John flicked the ball on for Hunt to head the ball past Bevis to put the Reds ahead.

In the second half, rather than go flat out to try and finish the game off, the Reds seemed content to sit on their lead and were nearly punished for it. Broadfoot was giving Ferns a torrid time down the right flank and on a number of occasions Yeats had to get over and help his teammate out.

However, despite all the effort of the Ipswich players, they were not well-blessed with skill and the Reds were able to absorb the pressure.

Liverpool still had their chances after the break with Hunt hitting a shot just wide, Callaghan forcing Bevis into a save at the foot of the post, and St John firing straight at the keeper from ten yards. They were coasting along though but with Broadfoot a particular danger, there was always the worry that the home side may find an equaliser. Despite Broadfoot's ability, there was nobody able to convert his crosses and if Ipswich were going to equalise, then a set piece was perhaps the most likely source and from one corner both Ferns and Gerry Byrne were forced to make goal line clearances.

As the game drew to a close, Ipswich began to wilt a little and Liverpool's superior fitness allowed them to resume total control. St John had a header well saved by Bevis and in the last minute Hunt was sent clear but his clever chip over the keeper bounced off the bar and over. It was a deserved win for Liverpool but perhaps should not have been as close a scoreline as it was, with Jack Rowe writing in the *Daily Post* the following Monday that he had hoped to see 'a little more urgency in putting the game beyond the hope of an Ipswich recovery.'

The win was Liverpool's fifth on the trot and lifted them up to third place. Their title chances were now as good as anybody else's as they were only separated from second place Manchester United on goal average. They were two points behind leaders Sheffield United but did have a game in hand. With the next three matches being against teams in the bottom half of the table there was no reason to believe that the Reds couldn't keep this winning momentum going, or was there?

Liverpool: Lawrence, Byrne, Ferns, Milne, Yeats, Stevenson, Callaghan, Hunt, St John, Melia, Thompson.

Ipswich: Bevis, Bolton, Compton, Baxter, Nelson, Elsworthy, Broadfoot, Blackwood, Moran, Hegan, Leadbetter.

Referee: Mr W. Handley (Cannock).

Attendance: 16,356.

2nd November 1963: Liverpool 0 Leicester City 1, Football League Division One

In the run up to the Leicester game there was a surprise when the Scotland side was announced for a forthcoming match with Norway. Despite Liverpool having been approached a week earlier about the availability of four of their players, none were selected.

Managers nowadays would breathe a sigh of relief at players being left out of international sides but Bill Shankly was livid that they had been overlooked, commenting: 'I can only say it is highly mysterious how none of our players have been included in the party. Try as I will I cannot understand it. I am sorry for the boys who are all in top form, this is all out of our hands.'[20] Shankly also suggested that the selectors were looking for more home-based players, but one player from the English League who was called up was Leicester's Frank McLintock, a right half who was also very good at getting into attacking positions. He was seen as one of the main dangermen in their side as they headed to Anfield, as well as striker Mike Stringfellow.

Liverpool had lost twice in the league to Leicester the previous season as well as in the FA Cup semi-final. Shankly though was quick to dismiss any suggestion that this was a grudge match, with Horace Yates reporting in the *Daily Post* on the Thursday before the game that he had said, 'So far as we are concerned there is absolutely no feud between the clubs. I expect to see a very interesting game of football. They had the breaks last year, who can say they will get them again?'

The five successive wins that had lifted Liverpool up to third in the table was causing excitement for both players and fans. A full house was predicted at Anfield for a game that could see Liverpool go top of the table if Sheffield United lost. Ian St John wrote in his *Daily Post* column on 29th October that this would mean a £40 per man crowd bonus and that 'these were great and rewarding days for Liverpool.' Like Shankly, St John felt things would be different this time around on the pitch:

> 'They are certain to turn on their defensive brand of play which tied us in knots last time. They would be foolish not to. This time I believe we have the remedy. We are much stronger on the wings than we were and indeed our wingers could be the match winners for who better to turn the defence? Moreover our finishing is so much better, I am dying to see how they react to being a goal down, something they have never experienced against us.'

Leicester's side was expected to contain ten of the players who faced the Reds in the FA Cup semi-final just over six months earlier, the only change being Len Chalmers at right back instead of John Sjoberg. Leicester had finished fourth in the league and spent big in the summer, breaking their transfer record to sign Bobby Roberts from Motherwell for £40,000, and also splashing out £20,000 on Sheffield United's Bill Hodgson. However neither had been able to command a first team place in a side that were twelfth in the league.

There were concerns in the days before the game over the fitness of right back Gerry Byrne, who was unable to train for the first part of the week due to an injured knee. Shankly told reporters on the Friday that a decision would be made on the morning of the game with Ronnie Moran on standby. Bob Paisley had been putting Byrne under a course of intensive physiotherapy and the swelling came down enough for him to pass a fitness test, meaning Moran boarded the coach with the reserves at noon to head to Old Trafford for a Central League fixture with Manchester United. Back at Anfield though, the bogey struck again as Liverpool lost to Leicester and failed to score in a game that saw crowd trouble at Anfield for the first time that season.

Back then teams didn't come out of the tunnel together and Leicester took to the field first, antagonising the crowd by heading straight to the Kop where they were met by a barrage of missiles, boos, gesticulating and chants of 'We Want Football.' The Reds won the toss and the first thing Tommy Lawrence had to do when he took up his position in goal was to clear the penalty area of debris, which included several items of fruit. Soon after the start, the Reds were awarded a free kick near the touchline but before Phil Ferns took it the referee was handed an object by the linesman that had been thrown from the crowd. Leicester were tackling tough and solid at the back but they did try to get forward too, Howard Riley skipping past Willie Stevenson only to see his shot blocked. Liverpool's first chance was from a corner but Ian St John's header was easily held by Gordon Banks.

It was not a good game to watch, with neither side creating any clear opportunities and the defences coming out on top. When the Reds forwards did manage to get behind the Leicester defenders, Banks was always quickly off his line to clear the danger. He did have one awkward moment though when a combination of both the sun and a crowd of defenders left him unsighted as Peter Thompson's shot found its way through but he still managed to dive on the ball just in time. Leicester then took the lead in the 29th minute after an error by Yeats, whose poor clearance was seized upon by David Gibson. He squared the ball to Riley who drove it into the box where Ken Keyworth stretched his leg out to stab the ball into the net with Lawrence and the Reds defence believing there was no danger.

Liverpool almost equalised soon after the game restarted but St John headed over, then nerves crept in for the rest of the half as players didn't take responsibility for the ball and looked to just get it up the field as quickly as possible with no composure. They were fortunate when Ferns misplaced a header just before half time and the ball went out for a corner, but there wasn't enough time for it to be taken.

As Banks ran towards the Kop goal at the start of the second half he had toilet rolls and fruit thrown at him but didn't have much to do early on as Richard Norman was a rock in defence. He did need to haul back Melia at one point though as the Reds forward got past him but the free kick was headed over by St John. The game continued to be a rough one, McLintock having needed treatment in the first half and now Yeats was tended to by Paisley after receiving a cut above his left eye. Despite their defensive tactics Leicester looked dangerous when they broke, with even right back Chalmers having the confidence to get forward and join the attacks.

The Kop were beginning to turn their disgruntlement towards their own team rather than Leicester, but the atmosphere changed when Banks was out of his goal only for Callaghan's shot to be headed off the line by Ian King. This led to a sustained period of Liverpool pressure with Banks making two great saves, firstly from Yeats's towering header and then from a Stevenson drive which he held onto magnificently.

In the 72nd minute a moment of blind panic in the Leicester penalty area saw Chalmers head the ball past Banks as he tried to get in the way of a Callaghan shot only for it to bounce off the crossbar. It summed up the day though when things just wouldn't go right. Too many crosses from Callaghan and Thompson were too high for the forwards to reach, and Milne had one of his least convincing displays in a Red shirt doing only one thing of note when a fine low shot forced a good save from Banks.

The Reds remained open at the back as they pressed for an equaliser and only a last gasp tackle by Stevenson on Stringfellow prevented the Leicester forward from being clean through on goal. Near the end St John had a volley that went well wide and Callaghan hit a shot that beat Banks but went just past the post. At the final whistle, Milne chipped the ball towards an unguarded goal only for it to spin away from the goal line and run past the post, an irony that wasn't lost on the Kop.

After the game there were some reports of Leicester fans being verbally abused in the Main Stand car park, with one female also claiming that a male got hold of her shoulders and that she had been hit on the head by a plastic bottle. It was also claimed that missiles were thrown at the coach that took Leicester's players to Central station causing dents, but the police confirmed there were no complaints and Chairman T.V. Williams said:

> 'I saw the Leicester directors and their wives to the coach. I shook hands with their manager Mr Matt Gillies on the steps of the coach and I waved them away. There were not more than a dozen people left in the car park at that time. What happened, if anything, outside the ground I do not know because I was not there but I saw them safely off our premises. I was amazed when I read what was supposed to have happened.'[21]

Writing in the *Liverpool Echo* the following Monday, Leslie Edwards commented that the behaviour of some fans only inspired Leicester to victory. He believed booing and gestures were part of the game but when it came to throwing missiles it was a different matter altogether and as such Leicester's players 'had their dander up from the first moment.' St John though disagreed, writing in his *Daily Post* column on the Tuesday that the players had jokingly asked Reds keeper Tommy Lawrence if he enjoyed watching the game and that for the most part it was Gordon Banks v Liverpool.

Ron Yeats agreed as he accepted responsibility for the Leicester goal but also commented 'after this Tommy Lawrence hardly saw the ball.'[22] Had Liverpool won, they would have gone up to second in the league but as it was defeat saw them drop to sixth, but their next game at struggling Bolton where they were sure to have a large following, was a great chance to make amends.

Liverpool: Lawrence, Byrne, Ferns, Milne, Yeats, Stevenson, Callaghan, Hunt, St John, Melia, Callaghan.

Leicester: Banks, Chalmers, Norman, McLintock, King, Appleton, Riley, Cross, Keyworth, Gibson, Stringfellow.

Referee: Mr R Windle (Chesterfield).

Attendance: 47,438.

9th November 1963: Bolton Wanderers 1 Liverpool 2, Football League Division One

Despite the defeat to Leicester, Liverpool were still handily placed in the league but they could have been a point clear at the top with a game in hand if they'd won just two of the four games that had been lost at Anfield so far. Leslie Edwards had said in the Echo on the Monday after the Leicester game that the passion of the home crowd had inspired the visitors to victory, while three days later an interesting letter from a fan was published explaining why it also did harm to the home team. Mr Clay from Wigan had written,

> 'So fanatical, loyal and indeed passionate are the Liverpool supporters that Liverpool players feel that they have to perform miracles to live up to the standards of idolisation which the crowd shows. Hence they no longer play it cool. The cohesion disappears and the eagerness to grab a bagful of goals overwhelms the logical tactic of first of all weighing up the type of football the opposition is playing. Liverpool have undoubted potential as regards football ability but psychologically they still need to mature in order to reach the pinnacles of the game.'

The defeat to Leicester certainly led to raised eyebrows when it came to the crowd's reaction. Defeats earlier in the season had been accepted in a sporting manner but the vitriol extended to the Leicester players was something that had not been seen at Anfield before. Mr Burke from Aigburth believed he had the answer. Writing to the Echo asking why the 'most sporting of all soccer crowds' had acted so out of character, he answered the question himself by concluding that it had 'simply been the crowd's memory of the mean, childish behaviour of certain members of the Leicester team' who he claimed had 'directed derogatory words and gloating gestures in the direction of the Liverpool players and sections of the crowd' after the preceding season's FA Cup semi final.

Liverpool had a great opportunity to put the defeat behind them against Bolton,who were one of the youngest sides in the league and struggling near the foot of the table. To try and bolster their attack they had just signed winger Jimmy Davison from Sunderland for £15,000, and he would be making his debut against the Reds where he was hoping to provide some ammunition for young forward Francis Lee.

That week it was revealed that the club had been taking electrical equipment to away games that allowed them to treat injured players. It was believed they were the only club in the league to do so and the wireless-sized device had helped Gordon Milne take part in the game against Ipswich a few weeks earlier. Bill Shankly said that it wasn't a 'magical cure-all'[23] but it was the best thing he had seen in the game, although he was leaving the actual operation of it to Bob Paisley and Joe Fagan. It didn't do any good for Gerry Byrne though, who was ruled out of the Bolton game on the Friday with an injured knee. Bill Shankly confirmed that Ronnie Moran would return to the side at left back with Phil Ferns moving over to the right, his third position of the season after trying out the combination in two practice games at Melwood that week.

The Reds didn't stay overnight due to the trip being a short one and they were followed by a large contingent of fans, many of whom arrived two hours before kick off to ensure they obtained entry. One group of youths had some fireworks confiscated,and had they managed to get them into the ground they would have probably provided far more spark than the Reds who laboured to victory despite having most of the possession.

Liverpool started brightly, with Peter Thompson giving right back Roy Hartle a tough time and Bolton retreated so much that Willie Stevenson became a sixth forward, forcing Eddie Hopkinson to make a low diving save while Jimmy Melia also had a shot comfortably held. Bolton's new signing Davison was largely anonymous as the Reds dominated, having a clear penalty appeal turned down after Roger Hunt appeared to have been felled by John Hulme.

In the 25th minute the opening goal came when Melia played the ball wide to Ian Callaghan and his cross was met by Hunt who headed past Hopkinson. Liverpool continued to have most of the play with Milne's shot from a Ferns corner only inches wide. It wasn't until after the half hour mark that Tommy Lawrence had to make his first save and he easily held on to a Wyn Davies header.

Six minutes before half time Bolton got an equaliser from an indirect free kick after Moran had obstructed Peter Deakin just inside the penalty area. Deakin took the kick himself, touching it to Dave Hatton who hit a low shot into the net through a crowd of players that left Lawrence unsighted. Liverpool had one chance to regain their lead before the break, when Callaghan who had been struggling after taking a knock to his left knee, managed to get in a cross but Hunt's shot was straight at Hopkinson.

Bolton started the second half strongly, with Deakin testing Lawrence and Francis Lee having a shot well wide. Liverpool managed to reassert their authority in midfield but they weren't linking well with the forwards. On one occasion, Stevenson passed the ball to Melia but wasn't anticipating the return pass and the ball ran out of play. The drabness of the game was matched by the weather with the floodlights being switched on at around 4.15pm due to the increasing mist that was descending on Burnden Park. Bolton had a great chance from a corner when Hatton's drive was headed on by Deakin but the ball went just over the bar.

In the 65th minute the Reds took the lead again, with Callaghan starting and finishing the move. Running from right to left he fed the ball through to Thompson who drew Hopkinson from his goal before playing the ball into Hunt. He tee'd up Callaghan who drilled the ball home from the edge of the box with Hopkinson still out of his goal.

Bolton hit straight back and Lawrence was forced to save from Hatton, before Ian St John had an angled shot that was well held by Hopkinson. Liverpool's inability to take a firm control of the game and increase their lead was summed up when St John and Thompson collided, leading to trainers of both clubs coming on to give them treatment. Both managed to resume and there were no more incidents of note in what was generally a dour game, but the two points gained meant that the Reds had now won more away games than in the whole of 1962-63. They had also won whilst not playing very well, a trait of champions and were now fourth in the table but with games in hand on all the teams above them.

Liverpool: Lawrence, Ferns, Moran, Milne, Yeats, Stevenson, Callaghan, Hunt, St John, Melia, Thompson.

Bolton: Hopkinson, Hartle, Farrimond, Hatton, Hulme, Lennard, Davison, Lee, Davies, Deakin, Butler.

Referee: Mr W Downey (Jarrow).

Attendance: 23,824.

16th November 1963 Liverpool 2 Fulham 0, Football League Division One

There were a number of players who suffered knocks in the Bolton game, one of them being Peter Thompson who was forced to pull out of the England Under-23 match against Wales at Bristol City's Ashton Gate due to an ankle problem. At a more junior level, Tommy Smith was available for selection by the England youth side who were touring the Canary Islands, and on Sunday 10th November he played in a 3-2 win over a Las Palmas XI.

The injury situation led to Bill Shankly instructing Ian St John to pull out of a testimonial game at Burnley for Tommy Cummings, although Roger Hunt was allowed to play for an All Star XI in a game that ended 10-10. St John believed that criticism of Liverpool's performance at Bolton was harsh, writing in the *Daily Post* on 12th November that it was harder playing against teams battling relegation than those who were comfortable in mid table. He also believed that the Reds had done well to bounce back from the Leicester game and that it underlined their title credentials.

> 'Our victory at Bolton shows we can take a defeat without losing our nerve and confidence. There were some who, before Saturday's game, tried to tell me we were lucky we "only had to go to Bolton." How wrong can anyone be! This was a battle. We expected to have to fight because Bolton are in such a position they have to snatch a point where they can. Often when teams are in that unenviable plight they are anything but sitting targets. Nor were Bolton. It is far better to play away from this atmosphere of desperation.'

On 12th November the city was stunned when one of the great characters of Liverpool politics, Alderman John Braddock, collapsed and died at a function at the Walker Art Gallery. Seventy-year-old Alderman Braddock was the Leader of Liverpool City Council and had come to the city shortly before the outbreak of the First World War, having been born and raised in Stoke. His wife Bessie, MP for Liverpool Exchange, was in the House of Commons when the news was broken to her and she took the midnight train back to Liverpool with funeral arrangements being finalised the next day. It was announced that he would be cremated at Anfield Crematorium on Friday 15th November and that the service would not be a religious one. If anyone wished to send flowers or donations, they should do so to any Liverpool hospital.

It was confirmed on the Thursday that Thompson's ankle was better and he would be able to face Fulham, but Gerry Byrne was continuing to struggle with his injury and he was ruled out on the Friday. Fulham had former Reds keeper Dave Underwood in their side and also a debutant in left winger Bobby Howfield, a new £6,000 buy from Watford. Shankly told Horace Yates that Howfield had been on Liverpool's radar at one time, but they felt he wasn't of the sufficient quality they needed in that position. The match against Fulham looked to be a home banker, with the London side having scored just three goals in nine away matches so far. A cautionary note though was that their one away win had come at Leicester, so if they could win there, they could easily win at Anfield, warned Horace Yates in the *Daily Post* on the morning of the game. His prediction was right, as Fulham took the game to the Reds and let them off the hook on a number of occasions before two goals in the last five minutes gave Liverpool both points.

The behaviour of the crowd was sure to come into scrutiny following the events at the Leicester game, with a Mr Airey suggesting to the *Liverpool Echo* that Billy Liddell should address fans before games appealing for good behaviour as he was sure to be respected. Leslie Edwards didn't believe it was necessary however, writing that the Leicester game was a 'special case.' However the club did go to the trouble of printing a plea for fans in the match programme to 'cut out the foolishness' and had former Chairman Mr R. L. Martindale address the crowd beforehand. He told spectators: 'We are here to see good football and good entertainment and you spectators can help. Will the many who don't want trouble help restrain the few who threw things.' The concern came not just from the Leicester game, but the fact that across the park at Goodison, Everton's last two games had also seen trouble. The previous week they had been beaten by Blackburn in a game that saw fruit thrown at the referee and a crowd of around 2,000 remaining in the road outside the ground after the game chanting 'We want the referee.'

It was a clear day at Anfield yet just twenty miles away in St Helens there was a dense fog with visibility less than twenty yards. Underwood was made Fulham captain for the day and was given a rousing reception form the Kop, even though he won the toss forcing the Reds to kick into their most vociferous support for the first half. Fulham looked nothing like a side near the bottom as they started brightly but Ron Yeats was equal to anything they tried down the middle, with centre forward Stan Brown having to move out to the wings to see any of the ball.

Liverpool's first chance came from Ian Callaghan who tried a drive similar to the one that found the net against Everton but this time it went well wide. Fulham then had a great opportunity from a corner that the Reds' defence failed to deal with, but Brown and Howfield ran into each other as they tried to turn the ball over the line. Johnny Haynes, England's first £100 per week footballer, was playing some nice touches and receiving sporting applause from the crowd and he set up a great chance for Brown, but he hurriedly skied his shot not realising he was unmarked and clean through on goal. Just a minute later Howfield took a corner and Haynes had a shot but Tommy Lawrence did brilliantly to hold it on the line.

Willie Stevenson came close for Liverpool with a shot that dipped just over the bar, then Callaghan had a deflected effort that went into the side netting but fooled many of the crowd into thinking it was a goal. Despite increasing their foothold in the game the Reds were still struggling to cope with Haynes, who was linking well with Alan Mullery and giving a good demonstration of the precision passing that Liverpool's players lacked. The Reds were not as hurried as they had been against Leicester and were taking their time, but sometimes Jimmy Melia and Hunt especially, dwelled too much on the ball with the former coming in for some criticism from the crowd. Fulham's Jimmy Langley rarely lost a tackle, more often than not going on to set up an attack after he had won the ball, and he was useful with the throw-ins too, projecting the ball up to thirty yards.

Towards the end of the first half play was stopped twice, firstly when Bobby Robson required treatment after a tough but fair challenge by Phil Ferns, and then after Underwood jumped into George Cohen after collecting a corner. When half time came it was Fulham who were the more satisfied with Haynes receiving a pat on the back from Maurice Cook as he headed towards the tunnel. During the first half it had clouded over and at half time it began to rain.

Early in the second half the Kop began to chant for the Reds for the first time in the game but it still didn't get the players going. Fulham were hungrier for the ball and Ron Yeats was forced to jump up and commit a deliberate handball to stop Brown running on to a pass that would have put him clean through on goal. A few minutes later Brown was allowed a great opportunity after a flick on by Howfield but his shot was well wide.

Haynes was getting better as the game went on, with the crowd continuing to show their appreciation even though it was looking like they would be going home disappointed at the result. There was some short-lived joy for Liverpool when Melia fired the ball into the net, but the referee disallowed the goal due to a foul on Robson. Haynes then nearly capped a fine individual display with a goal, stunning the defence with a clever backheel and then receiving the ball back, but his shot rose into the crowd. As the second half wore on Fulham began to sit back more as they appeared to settle for a point, leading to a barrage of shots on their goal that lifted the crowd. The best chance came when Underwood parried a Hunt shot back into his path but from the rebound Bobby Keetch managed to hook the ball clear. There then followed a period of passing and little penetration, which again caused the crowd to get restless.

Eventually with just five minutes left Liverpool took the lead and it was down to an Underwood error. Melia crossed from the right but the keeper failed to hold the ball and a scramble ensued. St John eventually managed to prod it into the net and despite Fulham protests the goal stood. Before play could resume Robson was briefly treated for an injury but straight from the kick off the Reds were awarded a free kick. Melia sent the ball into the box and Hunt headed it out of Underwood's reach to put the game beyond doubt. Fulham weren't totally beaten though and just before the final whistle Mullery hit a good shot from the right that went just wide.

It had been a cruel scoreline on the visitors who had put in one of the best performances of any side at Anfield so far and certainly didn't play like a side who were just outside the relegation zone. The Liverpool crowd were given praise for the sporting behaviour which was also replicated by the players and management. Before the game Shankly took Fulham's veteran full back Jim Langley his customary pre-match cup of tea, while afterwards he went to their dressing room to commiserate them in defeat, telling the Echo's Leslie Edwards that it was the first time he had ever done this. Some of Fulham's players also visited the Reds changing room to offer them all the best for the rest of the season, despite the obvious disappointment at such a late defeat.

Shankly admitted that he wasn't 'tremendously delighted' at Liverpool's performance, even though it had been enough to take them up to second in the table, just a point behind leaders Sheffield United with a game in hand. They would have to play far better if they were to maintain their title challenge, but there were positive signs in that the defence had been solid and if the attack could replicate their form of the last quarter of the game for ninety minutes in future, more goals would come.

Liverpool: Lawrence, Ferns, Moran, Milne, Yeats, Stevenson, Callaghan, Hunt, St John, Melia, Thompson.

Fulham: Underwood, Cohen, Langley, Mullery, Keetch, Robson, Key, Cook, Brown, Haynes, Howfield.

Referee: Mr R. Langdale (Darlington).

Attendance: 38,478.

Top of Table

		Pl	W	D	L	F	A	GA	Pt
1	Sheffield United	18	9	6	3	34	22	1.54	24
2	Liverpool	17	11	1	5	34	19	1.79	23
3	Blackburn	19	9	5	5	41	26	1.58	23

9

To the Top

Liverpool went top of the league for the first time that season on 23rd November when they won 1-0 against Manchester United at Old Trafford. Their rise to the summit though was overshadowed by events in Dallas, where President John F. Kennedy was shot the day before that game.

23rd November 1963: Manchester United 0 Liverpool 1, Football League Division One

After the Fulham game Liverpool's players were given a three day holiday at the club's expense to recharge their batteries. However it wasn't like the modern jaunts in mid winter to Dubai, instead it was a fifty mile trip to Blackpool. Bill Shankly told the press that it was solely a bonding exercise and no training equipment would be taken there, not even a ball. The boss himself though stayed at home to help wife Nessie who was recuperating from an operation. Another not making the trip was Gordon Milne, who had been selected to play for England in a British Championship game against Northern Ireland, while Gerry Byrne stayed to continue his treatment on his injury as he neared full fitness. The weather was not good and it was impossible to play golf, but the players didn't let it dampen their spirits and they socialised with players from Leeds and West Bromwich Albion,who were also taking a seaside break.

As well as England's game against Northern Ireland (in which Jimmy Greaves scored four in an 8-3 win), Scotland were in action against Wales but none of Liverpool's players were selected. Ian St John wrote in his *Daily Post* column on Tuesday 19th November that he couldn't understand the omission of Ron Yeats. 'Yeats is the best centre half in Britain today and I make no exceptions. It is not sufficient to say he almost got in to the side to play Wales tomorrow. There should have been no doubt about his selection. I know. I have played in the Scottish side and they just cannot afford to do without Yeats.'

St John also wrote how he believed that despite being lucky to beat Fulham there had been plenty of other occasions in the season when they deserved to win but didn't. This didn't please everybody though with a Mr Vines from West Derby, who didn't state if he was a Liverpool or Everton fan, having a letter published in the Echo two days later that said,

'He must be joking, otherwise how can he explain the following facts –

> Victory over West Bromwich who fielded five reserves and still deserved to win, Wolverhampton (ten changes on the day of the match), Ipswich (two gift goals against a team including a teenage reserve goalkeeper) and a narrow victory over Bolton "A" … another deflected shot after the goalkeeper, like Underwood, dropped the ball!'

There may have been praise for Liverpool's supporters after their sporting behaviour against Fulham, but Everton were coming in for criticism from the Football Association. On 21st November their chairman John Moores revealed that they had been given two stern warnings by the FA for failing to control fans. The first incident had occurred against Spurs the previous month when a dart was thrown, then this was followed by the missile throwing and crowd gathering outside the main entrance at the Blackburn game. Moores reminded the press that no fan had been prosecuted for an incident at Goodison for over twenty years but with the very real threat of ground closure, it was decided to take drastic action and close part of the terracing behind each goal. It was the terracing nearest the goal nets that was closed, meaning the keeper was not quite as close to missile throwers as previously. This temporary measure eventually became permanent and explains why television footage of famous derby moments such as Sandy Brown's own goal in 1969-70 and Emlyn Hughes's two strikes in 1972-73 were played out in front of curved terracing.

It wasn't just Everton who were having problems. The previous Saturday, Manchester United supporters had wrecked a train bringing them home from a game at Aston Villa and the Football League Management Committee held a special meeting that week to discuss increasing hooliganism, releasing a statement afterwards pleading with fans not to take frustrations out on referees if they didn't like a decision.

There was some movement in the transfer market that week with Liverpool's reserve keeper Jim Furnell agreeing to join Arsenal. Furnell had been unable to regain his place since suffering an injury the previous season and with Welsh amateur international Trevor Roberts also on the books, the Reds didn't stand in his way. He would get an immediate chance to become number one at Arsenal, with Jack McClelland out with a broken collar bone and his replacement, amateur Bob Wilson, struggling to capture any decent form. Furnell would go on to play for Arsenal for five years and when McClelland left at the end of 1963-64 he ironically took over the number one spot from ex-Red Dave Underwood at Fulham. Former Reds striker Dave Hickson was also on the move that week with current club Tranmere Rovers releasing him from his contract to take over as player-manager of Irish League side Ballymena United.

On the morning of Friday 22nd November, ex-Everton and Mansfield player Jimmy Gauld appeared at Rochdale Magistrates Court where he was fined £60 for bribery. The previous March he had offered money to Oldham Athletic players so that they could play badly against Mansfield. Gauld was arrested after Oldham's players contacted the police but it turned out this was just the tip of the iceberg as Gauld didn't know to quit when he was ahead. His greed in selling his story later in the season would lead to several more arrests and imprisonment for famous players.

With so much else going on, it wasn't until the Friday that local papers mentioned the crucial match with Manchester United, who were sixth in the table but just a point behind the Reds having played a game more. Liverpool's toughest opponent at Old Trafford would be Denis Law, whose development had been assisted by Bill Shankly when he was at Huddersfield. United were managed by former Liverpool captain Matt Busby, who had been there since 1946 and rejuvenated them.

Gone were the days when Liverpool went to Old Trafford hopeful of a precious point in their fight against relegation. Now they were going as title challengers but would still face a stern test and Leslie Edwards predicted in the *Liverpool Echo* the night beforehand that a draw would be a good result. It had been hoped that Byrne would be available again but Shankly announced on the Friday that he would not be risked having only managed to train in full for the first time on the Thursday after having fluid drained from his knee. Neither was he included in the reserves side to face Derby County at Anfield, and it meant Phil Ferns had a further chance to enhance his reputation as he was set to mark Bobby Charlton.

As Liverpool prepared for the big game, the world was stunned on the Friday night when John F. Kennedy was shot, news which would dominate the papers the next morning. He was assassinated at 6.30pm British time with tributes soon being made on this side of the Atlantic where some cinema performances were interrupted to flash the news on their screens. The Lord Mayor of Liverpool, Alderman John McMillan, was attending a dinner of the Liverpool Society of Chartered Accountants and he told those present, 'I am sure everyone in this room and the city will want to join me in expressing sympathy to Mrs Kennedy and her family on this tragic bereavement. President Kennedy's death is a great loss to the Western world. He was a great man. He will be sorely missed.' The American Consul in Liverpool, George H. Steuart Jnr, said of him,

> 'Few before him have worked so vigorously to remove the barriers to complete equality for all people in our country. His relentless pursuit of peace and understanding between nations is known throughout the whole world. Probably few men in our country will ever leave such an imprint on our history in such a short space of time.'[24]

A *Daily Post* journalist was dispatched around some pubs in the city centre to get some opinions and was told by one drinker, 'You feel as if you knew him personally. It's hard to believe that such a thing could take place.' Another said, 'The utter stupidity of it all. What good can possibly come from such idiocy.' One pub goer who thought he could bring a humorous touch to the event failed to do so. A planned screening of serial *Emergency Ward 10* on ITV was cancelled, leading to a man to comment that they should have left it on as the doctors may have been able to help. The Post reported that, to the cheers of others, he was knocked off his barstool by a left hook from another regular.

On the River Mersey ships flew their flags at half mast but life went on and there were no cancellations of the planned football matches, although a period of silence was held at all First Division games. The shooting did have an effect on the attendance at Old Trafford though as more than 60,000 were expected but just 54,654 turned out to see Yeats score his first goal for the club as Liverpool won 1-0 to go top of the league for the first time since promotion.

The Reds sat back early in the game and Peter Thompson almost gifted United an opportunity when he tried to play a ball upfield but instead sliced it across the edge of the penalty area. Thankfully Law and Charlton were taken too much by surprise to capitalise on it. United's game plan to stop Liverpool seemed to be to stifle Roger Hunt, which gave Willie Stevenson some space and his hard low shot was only just tipped around the post by Harry Gregg. United hit back with Albert Quixall having a shot go just over the bar and another pushed away by Lawrence within the space of a minute. Ronnie Moran then misplaced a pass into the path of Paddy Crerand, whose cross was headed inches wide by Law.

Most of Liverpool's attacks were coming from the back, with Hunt dropping deep on one occasion and undertaking a thirty yard run, but Jimmy Melia failed to take advantage when the ball was laid off to him and he shot well wide. The Reds had another great chance when St John prodded the ball past Gregg but as it slowly dribbled towards the goal the United keeper managed to recover and get to it before Hunt could help it over the line.

United were continuing to look dangerous, with Charlton giving Ferns a hard time and Quixall trying a shot at every opportunity. They came close to taking the lead in comical fashion when Milne's attempted clearance looped over Lawrence's head but the keeper managed to get back acrobatically and tip the ball over the bar. United then strongly appealed for a penalty when Yeats tackled David Herd on the edge of the area but the referee waved their claims away.

After surviving the first half onslaught Liverpool almost took the lead shortly before half time when Thompson took a corner which was headed goalwards by Yeats but cleared off the line by Maurice Setters, who clattered into the post. The game was stopped while both Setters and Gregg, who had been knocked out by Yeats, received treatment with Bob Paisley lending a hand. Gregg was stretchered off the pitch with Herd taking over in goal but Setters was able to carry on. Yeats was booed by most of the crowd when he touched the ball for the first time and after the half time whistle went, Gregg continued to receive treatment for a couple of minutes at the side of the pitch before he was able to get up and walk to the dressing room.

When the second half began Liverpool adopted a more attacking approach as they sought to utilise the extra man advantage and United's lack of a regular keeper. Thompson put in a dangerous cross from the left which was knocked down by Ian Callaghan to Melia but his shot was deflected wide by Noel Cantwell. Thompson then cut inside after Hunt had drawn some defenders away from him but his shot was skied well over the bar. After Liverpool's initial flurry United managed to get to grips with the numerical disadvantage with Quixall posing a significant danger. Ferns was still struggling and hauled back the United winger,leading to calls for his dismissal from the crowd, but the referee had a word with him and nothing more.

Liverpool's best chance came just after the hour mark when St John's pass got behind Bill Foulkes and gave Hunt a clear run on goal, but his effort was weak and gratefully gathered up by Herd. The stand-in United keeper then had a let-off when Crerand hit a poor back-pass but he managed get out of the box and clear the ball before St John got to it. Herd had to make his first save when Melia hit a low shot near the post following a cross by Callaghan. With fifteen minutes remaining Liverpool took the lead through Yeats, who came forward for a corner and ran onto the ball, stooping low to head the ball past Herd and claim his first goal for the club.

United almost got straight back into the game when Setters tried a long range effort but it went just wide of the post, but Liverpool had two good chances to double their advantage with St John and Thompson hitting shots over the bar. With nine minutes left the crowd was stunned when Gregg re-appeared with his arm strapped to his chest to take his place on the right wing. As he went on to the pitch the Liverpool players joined in the applause for a player who turned out to have a fractured collar bone. Gregg only touched the ball once, but Moran was able to tackle him without making bodily contact as the Reds held on for victory.

As the Liverpool players journeyed home that night, a twelve-year-old boy disappeared from the market at Ashton Under Lyne, eight miles east of Old Trafford. The abductors knew that with much of the news focus being on Kennedy there would not be as much press coverage as usually would be the case. The boy was John Kilbride, who became the second victim of Moors Murderers, Ian Brady and Myra Hindley.

Cynics may have pointed out that Liverpool had only won the game due to Gregg's injury, but in his analysis in the *Daily Post* on 25th November, Horace

Yates commented that he doubted United could have fought any harder even with eleven men. He also believed that Yeats' header was so powerful that even Gregg wouldn't have saved it. Shankly afterwards pronounced that the Reds scorer was the greatest centre half in the world, while any suggestion that he had been responsible for Gregg's injury was ridiculed by Yates. He wrote that 'only the nincompoops' thought he should take any blame with Yeats himself saying 'it was just one of those unfortunate things.'[25] Liverpool were now top of the league but only just, with the top four teams being separated only by goal average.

Liverpool: Lawrence, Ferns, Moran, Milne, Yeats, Stevenson, Callaghan, Hunt, St John, Melia, Thompson.

Man Utd: Gregg, Dunne, Cantwell, Crerand, Foulkes, Setters, Quixall, Moore, Herd, Law, Charlton.

Referee: Mr E. T. Jennings (Stourbridge).

Attendance: 54,654.

30th November 1963 Liverpool 2 Burnley 0, Football League Division One

The victory over United meant that Liverpool had 25 points from eighteen games and led second placed Blackburn, who had played two games more, on goal average. Also on 25 points were Tottenham who had also played eighteen games and Arsenal who, like Blackburn, had played twenty games. It was so tight at the top that just three points separated the top nine teams. This was in contrast to the corresponding weekend in 1962-63 when ten points separated the top nine.

A year previously, eventual champions Everton had accumulated 27 points from their first eighteen games, as had Tottenham who would eventually finish runners up. It suggested that the 1963-64 champions would need less points to win the league and that the title race could involve more teams, but anyone who could put a consistent run of victories together had a great chance of pulling away from the chasing pack.

Liverpool were now dominating the sports pages locally, with the *Liverpool Echo* proclaiming that their rise to the top of the First Division in only their second season after promotion was 'the greatest success story in Liverpool's long history.' Horace Yates wrote that Liverpool had been involved in a tussle at Old Trafford but on gaining the numerical advantage had 'seized their opportunity like champions' and reduced the United attack to 'the point of despair in trying to achieve a shooting sight of goal.'[26]

In his *Daily Post* column on the Tuesday following the United game, Ian St John said that it was a 'marvellous feeling' to be at the top of the league and that 'we don't intend it shall be a fleeting acquaintance with glory.' He also revealed how Paisley had displayed his tactical acumen to give some advice to Yeats about corners, which led to the captain's first goal for the club. Yeats had once stood around where he expected the ball to drop for corners, meaning that he could be jostled out of the way, but on Paisley's advice he was now taking up position on the edge of the area and running onto the ball. This gave him a great advantage with St John explaining that a six foot two, fourteen stone man at full flight is quite a handful to contend with. However, he also managed to get a quip in because it had taken Yeats more than two years to score for the Reds. He joked that when he found the net it was usually an own goal. This didn't stop Yeats talking about it to teammates at every opportunity though, although he did admit that 'my one regret is that it had to be against a substitute goalkeeper.'[27]

The news continued to be dominated by events on the other side of the Atlantic. On Sunday 24th November, Lee Harvey Oswald, who had been arrested for Kennedy's murder, was being transferred from the city gaol in Dallas to the county gaol when he was shot by striptease club owner Jack Ruby, who inexplicably managed to get within just a few feet of him. The drama happened at 7.07pm British time and was captured by television news crews in America. Ruby, who said he did it for Kennedy's widow Jackie, was overpowered and placed in the same cell that Oswald had vacated a few minutes earlier, while Oswald died within an hour at the Parkland hospital. On 29th November a memorial service for Kennedy was held at Liverpool Cathedral, attended by several hundred people including the Lord Mayor and consular officials.

The shooting of Kennedy may well have led to a calmer atmosphere at English grounds that week, with no crowd trouble being reported in the First Division in the games that took place the day afterwards. There was an arrest in Tranmere's game away to Chesterfield however, when an apple was thrown at the Rovers' keeper. There was also a bizarre incident at Goodison where a male shouted 'Long Live Kruschev', in homage to the President of the Soviet Union, during the period of silence for Kennedy. James Downey, a 24-year-old from Norris Green was surrounded by spectators and punched before being handed over to police. After appearing at court he was bound over to keep the peace after admitting 'using abusive and insulting language whereby a breach of the peace was likely to be occasioned.'

Although Everton had taken some pre-emptive action themselves to combat trouble at Goodison by closing areas of terracing closest to the goals, this still wasn't enough to satisfy the Football League and that week they were fined £100 and ordered to post warning notices about behaviour around the ground in relation to recent incidents.

On Wednesday 27th November, Anfield hosted an England Under-23 international against West Germany, a game for which Reds winger Peter

Thompson was called up. The day before the game the international players trained at both Goodison and Anfield then played a practice game against Liverpool at Melwood, which allowed Gerry Byrne to have a first half run out. A crowd of 26,472 attended the main event which England won 4-1 against a side that contained Günther Netzer, who played against Liverpool in the 1973 UEFA Cup final for Borussia Mönchengladbach.

Although Byrne had played in the practice game, Shankly continued to express caution concerning his knee injury, with Horace Yates reporting in the Post the day before the Burnley game that he had said, 'I would not like to say at this moment that Gerry is fit enough for league football.' He was Liverpool's only injury worry with Burnley, who had finished third the previous season and been champions in 1960, having a number of problems. Centre forward Ray Pointer had been out with an ankle problem since early September but it was hoped he would return, having come through three reserve outings, although manager Harry Potts said it would depend on how soft the pitch was. Definitely out were winger John Connelly, who was recovering from an appendix operation, midfielder Jimmy Adamson who had a knee injury, and full back Alex Elder who broke his ankle in pre-season training. This, coupled with Liverpool's position at the top of the table, led to Yates having the confidence to write on the morning of the game that it was a 'home banker.' Liverpool did win as he predicted, but it wasn't as easy as Yates anticipated and they didn't finish the game off until the closing stages.

Burnley were given a boost when Pointer was declared fit to play and started brightly. Early on he was sent clear on the wing and put in a dangerous cross that Jimmy Robson only just failed to connect with. He then had a shot blocked by Ron Yeats as the Reds were forced to play most of the game in their own half for the first few minutes, with Yeats heading quite a few crosses clear. One that did manage to evade him found Trevor Meredith but thankfully his header was narrowly wide. Yeats was also spoken to by the referee after using his hand to stop a cross, while at the other end Liverpool's first attack saw Ian St John appear to be impeded by John Talbut, but no foul was given leading to St John being spoken to for dissent. Lawrence was then forced to make a good diving save from Meredith as the Reds struggled to get any foothold in the game.

Liverpool's first chance fell to St John but his header from Roger Hunt's cross was straight at Adam Blacklaw. Some good football was being played but when Walter Joyce clattered into Ian Callaghan after the ball had gone out of play the referee made it clear that one more blatant infringement of the rules by any player would lead to a sending off. Callaghan showed no sign of being in discomfort and he was involved in the best Liverpool move of the game so far when he collected a pass from Melia and hit a shot that beat Blacklaw but went just over the bar. The Reds were now beginning to get on top and from a corner, Blacklaw punched the ball out but only as far as Hunt whose goalbound volley was blocked close to the line by Brian O'Neil. Burnley then almost got a breakaway goal when Yeats missed the ball in midfield and Pointer seized onto it, but after running clear of Willie Stevenson his shot went just wide.

The Reds finished the first half much the stronger of the two teams with Hunt firing straight at Blacklaw after an excellent cross by Callaghan. Yeats then showed he was not one to shy out of a challenge and after he and Pointer raced thirty yards after the ball, the Burnley striker ended up tumbling into the crowd but he was unhurt.

The second half saw Liverpool begin where they had left off with Hunt hitting straight at Blacklaw after being set up by Gordon Milne. For all their dominance, they couldn't get past Talbut who was proving just as effective a centre half as Yeats was for Liverpool. Hunt was not having one of his better days, his shots being easily dealt with by Blacklaw, and after changing track when played in by Melia his lob went hopelessly wide. It was then St John's turn to mess his shot up when Melia crossed for him but he only succeeded in slicing the ball into the side netting. Despite Liverpool's dominance, Blacklaw was rarely tested, with Burnley packing the penalty area with enough defenders to block any shots that went in.

The breakthrough finally came in the 69th minute when Callaghan crossed and as Hunt and Blacklaw jumped up together the ball bounced off the Burnley keeper into the path of St John who scored from a tight angle. Lawrence was then called into action for the first time in the second half when he had to react quickly to save a surprise shot from Pointer. Johnny Price then had a shot that Lawrence held on to before they had a great opportunity after Yeats got caught in possession. He had run half the length of the field before misplacing a pass and from the breakaway, Brian Miller's shot was turned onto the post by Lawrence and thankfully the ball bounced the right way out of danger. Ronnie Moran then broke up another Burnley attack and ran with the ball before unleashing a thirty yard shot that deflected wide of the post.

With four minutes left Liverpool sealed the victory when they were awarded a penalty after Joyce brought down Callaghan. Captain Yeats called upon Hunt to take the penalty rather than the usual taker Moran, who had missed three earlier in the season and indicated his desire not to take any more. Blacklaw guessed right and got a hand to the ball but he only succeeded in pushing it into the roof of the net. It was a deserved victory for Liverpool on the whole, but Burnley had to be congratulated for making a game of it. Tottenham drew and Arsenal lost, but Blackburn won their game with the result that Liverpool were still only top on goal average, although they had two games in hand on their Lancashire rivals.

Liverpool: Lawrence, Ferns, Moran, Milne, Yeats, Stevenson, Callaghan, Hunt, St John, Melia, Thompson.

Burnley: Blacklaw, Angus, Joyce, O'Neil, Talbut, Miller, Meredith, Robson, Pointer, Harris, Price.

Referee: Mr A. Holland (Barnsley).

Attendance: 42,968.

Top of Table

		Pl	W	D	L	F	A	GA	Pt
1	Liverpool	19	13	1	5	37	19	1.95	27
2	Blackburn	21	11	5	5	48	28	1.71	27
3	Tottenham	19	11	4	4	54	36	1.50	26

10

The Rise of the Mersey Sound

Liverpool FC's rise to the top of the First Division occurred roughly as The Beatles rose from being a local band playing the clubs of Liverpool to becoming the most famous group in the world. Just as some of the players who had been Second Division regulars were moulded by Bill Shankly into a team that could compete at the top of the First Division, John, Paul, George and Ringo were taken on by Brian Epstein who masterminded their takeover of the British pop charts, followed by the world. It wasn't just The Beatles who rose to fame. There were also plenty of other Liverpool bands taking over the pop charts at that time as well, one of which would release a song that season which would become synonymous with Liverpool FC.

When Bill Shankly took over at Liverpool in December 1959 The Beatles consisted of just John Lennon, Paul McCartney and George Harrison and were known as Johnny and the Moondogs. In August 1960, after being known as the Silver Beatles, The Beatles was finally settled on. By then they had also recruited Stu Sutcliffe, Lennon's friend from art college, and also auditioned for a drummer, successfully recruiting Pete Best. Then they went to Hamburg for their first stint there and remained until November.

Another stint in Hamburg followed but it was January 1962 when an appointment was made that would change the course of music history. Local record shop owner Brian Epstein became their manager and he set about securing a record deal for what was now a four piece band. Sutcliffe had left the previous summer to continue his art studies in Hamburg after falling in love with Astrid Kirchherr, but tragically died of a brain haemorrhage in April 1962.

The Beatles were signed to the Parlophone label in May 1962, the month after the Reds had been crowned Second Division champions. A few months later, Pete Best was replaced as drummer by Ringo Starr and the first single *Love Me Do* was released in October, peaking at number seventeen in the charts on 29th December. This coincided with Liverpool's adjustment to life in the First Division as they ended the year in fifth place following seven successive wins that saw them pull away from the edge of the relegation zone.

Please Please Me was released in January 1963 and peaked at number two on 16th March, the same weekend Liverpool won 2-1 at Arsenal in the 5th round of the FA Cup. The week after the Reds lost to Leicester in the FA Cup semi final, they got to number one for the first time with *From Me To You*, a song which stayed there for seven weeks. They replaced fellow Liverpool band Gerry and the Pacemakers at the top after their first single *How Do You Do It* had been there for three weeks. Gerry and the Pacemakers' second single, *I Like It*, then took over from The Beatles in the middle of June and stayed top for four weeks. Liverpool's fourteen week reign at the top was eventually broken by Coventry's Frank Ifield with *Confessin'.*

In early August another Liverpool group, The Searchers, went to number one with *Sweets For My Sweet* and on the opening day of the season Bootle's Billy J. Kramer was number one with *Bad To Me*, although his backing group The Dakotas were from Manchester. The Beatles' second number one was *She Loves You*, which topped the charts for four weeks in September and October. Brian Poole and the Tremeloes, who Decca had taken on instead of The Beatles, then had three weeks at the top with *Do You Love Me*. For the last nine weeks of 1963 though the top spot was swapped between The Beatles and Gerry and the Pacemakers. It seems quite fitting, so many years on, that the number one song when Liverpool hit the top of the table for the first time was *You'll Never Walk Alone.*

Gerry and the Pacemakers made chart history by getting to number one with their first three record releases, something that would be emulated in 1984 by another Liverpool band, Frankie Goes To Hollywood. However it was The Beatles who were making the most headlines. The term 'Beatlemania' is believed to have been coined by Scottish promoter Andi Lothian when they played at Caird Hall in Dundee on 7th October. Incredibly that was their 178th live performance of 1963, with the band often playing two concerts in different venues on the same day. They had enjoyed a rapid rise to the top but manager Brian Epstein insisted on honouring all bookings, meaning they were playing a wide range of venues. An example of this came in mid-September when they played the Northwich Memorial Hall one night and London's Royal Albert Hall the next.

Despite the large number of concerts there was still an overwhelming demand for tickets. Six shows were booked for the Finsbury Park Astoria over Christmas but queues still formed four hours before tickets went on sale on 22nd October. The following month queues began to form in Southend on the night of Thursday 14th November, even though the box office didn't open until the Sunday. Police were forced to close a road and the estimated cost of maintaining order was £400.

The most chaotic scenes though were reserved for Liverpool a week afterwards. On the day the Reds went top of the league for the first time, coaches from Manchester weren't just bringing football fans back, they were also bringing Mancunian teenagers too. They were amongst an estimated 12,000 that descended on the Liverpool Empire to queue overnight for tickets for the 'One Night Stand' Christmas show on 22nd December. Over fifty people were treated for fatigue and the effects of the cold and several streets were closed. The Chief Constable was not impressed at having to deploy 100 officers to maintain order in the mile-long queue and called for all future ticket sales to be by postal application only.

At the concerts themselves fans went wild. At the Birmingham Hippodrome on 10th November they were showered with teddy bears, sweets and carnations from the audience, many of whom had waited outside beforehand to get a close up glimpse of them arriving. The four lads had fooled them though, wearing policeman's smocks and helmets to get into the theatre unnoticed. This had come a week after appearing in the Royal Variety Performance at the Prince of Wales theatre in London, when John Lennon said his famous line about people in the cheap seats clapping their hands and the rest rattling their jewellery.

It wasn't just in the United Kingdom where Beatlemania was taking off either, as the group were mobbed in October during a five gig tour of Sweden, their first foreign trip with the exception of the Hamburg jaunts. In their last concert, in Eskilstuna, girls swarmed the stage and had to be removed by police but John Lennon didn't seem to mind, saying he'd be happy to stay in the country another week if he could. It was certainly a special time to be a Liverpudlian with Liverpool FC fighting for the title and the city's pop groups taking over the charts. One of them, the Swinging Blue Jeans, were even used as part of the plot line for the Christmas special of Merseyside-produced police television drama *Z Cars*. Going into 1964, things were going to get even better.

11

Christmas Bonus

If there is an old adage that getting to the top is easy – staying there is the hard part, then Liverpool had the chance to find out if that was true in December, when the first half of the month saw them faced with a tricky fixture at Arsenal followed by a home game with fellow Lancashire challengers, Blackburn. Then came the tough festive programme that had them scheduled to play Stoke City twice in three days.

7th December 1963: Arsenal 1 Liverpool 1, Football League Division One

Liverpool's first game as league leaders was away to Arsenal, who were just two points behind in fourth place having played two games more. They also had an excellent home record having won eight of their eleven games at Highbury, but then Liverpool's record on the road was just as good, with six wins out of eight.

It was confirmed on the Thursday that the team would be unchanged with Gerry Byrne still not being fully fit, while former Liverpool keeper Jim Furnell was expected to be in goal for Arsenal. Furnell had endured a torrid afternoon the previous weekend at Blackburn where the Gunners lost 4-1. One of the goals had come after the ball hit a divot and deceived him, but it was at wing half where the changes were made with John Barnwell and John Snedden both coming into the side.

While Bill Shankly could be pleased that, on the whole, he had a settled side brimming with confidence, he was not impressed with England manager Alf Ramsey's announcement on 5th December. Ramsey stated that he would be holding monthly get-togethers lasting three days a time. This was to make sure the players continued to be familiar with each other due to the next international against Scotland in the British Championship being four months away. The first session would be at Birmingham University from 16th to 18th December and Roger Hunt, Gordon Milne and Peter Thompson were selected. Shankly told Horace Yates of the *Daily Post* that 'this is not the time of the season when extra training is either necessary or welcome.'

As Liverpool's players began their journey to London on the Friday, Christine Keeler was sentenced to nine months imprisonment for perjury with her barrister saying that there were 'wicked people who want to see this young woman sent away.' Coincidentally, her first appearance in court exactly three months earlier had come on the day that the Reds had last travelled to London for a game against Chelsea, but whereas on that occasion they had returned with both points, this time they would have to settle for one.

Due to the colour clash Liverpool wore white, while Arsenal manager Billy Wright allowed Furnell to have the captain's armband. The game started quietly with Arsenal having slightly the better of the play and Tommy Lawrence was the first of the two keepers to be called into action when he easily held on to a Jimmy Magill shot. Centre forward Joe Baker then went close when his header hit the bar from a free kick following a foul by Ronnie Moran. The Reds appeared nervous and were making mistakes due to the intensity of Arsenal's tackling, but Peter Thompson spotted a potential weakness in left half John Snedden, who was carrying some extra weight. He moved over to the same flank and combined well with Ian Callaghan to start creating attacks, but too many times the Liverpool forwards seemed scared of taking responsibility when the ball came their way.

Geoff Strong, who would go on to become a fine utility player for the Reds, was playing at inside right and his header from a John McLeod cross hit the angle of post and bar. He then had a goal disallowed from a corner after the referee adjudged that he had punched the ball over the line. Liverpool's first real chance came shortly before half time when Milne hit what looked like an unstoppable volley. It was described by Leslie Edwards in the Echo as '30 to 1 on' to beat Furnell but the keeper stretched to tip the ball round the post to the applause of his former team mates. The game then limped along to half time with neither side testing the other's keeper again in what was on the whole a disappointing first period.

The second half began along the same lines as the first with both sides passing the ball poorly, the damp surface not helping either team. Hunt tried a long range shot but it had no power and Furnell easily gathered, then at the other end Barnwell's powerful drive went wide. Billy McCulloch then took a long throw that deceived everybody and very nearly ended up in the net, such was the unwillingness of both sets of players to attack the ball. Arsenal's failure to take advantage of Liverpool's sloppiness was leading to the home crowd getting on the players' backs.

When the deadlock was finally broken after an hour, it was down to over confidence of Arsenal's defenders that led to a Liverpool goal. Thompson's long ball down the left flank was allowed to run towards the by-line but Hunt sensed he may be able to keep it in and gave chase. He then cut into the box and hit a shot that Furnell managed to block but only into the path of Callaghan who had the simple task of tapping the ball into the net. The Reds almost had a second a few moments later when there was panic in the box, but Ian Ure managed to hook the ball away for a corner.

With twenty minutes remaining Arsenal managed to get an equaliser when Baker fired in from a tight angle after George Eastham had crossed.

Ian St John scores against Aston Villa at Anfield

Captain Ron Yeats at Melwood

Roger Hunt makes it 5-0 against Ipswich at Anfield

Ian Callaghan, one of three players who didn't miss a league game in 1963-64

Full back Gerry Byrne made 33 appearances in 1963-64

Tough tackling full back Ronnie Moran

Keeper Tommy Lawrence

Roger Hunt scores Liverpool's second goal against Stoke on Boxing Day

Ian St John in action against Spurs at White Hart Lane on Good Friday

Alf Arrowsmith, who got 15 goals in 20 league appearances

Programmes left to right: From the fourth home game of the season against Wolves, the Reds won 6-1 to record their first win of the season at Anfield. From the first game of the season away to Blackburn Rovers. The match at Old Trafford on 23rd November when Ron Yeats scored his first Liverpool goal in a 1-0 win that put them top of the league. And from the 2-0 win at Leicester on 28th March 1964

Inside forward Jimmy Melia who was sold to Wolves in March 1964 after losing his place to Alf Arrowsmith

Reserves captain Phil Ferns who made 18 league appearances as a stand in full back and half back

Young defender Chris Lawler made only 6 league appearances as cover for Ron Yeats but showed why he would go on to play over 500 games for the Reds

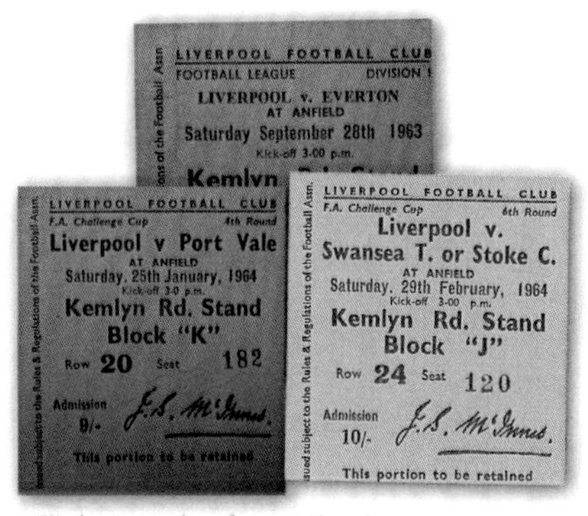

Ticket stubs from the league game against Everton and the FA Cup games against Port Vale and Swansea (courtesy Rob Gowers)

Chairman Tom Williams

Reds boss Bill Shankly

Trainer Bob Paisley

Reserves trainer Joe Fagan

Trainer Reuben Bennett

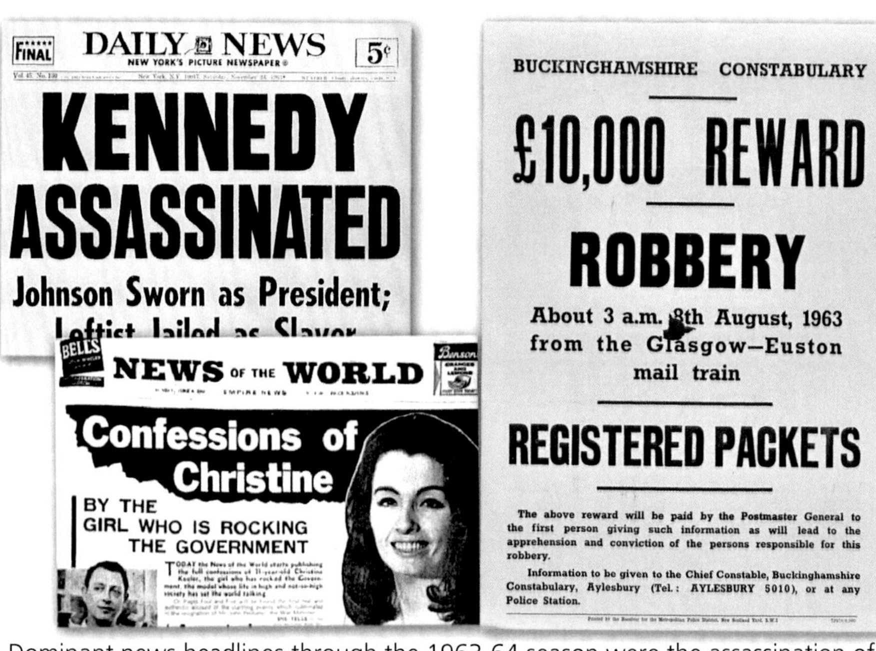

FINAL DAILY NEWS 5¢
NEW YORK'S PICTURE NEWSPAPER

KENNEDY ASSASSINATED

Johnson Sworn as President;

NEWS OF THE WORLD

Confessions of Christine

BY THE GIRL WHO IS ROCKING THE GOVERNMENT

BUCKINGHAMSHIRE CONSTABULARY

£10,000 REWARD

ROBBERY

About 3 a.m. 8th August, 1963
from the Glasgow—Euston
mail train

REGISTERED PACKETS

The above reward will be paid by the Postmaster General to the first person giving such information as will lead to the apprehension and conviction of the persons responsible for this robbery.

Information to be given to the Chief Constable, Buckinghamshire Constabulary, Aylesbury (Tel.: AYLESBURY 5010), or at any Police Station.

Dominant news headlines through the 1963-64 season were the assassination of President Kennedy, the Profumo Affair and the Great Train Robbery

Roger Hunt makes it 5-0 against Ipswich at Anfield

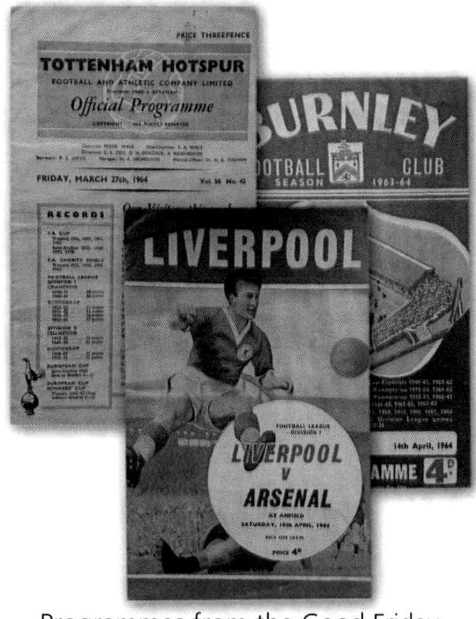

Programmes from the Good Friday encounter at White Hart Lane when Roger Hunt scored a hat trick in a 3-1 win. The 2-0 win at Burnley on 14th April that put the Reds on the brink of becoming champions. And the title clinching game against Arsenal

Ian St John scores the first goal in the 5-0 win over Arsenal that clinched the title

Alf Arrowsmith makes it 2-0 in the title winning game against Arsenal

Willie Stevenson with the makeshift trophy after securing the league title in the victory over Arsenal

The players celebrate in the dressing room after clinching the title against Arsenal
Copyright PA Photos

Ron Yeats with the Championship trophy prior to the start of the following season
Copyright PA Photos

The crowd now encouraging rather than deriding them, Arsenal sensed a winner was a possibility and when Eastham managed to evade Ron Yeats it was fortunate for the Reds that his cross went across the face of goal with nobody there to turn it home. A stoppage due to an injury to Milne took the pace out of their game and when play resumed, Liverpool managed to get playing again. In injury time Ian St John almost snatched both points when his shot slipped under Furnell's body but the Arsenal keeper managed to get back to gather the ball with Hunt closing in. Hunt then had another glorious chance when he was played in by Jimmy Melia but he didn't realise how much time he had to line it up and the shot was hurried and weak, easily gathered by Furnell. There was no further action and the draw kept Liverpool on top of the table but only on goal average from Blackburn and Tottenham, all three sides now being level on 28 points.

There had been a good Reds following at Highbury and Leslie Edwards concluded in his *Daily Post* report the following Monday that they 'must have been a little disappointed' by what 'was not a champion show.' In his analysis for the *Liverpool Echo* that evening, he still raved about Furnell's save from Milne's volley, describing it as 'out of this world' but on the whole felt the Reds were too defensive. He did say however that a point in London is a respectable result and that fans had perhaps become to blasé after the attacking performances at Anfield. He felt that the next game, at home to second placed Blackburn, would see 'all out offence' in what would be a 'clash of the gladiators.'

Liverpool: Lawrence, Ferns, Moran, Milne, Yeats, Stevenson, Callaghan, Hunt, St John, Melia, Thompson.

Arsenal: Furnell, Magill, McCulloch, Barnwell, Ure, Snedden, McLeod, Strong, Baker, Eastham, Armstrong.

Referee: Mr L. Callaghan (Merthyr Tydfil).

Attendance: 40,551.

14th December 1963: Liverpool 1 Blackburn Rovers 2, Football League Division One

Although Liverpool's next game would see them come up against second-placed Blackburn Rovers at Anfield, it was the FA Cup that captured more coverage in the local press in the week leading up to it, demonstrating just how highly regarded the competition was then. On Monday 9th December, the draw for the third round was the main headline on the front page of the *Liverpool Echo*, informing readers that the Reds would be at home to Second Division Derby County.

As Liverpool savoured life at the top of the league, a fan wrote to the Echo pointing out what had happened last time they occupied pole position. Mr Birks from Whiston recalled how the Reds had been top for the early part of 1952-53 before slipping to third after a 2-2 draw at Bolton in their twelfth game. They never regained top spot and ended up in a relegation battle, only avoiding the drop with a 2-0 win over Chelsea on the last day of the season.

Over at Goodison, the behaviour of fans was coming under the spotlight again with rumours of an incident at Everton's home game with Chelsea the previous Saturday. Chelsea manager Tommy Docherty was reported to have been struck by a missile at the end of the game and had been seen running towards the crowd before being pulled back by his trainer. However he refused to confirm or deny the reports saying no more than, 'Whatever happened I reported it to Harry Catterick, the Everton manager, immediately after the game. So far as I am concerned that is as far as it is going.'[28] However by the end of the week the FA had received an official report and there were fears that part of the ground could be closed as punishment.

Tuesday's local press continued to focus on the FA Cup, even though the third round would not take place until 4th January, with four league games still to come before then. More focus was on Everton's potential banana skin at Third Division Hull City, who were anticipating a record crowd for the tie. Liverpool's game with Derby was secondary in the reports and their manager Tim Ward seemed to admit his side had little chance, saying that 'if we had to be drawn away it may as well be somewhere where we'll get a good gate.' He did add, however, 'and you never know in this game.'

It was not until the Thursday that there was any reference to the Blackburn game and even then it was more to do with the team than the importance of the fixture. The Post reported that Bill Shankly had ruled Gerry Byrne out of the game, saying that he would not play again until he was 'absolutely ready.' That evening the Echo advised fans that there were no stand tickets remaining and that the team would be unchanged, although Byrne was progressing well. Blackburn had no injury worries either, with keeper Fred Else having recovered from a slight groin strain. It was revealed that the sides would be wearing black armbands as a mark of respect to Blackburn secretary Reg Taylor, who had died earlier in the week. Mr Taylor had been secretary of Preston when Bill Shankly joined them as a player and was described by the Reds boss as a 'grand man.'[29]

Writing in the *Liverpool Echo* the night before the game, Leslie Edwards said that Blackburn's orthodox style of football meant that the Anfield crowd could see the game of the season, but he was still not taking the visitors' title chances seriously despite their run of six unbeaten away games. He wrote that Liverpool and Tottenham remained the main contenders and this game was the perfect opportunity for the players to show the fans that this could be their year. It wasn't to be the case however, as Blackburn put on a fine attacking display to take both points and leapfrog the Reds to the top of the table.

It was a drab day and the floodlights were switched on before the game.

The crowd gave Ron Yeats a tremendous reception as he took the field as he was playing his 100th league game for the club. He lost the toss though and the Reds were forced to kick into the Kop for the first half, where they missed two golden chances within the opening few minutes. Firstly Ian St John sent Jimmy Melia clean through with a clever lob but the inside right chested the ball down too far and it ran out of play. Roger Hunt then missed a golden chance when Ron Clayton completely missed his header as he tried to clear Melia's long ball, leaving the centre forward with just the keeper to beat but he shot tamely at Fred Else.

The Reds were made to pay for the missed chances in the tenth minute when John Bray played the ball to Andy McEvoy who was on the right hand edge of the area. With everybody expecting him to cross the ball goalwards, he instead took the ball past Yeats and hit a low shot that crept past Tommy Lawrence into the goal. Blackburn didn't sit back on this lead and McEvoy and Fred Pickering made sure that Yeats had plenty of defending to do with Pickering going on a forty yard run but his shot went across the face of goal. Liverpool had plenty of the ball but weren't using it properly, whereas when Blackburn attacked they did so clinically and looked like extending their lead. One such occasion was when Mick McGrath played a thirty yard pass to McEvoy who shot just wide of the post.

Liverpool did wonder how they failed to score during a frantic goalmouth scramble that saw St John prod the ball past Else only for Mike England to clear it off the line. However the ball rebounded off Else into the path of St John but as he stuck a leg out to poke the ball goalwards, Else managed to get his hands to it and turn it around the post. The corner was then wasted when Ian Callaghan's kick was turned high over the bar by St John. As half time drew near the Reds were now well on top and Lawrence didn't touch the ball for the last fifteen minutes of the half, the final action of which saw Yeats go forward for a corner and head the ball just wide.

The surface was quite hard and the bounce of the ball was deceiving players at times. The first action of the second half saw St John play the ball into the area where it was missed by both Else and Keith Newton, but Hunt was so surprised by this that although he got a foot to the ball it went wide. Liverpool were then made to pay again when Blackburn went 2-0 up in the 52nd minute. McEvoy was again the scorer, collecting the ball from Bryan Douglas on the edge of the box and hitting a fine shot that left Lawrence rooted to the spot.

Melia was having one of those days where nothing went right for him and when he was presented with a great shooting opportunity after a lucky deflection he dwelled on the ball too long, allowing Bray to block his shot. The ball went out for a corner which Melia took, but he hit it straight into the side netting. In their desperation to get a goal back, Ronnie Moran and Yeats were both joining in the attacks with Yeats heading just wide from a corner.

St John then missed with a hard shot but on the whole Liverpool seemed to be panicking too much and not building up attacks with any clear precision. Blackburn, on the other hand, remained composed and Mike Harrison forced a good save from Lawrence before McEvoy hit a shot wide.

Callaghan almost got a goal back when he hit a fine effort that Else did well to hold but at midway through the half it was the first time in the game that the opposition keeper had been seriously tested. In the 74th minute they finally got one back when Melia, in his best move of the game, went on a run down the left and pulled the ball back to Peter Thompson whose cross was headed into the net by Hunt. Within a minute the Reds were almost level when Thompson again crossed for Hunt but this time Else made a brilliant save.

The crowd were now right behind the Reds by roaring every touch of the ball and Melia had overcome his earlier poor form. A brilliant run down the left ended with a cross that Else managed to get out of his goal to intercept. Blackburn were dangerous on the counter attack though and Phil Ferns blatantly brought down Mick Ferguson to stop him having a clean run on goal, leading to the referee having a word with the Reds' defender. The free kick was cleared but a few moments later Douglas went down in the area after being challenged by Moran and Yeats but with hearts in mouths, the referee waved play on. There was no time for Liverpool to launch another attack though and the defeat meant they were no longer league leaders. Blackburn had replaced them and results elsewhere meant the Reds had now dropped to fourth.

Despite the defeat the home crowd were extremely sporting, but there were reasons to worry after this performance. All of Blackburn's forwards had played well, but the same couldn't be said for Liverpool's. Writing in the *Daily Post* the following Monday, Horace Yates said that Blackburn's centre forward Pickering was put in a straightjacket by Yeats, likewise Hunt by the visiting defence. The big difference was that whereas St John and Melia struggled, Blackburn's inside forwards took advantage of the extra attention given to Pickering and created opportunities for themselves. He concluded that Liverpool's forward line was 'suspect' and that the 'chapter of misses threw the problem up into such sharp focus that the cause of the reverse eluded nobody.' Yeats accepted that Liverpool only had themselves to blame, but promised fans 'we shall be back.'[30]

Liverpool: Lawrence, Ferns, Moran, Milne, Yeats, Stevenson, Callaghan, Hunt, St John, Melia, Thompson.

Blackburn: Else, Bray, Newton, Clayton, England, McGrath, Ferguson, McEvoy, Pickering, Douglas, Harrison.

Referee: Mr H Horner (Coventry).

Attendance: 45,182

21st December 1963: Blackpool 0 Liverpool 1, Football League Division One

It was confirmed at the beginning of the week that Liverpool had accepted an invitation to tour the United States and Canada at the end of the season, playing ten matches. It was described as a 'splendid bit of news' by captain Ron Yeats who said, 'There will be a lot of competition amongst us to get into the list of those to travel because this can be nothing but a wonderful experience for those fortunate enough to be selected.'[31]

Crowd trouble continued to make the headlines that week. Everton received a letter from the FA asking them for their observations about the incident involving Tommy Docherty who claimed he had been struck in the face by a missile, believed to be a screwed up cardboard carton. As they sweated over whether the FA would close parts of Goodison Park, Everton officials revealed they had been the victims themselves of disorder on 14th December during their away game at Fulham. They reported to the FA that captain Derek Temple had been struck on the neck by a staple thrown by the crowd during the second half, and that George Heslop was hit by a stone as he left the field at the end of the game. In contrast to the disorder elsewhere the *Daily Post* reported on 16th December that the crowd at Anfield had behaved 'wonderfully well' despite the defeat.

It was now more than a year since the Cuban Missile Crisis and some further indication that the Cold War was thawing a little came when it was announced that week that the Berlin Wall would open for the first time since it was erected in August 1961. The East German authorities stated that 100,000 one-day passes would be available to those in the West to visit relatives in the run up to Christmas. However the West German Government in Bonn stressed that this did not mean that they recognised the state of East Germany, and that the agreement to allow people across the Wall had been made solely for the purposes of humanitarianism.

On 18th December, the *Daily Post* reported that contrary to previous plans, the club were now giving serious consideration to expanding Anfield again the following close season. Horace Yates wrote that a double decker stand at the Anfield Road end at the cost of over £100,000 was in the pipeline and could be completed in time for the following season. This would take the capacity of the ground back above 55,000, the belief being that despite the league position, one of the reasons for the relatively low crowds at Anfield so far this season was that many fans didn't go due to the risk of being locked out. The economic situation was certainly not a factor as unemployment figures released that week revealed that the figure in Liverpool was just 2.5%, compared to the national average of 2%.

Those fans that were going to matches, this being in the days before even highlights were shown on television, continued to debate the reason for Liverpool's poor home form. A Mr Sinnott from West Derby had a letter published in the *Liverpool Echo* the same evening saying that the lack of a good old-fashioned centre forward was the problem. He wrote,

> 'Ian St John is a fine player but seven goals in nineteen matches speaks for itself. St John likes to roam and would in my opinion be a better inside forward. Liverpool seem to rely too much on the goalscoring of Hunt and when he is off form, as he has been of late, who else is there to take over from him? The fact that all Liverpool's home defeats have been by the odd goal suggests that it is the attack that is the weakest link in the Anfield supply chain.'

One of the reasons for St John's poor form of late was the fact that his wife had recently given birth to a baby boy, also named Ian, who would need to remain in hospital until after Christmas. Yeats had written in his Echo column the previous weekend, 'His wife and baby are now doing well and he can concentrate on scoring goals again.' St John himself was philosophical about the fall from the top of the table, writing in his *Daily Post* column that week,

> 'If it is easy to slip, it's just as easy to rise. We intend to put the rising theory into practice as early as possible. You know, it almost hurts to look at the league table these days. There we are with only one league defeat away from home in nine games. If only we had fared as well at Anfield as we have at other grounds, the Championship race would be nearly over. It is a failure up front that is responsible for our worries. How can we hammer it out? If we were not creating chances we could not be blamed for not accepting them. But we are making chances, a lot of them, but our goalscoring record bears no sort of tribute to that feat. It is very upsetting because this is the opportunity of a lifetime. Our aim is to win the Championship. Magically and without explanation the goals could start flowing again anytime. Once they do I think they will come in a flood.'

It wasn't just at first team level where the strikers were struggling. On 17th December Liverpool's youth team crossed Stanley Park to take on Everton at Goodison in the FA Youth Cup in front of over 10,000 fans and went down 1-0. The following day's Echo reported that it was only a fine goalkeeping display by Rodney Swindlehurst that kept the score down in a game that 'Everton's greater forward skill told.'

Although St John's personal worries were reducing, he now had an injury to contend with, having taken a knock on the leg in the Blackburn game and joining Gerry Byrne on the treatment table. Byrne was referred to a specialist that week but Bill Shankly said he was still improving, telling Horace Yates, 'I consider he is better now than at any time since his injury became apparent.'[32] The visit brought good news, the specialist confirming that the injury was now clear and it was just a case of working back to fitness. If St John failed to recover from injury to play his 100th league game for the club, Alf Arrowsmith was ready to deputise. Under normal circumstances Arrowsmith would have been on his honeymoon but there was no way Shankly was giving him time off for that. In fact, such was Arrowsmith's fear of upsetting the boss that after getting married the previous Saturday morning, he joined his teammates at Maine Road where he scored in the reserves 4-2 defeat at Manchester City.

With Roger Hunt, Gordon Milne and Peter Thompson all away at Alf Ramsey's training camp there weren't too many players out on the pitches at Melwood that week, but thankfully for Liverpool the trio brought no fresh injuries when they returned on the Friday. On that day a special practice match was arranged to test St John's fitness and he came through it with no problems, leading to Shankly confidently saying, 'It would appear that St John will be ready to play.'

With a touch of sarcasm, given his unhappiness about Ramsey's sessions, he added, 'It made quite a change for us to have all our players together for training.'[33] Some of those players that had remained in Liverpool went to an Orphans Christmas Party where Yeats was an unconvincing Santa Claus as afterwards, children pointed out that he hadn't changed his shoes and socks.

Although St John had proved his fitness, Shankly stopped short of confirming the side, saying he would name it on the Saturday This led to Horace Yates speculating in the Post on the morning of the game that a change was still being considered as his satisfaction with the forward line must be 'wearing thin.' In the previous evening's Echo, Leslie Edwards suggested that it wasn't necessarily personnel changes that were needed, more a change of plan as too many times forwards weren't shooting. As Shankly continued to ponder his selection, Blackpool confirmed that right back Jimmy Armfield was unavailable due to a bruised foot, his place being taken by Tommy Thompson. In the end, Shankly decided to stick with the same side and St John, playing his 100th league game for the Reds, repaid the faith shown in him with the only goal in a 1-0 win.

It was a bitterly cold day, the coldest of the winter so far with temperatures dropping to minus four overnight and it was not one for watching football in a largely open ground just a few hundred yards from the Irish Sea. This only deterred the home fans though. Liverpool's following, many of whom paid 7s 6d (37.5p) to travel on special trains from Exchange Station that called at Kirkdale and Orrell Park, were believed to have made up around three quarters of the meagre 13,254 crowd. There was an early scare for the travelling Reds when Phil Ferns hit a poor backpass that Graham Oates almost latched on to but Tommy Lawrence got there just in time. The hard ground made it difficult to control the ball at times and Blackpool's defenders made a couple of errors of their own, keeper Tony Waiters having to come to the rescue when Thompson and Ian Callaghan took advantage of them.

After those early scares Blackpool took control of the game for the first quarter, with Ray Parry having a shot well held by Lawrence, then hitting one just wide from a corner. But Liverpool got into it with St John turning a Milne cross just wide, Callaghan having a shot blocked by Barrie Martin, and Melia's long ball just bouncing away from St John. There was a familiar pattern developing though as Liverpool had plenty of the ball but took too long to get their shots in, allowing Blackpool's defenders to re-group and close them down. There was one exception though when Milne hit a snapshot from just outside the area which Waiters did well to get a hand to and turn it over the bar.

Ferns was not having as solid a game as in previous weeks and when he hit another poor backpass Lawrence had to resort to leaving his area and kicking clear. Yeats then slipped leaving Ray Charnley with a great shooting opportunity but his effort went wide. These mishaps aside, Liverpool had taken total control by the half hour mark, with Melia putting on his best display for some time. He started and finished one move that ended with his shot not being held by Waiters but Tommy Thompson managed to kick the ball clear as it bobbled towards the line. Melia was then involved in a good move where he linked with Willie Stevenson, but the final killer pass to St John, who would have had an open goal, was intercepted by Martin. Unfortunately for Melia he then injured his knee and was forced to move onto the wing, with Thompson coming inside. Lawrence also needed treatment after taking a kick when he went down at the feet of Charnley.

Despite the positional change, Liverpool continued to dominate with Stevenson helping out in attack while Melia was struggling. A brilliant ball from him to St John was laid off to Hunt but his shot went wide, then Callaghan had an effort well saved by Waiters. The Blackpool keeper then made a scrambled double save from Hunt just before half time, with Parry on hand to hook the ball clear before the Reds' striker could force the ball over the line. After shaky start it had been a good first half for Liverpool and their rhythm hadn't been disrupted by Melia's injury. He took up position on the wing for the second half which began as the wind was beginning to get stronger. The first two chances for either side from St John and Parry both went well wide.

Melia wasn't running about as much but his vision remained good and he was using the ball well. One pass to Thompson resulted in a shot that went well wide and a cross to St John was headed down to Callaghan who slipped when he was just six yards from goal. Perhaps spurred into action by this let off, Blackpool attacked and Oates had one shot tipped over the bar by Lawrence and another that shaved the post. The game was now really opening up with Yeats getting forward for Liverpool, playing a good ball out to Melia who crossed it back into the box but his header was well held by Waiters.

In the 61st minute Liverpool took the lead which on balance was deserved. Milne played the ball to Hunt down the right and he hit a low cross to St John who turned it into the net. Hunt almost added to the lead a few moments later but Waiters saved his low shot. Blackpool hit back but they struggled to deal with the wind with Steve Hill hitting two shots well over. They almost had better luck when Hill crossed for Parry whose shot beat Lawrence but Ferns, now playing with far more confidence, managed to clear the ball off the line.

Yeats then displayed his strength when a shot from Oates struck him in the chest but he hardly flinched. Blackpool were throwing all their men forward in search of an equaliser but like the Reds the week before, they weren't composed enough. Liverpool on the other hand didn't panic and Stevenson was very good at moving the ball out of defence while Melia, despite his injury, distributed the ball well when it came to him.

The Reds moved up to third in what had been a fantastic end to end game that was worthy of more than one goal. Only the great goalkeeping and some wayward shooting not helped by the weather kept the score down. Liverpool's half backs had played magnificently in both defence and attack, while the injury to Melia did not disrupt their pattern. Horace Yates wrote in the *Daily Post* the following Monday that 'given the ordinary run of the ball they could have had three or four' while in that evening's *Liverpool Echo* Jack Rowe wrote, 'The margin of Liverpool's victory did not completely reflect their superiority.' With two Christmas games against relegation threatened Stoke coming up, the Reds had every reason to be confident of regaining top spot by the New Year.

Liverpool: Lawrence, Ferns, Moran, Milne, Yeats, Stevenson, Callaghan, Hunt, St John, Melia, Thompson.

Blackpool: Waiters, Thompson, Martin, Crawford, James, Cranston, Hill, Ball, Charnley, Parry, Oates.

Referee: Mr J Parkinson (Blackburn).

Attendance: 13,254.

26th December 1963: Liverpool 6 Stoke City 1, Football League Division One

Liverpool's win at Blackpool meant that they had the best away form in the First Division and picked up sixteen points on the road, one more than they had in the whole of 1962-63. If that could have been replicated at home they would have had a comfortable lead at the top. The title race was turning into an exciting one, with just seven points separating the top eleven teams compared to twelve at this stage the season before.

Liverpool city centre was boasting its busiest Christmas ever, the Echo reporting on Christmas Eve that Eric Cockerham, Chairman of the Liverpool Stores Committee believed that more money had been spent there than ever before. He also stated that the Christmas lights, which were far brighter than the year before, made the city a 'gay and bright place to shop in' and had helped increase visitor numbers. Records were a popular present, with one leading record store reporting that the Beatles L.P. *With The Beatles* had sold more than the Christmas number one single, an extremely rare phenomenon.

The main selection concern as they got ready for the Boxing Day game with Stoke City was Jimmy Melia's knee injury, which saw him attend Anfield on the Sunday for treatment. There were no papers on Christmas Day or Boxing Day so Bill Shankly was unable to confirm to the press beforehand whether or not he would be available for the game. Stoke's Stanley Matthews though, who was still entertaining the crowds at 48, was expected to be fit again after missing his side's match the previous Saturday. In his preview in the Echo on Christmas Eve, Leslie Edwards called him the 'most compelling figure in the game'

The expected appearance of Matthews at Anfield for the first time since December 1953 helped put a few thousand on the gate but they were to be disappointed as he was ruled out of the game. Melia failed to recover from his knee injury, meaning Alf Arrowsmith was given another opportunity. This must have pleased Mr Hagerdorn from Allerton who had a letter published in the Echo that week saying: 'Why Arrowsmith can be continually ignored at the present critical time when the team is in the middle of a goal famine is beyond me to say the least. We know he is no polished international but he does at least shoot on every possible occasion and from every angle.' The thirty goals a season reserve striker was on the mark and Roger Hunt struck four as Liverpool clicked into gear after half time, hitting Stoke for six and putting their recent scoring woes behind them.

On a hard but greasy pitch, the Reds got off to a good start and in the ninth minute Peter Thompson's cross was nodded down by Hunt to Ian St John who stooped low to head the ball past Lawrie Leslie into the Kop goal. However, an anticipated onslaught never came as Gordon Milne and Willie Stevenson struggled to create attacks, and for all their best efforts, the ball rarely ran well for Arrowsmith and St John. In contrast Stoke moved the ball around and Tommy Lawrence twice had to make good saves, first holding on to a powerful downward header from George Kinnell, and then turning a Calvin Palmer shot round the post. Poor finishing also thwarted Stoke but when they did find an equaliser in the 35th minute it was no more than their efforts deserved. After some good build-up play, John Ritchie hit a hard shot into the bottom corner that gave Lawrence no chance.

There was every reason to be apprehensive as Liverpool began the second half kicking towards the Anfield Road end but Stoke were blown away in a devastating six minute spell. In the 47th minute Thompson beat a man and got into the area, chipping to Hunt at the far post who headed the ball home. Two minutes later Thompson was the provider for Hunt again, taking the ball from Arrowsmith and then crossing for him to head past Leslie. In the 53rd minute the victory was all but secured when Hunt ran down the left and pulled the ball back to Arrowsmith,whose shot took a deflection and went in. With Liverpool rampant, Stoke pulled everyone back behind the ball and went for damage limitation as Lawrence remained a spectator.

Arrowsmith should have got his second when he found himself with a shooting position from three yards out but he somehow managed to put the ball over the bar. In the 73rd minute however, it was 5-1 when Hunt completed his hat-trick, sliding Milne's pass past Leslie. Eight minutes later he completed the rout, controlling the ball perfectly just inside the box before slamming it into the net. The Kop voiced their appreciation at this point, singing 'We Love You Yeah Yeah Yeah,' a variation of the Beatles song that had been Number One in the charts at the beginning of the month.

On the whole Stoke probably hadn't deserved to lose 6-1, their woeful defending at the start of the second half contributing to their collapse. Had Keith Bebbington been confident enough to run at Phil Ferns more he may have been productive, and Lawrence's two fine first half saves ensured the Reds were still in the game at half time. Still, there had been plenty of other games in the season where the Reds had lost when they didn't deserve to and it had been sensed that it would only be a matter of time before the goals went in. It may not have been a coincidence either, that this was Arrowsmith's third appearance of the season and the Reds had hit six in two of those. The victory kept Liverpool in third, a point behind Tottenham with the same number of games played, and two behind Blackburn who had played two games more.

Some Stoke fans didn't take the defeat too well, with the charter train from Lime Street being delayed for ten minutes after somebody pulled the emergency cord. When the train arrived at Runcorn the guard refused to take it any further until police went on board, meaning it had to wait until officers arrived from Liverpool. It wasn't just the football train departing Lime Street that had problems, as the train carrying Everton fans back from Leicester was found to have 36 broken light bulbs, four broken windows and one door off its hinges. The *Liverpool Echo* reported on 27th December that 'the whole question of football specials is constantly under review.'

Two days later Liverpool were due to travel to Stoke to play them at the Victoria Ground, but the Echo announced on the Friday evening that the game was in serious doubt. Liverpool's reserves had been due to play there on Boxing Day but they were given the news that the game was off whilst having lunch at a hotel near Knutsford. Stoke's groundstaff spent the Friday clearing ice patches from the pitch and the game was given a 50% chance of going ahead providing there was no further frost. Referee Harold Hackney travelled over from Barnsley to make an evening inspection between 6 and 7pm but didn't hold out much hope, saying he would have a further look the next morning. However when he did so, he concluded that there was too much surface water on the pitch which was unable to drain away due to the ground underneath being rock hard. He made his decision at 9.30am and telephoned Anfield where the Reds team were sat on the bus waiting for news as to whether they could set off.

Two members of the club staff spent much of the morning answering the phones to confirm to fans who were seeking confirmation that the game was indeed off, while Shankly tried his best to persuade Hackney to think again. He asked if holes could be drilled into the pitch to help drain the water and even offered to set off for Stoke anyway getting a further update at lunchtime, but the referee refused to change his decision. A frustrated Shankly told the Echo:

> 'I think our game could be the only one off in England. I think more could have been done yesterday and on Boxing Day. Last week before Stoke's game with Wolves there was ice on the pitch but Stoke put braziers on the pitch on Friday and the game was played. If Stoke would have done the same yesterday, anticipating the thaw, the ice would have melted earlier and given the groundstaff more time to fork the pitch and let the water drain away. We are so closely engaged at the top with Blackburn and Spurs that I don't like to see them increasing their lead at the top today while we are unable to play.'

Although most of the Liverpool players returned to their families, there was no way Shankly was doing this on a free Saturday. He immediately set off for Derby where the Reds' FA Cup opponents were taking on Middlesbrough. It gave him the chance to have a first hand look at the opposition and also run the rule over a Middlesbrough player, although he wouldn't reveal who it was. Captain Ron Yeats took in a match too, going over to Goodison to watch Everton take on Leicester.

The postponement meant that Liverpool missed the chance to return to the top of the table as both Blackburn and Spurs lost, but as 1963 came to a close it was fair to say that Liverpool were happy at their league position. Ian St John said in his final *Daily Post* column of the year, 'The table could hardly look more promising form Liverpool's point of view. True we are only occupying third place but I would not swap records with anybody in the table.' Before looking to get back to the top of the league though, it was time to turn the attention to the FA Cup as the Reds looked to go one better than the previous season.

Liverpool: Lawrence, Ferns, Moran, Milne, Yeats, Stevenson, Callaghan, Hunt, St John, Arrowsmith, Thompson.

Stoke: Leslie, Asprey, Allen, Palmer, Stuart, Skeels, Viollet, Kinnell, Ritchie, Dobing, Bebbington.

Referee: Mr J. Carr (Sheffield).

Attendance: 49,942.

Top of Table

		Pl	W	D	L	F	A	GA	Pt
1	Blackburn	26	14	6	6	61	34	1.79	34
2	Tottenham	24	14	5	5	65	45	1.44	33
3	Liverpool	23	15	2	6	46	23	2.00	32

12

Shooting Arrows and a Valiant Effort

Before they could build on the Boxing Day rout of Stoke, Liverpool turned their attentions to the FA Cup. After going so close in the semi final the previous season, Liverpool were determined to go one better this time around and get to Wembley as they sought to win the FA Cup for the very first time. January also saw them with two league matches but they would have to make do without Ron Yeats due to injury.

4th January 1964: Liverpool 5 Derby County 0, FA Cup Third Round

The Reds may have been in the hunt for the league championship but back then the FA Cup was just as important, as emphasised by the amount of press coverage it received, the fact that admission prices remained the same, and that there was no squad rotation. Liverpool's failure to win the cup in their 72-year history was the source of many jokes amongst fans in the city at the time, with Leslie Edwards writing in his *Liverpool Echo* preview on the day of the game,

> 'Liverpool's failure to win the FA Cup in all their long history has tempted many to suggest 'This must be their year.' We have long ceased conjecture on these lines, saying that we'll believe it when we see it. Thousands who vowed they'd break teetotal if it ever happened have long since passed on. Countless thousands of others would die happy if their side ever reached Wembley and won there.'

Interest in the cup amongst fans could be demonstrated by the fact that the draw for the third round was the main headline on the front page of the *Liverpool Echo* on the day that it occurred, while more areas of the ground were ticketed than normal. There was no cash admission to wing sections of the Main Stand on the day for example, while tickets were also required for the Paddock. There was no such enthusiasm from Derby County's supporters though, as they revealed the week before Christmas that they had sold only 200 of the 2,000 tickets allocated to them.

Bill Shankly confirmed on the Thursday that the team would be unchanged, a move that Horace Yates described in the *Daily Post* as one that led to Liverpool supporters 'scarcely batting an eyelid.' Jimmy Melia and Gerry Byrne were still some way off match fitness, but there was some experimentation as Shankly revealed that Alf Arrowsmith would play at centre forward with Ian St John moving to inside left. This experimentation meant that neither Melia nor St John could be certain of their place in the side as Shankly started moving the forwards around. The day before the game Yates wrote that 'the infusion of Arrowsmith's youth, drive and finishing power into the forward line will have destroyed any sense of complacency there may have been by what had come to be regarded as automatic selection.'

Derby may have been in the Second Division but Yates warned against it being assumed that the Reds had an automatic ticket to the next round, saying it would be a folly to do so. Liverpool's home form was nowhere near as good as it should have been and Derby had a good away record. Shankly was only too aware of the potential for an upset, telling fans,

> 'There have been some tremendous surprises in the cup in the past. It is certain there will be others in the future. We just want to steer clear of them. Derby will be given the same respect as we gave to Burnley, Arsenal, West Ham and Leicester last season. Our preparation has been along similar lines and it was good enough to take us to the semi final. I don't think there is any doubt we have proved ourselves cup fighters.'

Derby's team contained some youngsters, Ron Webster and Mick Williamson, who were making their cup debuts but their manager Tim Ward had faith in them. He preferred to use players in their regular positions rather than moving an experienced player to an unfamiliar role telling Yates, 'We haven't an experienced inside forward on the books who could do better. I know they will give me everything they have and work hard and chase for ninety minutes. It will be a tough game but we shall be fighting all the way.' In the end the scoreline looked comfortable for the Reds as they hit five without reply, Arrowsmith justifying his inclusion with four, but they were made to work hard for it by a resilient Derby side.

It was a misty day but otherwise perfect conditions for football with no wind or rain. *She Loves You* was played over the public address system before the teams came out, which led to the Kop singing 'We Love You Yeah Yeah Yeah' line as they swayed from side to side. Described by that night's Echo as 'the unusual prelude to the teams coming out,' this was the game that the Kop began to assert itself as a different type of football crowd as it was now becoming clear that the singing of 'We Love You Yeah Yeah Yeah' towards the end of the Boxing Day game was no one off.

After losing the toss the Reds were forced to kick into the Kop for the first half, during which Derby started slowly and unadventurously, seeming scared of making a mistake. However they gave away a free kick in a dangerous position when Ron Webster fouled Roger Hunt. Ronnie Moran took the kick which deflected and went just past the post for a corner. Shortly after this Ian Callaghan crossed and Hunt collided with keeper

Reg Matthews, the ball spilling loose but being cleared away. Derby had a chance when Gordon Hughes crossed to Jack Parry but his header was so weak that Phil Ferns was confident enough to stop the ball then pass it to Tommy Lawrence.

Willie Stevenson came close to putting Liverpool in front, his shot from outside the area being well saved by Matthews at the foot of the post. Derby then had two fantastic opportunities to take a shock lead. First Phil Waller, with a clear sight of goal from the edge of the area, mis-kicked and his shot spun wide, then Callaghan's weak backpass was intercepted by Micky Williamson but somehow he shot wide.

In the 23rd minute though, Callaghan made up for his error when he beat Bobby Ferguson and crossed into the penalty area. Although the ball was cleared it fell to the feet of Arrowsmith who hit a low drive into the net from the edge of the box. Just a minute later it was almost 2-0 when Arrowsmith played in Callaghan but his shot went just over the bar. The second goal came in the 38th minute when Arrowsmith played the ball to Thompson on the wing and he crossed back into the box, where the Reds centre forward was on hand to hammer it past the keeper.

Derby came out for the second half in a deflated state, with Liverpool taking the game straight to them in search of the goals that would confirm their place in the next round. Arrowsmith was on a mission to find his hat-trick and was running everywhere but it was Milne who had the best chance early on, his effort being held by Matthews at the second attempt. Sensing all may not be lost, Derby began to get back into it and had a great chance when Webster passed to Williamson, but his low effort went straight at Lawrence.

Shortly after this, Williamson and Ron Yeats chased after the ball and the Reds' captain went down holding his leg, but after being treated for several minutes by Bob Paisley he was able to continue. Bill Curry then found himself clean through on goal but his shot was beaten out by Lawrence back to him but he was unable to connect with his head and Liverpool had survived a lucky escape.

Derby's defence was well organised and restricted Liverpool to long shots, a couple of which were well saved by Matthews. In the 63rd minute the Kop's nerves were eased when Milne passed to Hunt and he hit a hard, low shot with his left foot past Matthews. The visitors didn't give up and had plenty of possession around the Reds' area, having a good penalty shout for handball when a shot was deflected wide but the referee only gave a corner. There was a concern for Liverpool with Stevenson moving into the middle and Yeats going onto the left flank as he continued to struggle with his leg injury. In what was now an anti-climatic game it seemed likely that Derby would get a goal back so it was a surprise when the Reds broke clear and Arrowsmith claimed his hat-trick in the 73rd minute. St John played him in and as Matthews advanced off his line, Arrowsmith kept his cool and slotted the ball home.

Derby never stopped looking for a consolation goal and were unfortunate not to be awarded a penalty when St John appeared to bring down Curry in the area. Lawrence then had to be at full stretch to turn a Hughes shot around the post. It didn't come though and after Matthews had needed treatment when he injured himself making a full length save from Hunt, Arrowsmith got the fifth with two minutes to go when he converted Milne's low cross. At the end of the game Arrowsmith got a tremendous ovation from the Kop, as did Matthews who had made some fine saves and also shown bravery to carry on at the end.

Liverpool: Lawrence, Ferns, Moran, Milne, Yeats, Stevenson, Callaghan, Hunt, St John, Arrowsmith, Thompson.

Derby: Matthews, Barrowcliffe, Ferguson, Waller, Young, Parry, Hughes, Webster, Curry, Williamson, McCann.

Referee: Mr M. Fussey (Retford).

Attendance: 46,460.

11th January 1964: Liverpool 2 Chelsea 1, Football League Division One

On the Monday after beating Derby, the Reds were handed a favourable home draw in the FA Cup as they were paired with a Third Division side, Port Vale. The bookmakers responding by making them 15/2 joint favourites along with holders Manchester United. Liverpool and Vale had met in the Second Division three seasons running in the mid 1950s with the Reds twice winning 4-1 at Anfield, but since then they had gone in opposite directions.

Vale were one of the few teams left in the draw that hadn't been scouted recently, a situation that Horace Yates predicted in the *Daily Post* would soon be rectified. Bill Shankly made it clear they would not be treated any differently to top flight opposition, telling Horace Yates,

> 'Any draw at home is a good draw. But Port Vale will be given the royal treatment as far as we are concerned. Whether they are named Arsenal, Burnley or Port Vale makes no difference to us. We will make our plans to win from strength. We do not rely on any form of co-operation from team weaknesses in the opposition. Port Vale have many very experienced players, not forgetting Billy Bingham who used to be with Everton, and their record is worthy of respect.'

Before the cup tie there were two league games to play, the first of which was at home to Tommy Docherty's young Chelsea side, who were in mid table but playing some attractive football. Liverpool looked like they would have to make do without captain Ron Yeats, who was receiving intensive treatment on his ankle following the Derby game and wasn't training, while

Gerry Byrne and Jimmy Melia were still working their way back to match fitness. Another injury was to Shankly himself, who wrenched his knee in training on the Monday and joked afterwards, 'I don't think I can be 100% fit for Saturday. Still we will probably get by all right as you may have noticed the chap playing right half now isn't doing too badly.'[34]

The city was awash with rumours that Shankly had had a bust up with Ian St John, who wore the number ten shirt for the Derby game and played at inside left while Alf Arrowsmith took over in the middle. St John was quick to quash the gossip, describing it as bunkum. In his *Daily Post* column on the 8th January he wrote,

> 'Mr Shankly asked me how I felt about switching positions. I had no hesitation in giving my reply. If it was for the good of the team, I said I would play inside left. In Scotland I have played inside right quite often. Inside left is new to me but as professional footballers we must realise that we have obligations to the club. Someone had to move over to make way for me, it is the natural sequence of promotion.'

The burst of goals since 21-year-old Arrowsmith had come into the team meant the Mancunian, signed from Ashton United for just £1,500 in 1960, was the name on all supporters lips. In the Echo, Leslie Edwards posed the question of where this left Melia who would normally expect to regain his place with St John moving back to centre forward. However, in the three home games in which Arrowsmith had played this season the Reds had scored a total of seventeen goals, a fact that couldn't be ignored. It was unthinkable that St John could not be accommodated in the team so Melia, so often the crowd's scapegoat when things went wrong, was now in danger of being left out for the time being.

By the middle of the week speculation was rife that Melia had asked for a move, with Blackpool and Burnley said to be interested. Shankly rubbished the claims, telling the Echo on the Wednesday, 'Ridiculous, Jimmy has not asked for a move and we as a club have never discussed such possibilities. You must remember he was not absolutely fit for the cup tie against Derby.' Shankly did concede though that Melia was too good for Central League football and that 'if he was out of the team when fully fit the situation would be different.'

When it came to money, the win bonuses and 40,000 plus crowds at Anfield meant the players were living quite comfortably on up to £100 a week, but this was small change compared to those involved in show business. On 8th January the Post ran a 'day in the life' feature on comedian Ken Dodd and reported that he was earning £1,500 a week. Despite this he still lived with his mum and dad in Knotty Ash and spent frugally, buying black pudding from St John's market.

Dodd's wealth appeared to contrast somewhat with that of ex-Liverpool centre half Laurie Hughes, who had become the first Reds player to appear in the World Cup in 1950. On the day Dodd was featured in the Post, Hughes was in court charged with receiving stolen goods. Now running a grocery store, Hughes and his business partner were accused of buying food that was actually the property of Woolworths. Represented by famous local solicitor Rex Makin, Hughes was described in court as being in a business he knew nothing about and that he had been a fool. The Magistrates agreed and took a lenient view, imposing a fine of just £20 on him.

Chelsea sent a warning to Liverpool in midweek when they knocked Tottenham, seen by many as the favourites for the league title, out of the FA Cup in a replay that was watched by over 70,000 at Stamford Bridge. Docherty warned that they weren't focusing just on the cups and believed his side could still work their way into the title race. He told reporters that his side were 'a far different proposition than when they beat us 3-1 at Stamford Bridge in September.'[35] Chelsea were now unbeaten in eleven games and had firmly adapted to life in the First Division, meaning it would be intriguing to see if Liverpool's forward line could continue to score so freely.

It was clear by the end of the week that Yeats would not be able to play, a wax bath administered by Bob Paisley failing to improve his ankle. He had an x-ray on the Thursday that revealed no breaks and that the only option was to rest for a few weeks. The Post reported on the Friday that various options were available for Shankly, as Byrne had come through a couple of practice games in the week with no reaction. He could go back into the side at right back with Phil Ferns moving up to right half and Willie Stevenson covering in the middle. Another possibility was reserve centre half Chris Lawler coming in as a straight replacement for Yeats. On the Friday afternoon though, Shankly sprung a surprise when he made another change in addition to the one that was enforced on him. Lawler was confirmed as in, but he also dropped Ferns and replaced him with 24-year-old Bobby Thomson, who had played four league matches the previous campaign. Ferns had been off form of late and Shankly blamed the press for this, telling journalists, 'Ferns has been so greatly affected by the criticisms that I had to take him out for his own good. He is now no more than a shadow of his former self.'

With the defence sorted out, Shankly now just had to take a final check on St John, who had felt twinges in his ankle the last few days. He declared himself fit on the Friday night, meaning Melia would have to make do with a reserve outing but he said he would not be doing anything drastic as he knew his chance would come again. 'I did not expect to get a game this week. I am prepared to bide my time, my chance will come and there will be no foolish requests from me.'[36]

Chelsea had a reputation as a lively attacking side but Shankly was confident his inexperienced defenders could cope. Horace Yates was not so sure, writing on the morning of the match, 'With Yeats in the team I would have been confident of victory. Without him I am merely hopeful.' He predicted that Chelsea would be at their most dangerous in the first twenty minutes and was proved right as they took an early lead. However his hopes were realised as the Reds came back to take both points with Arrowsmith hitting a stunning late winner in a game of two halves.

It had been expected that Ronnie Moran would captain the side in the absence of Yeats but instead, Shankly handed the armband to Gordon Milne which was a deserved honour given what he had contributed to the club since joining in 1960. Arrowsmith was immediately in the action, playing a great pass out to Peter Thompson who put in a dangerous cross but St John just failed to connect. Liverpool continued with the early high tempo and a good move ended with Roger Hunt hitting a tame shot that was easily gathered by John Dunn. Chelsea hit back and forced three corners in quick succession, before Barry Bridges appealed for a penalty after going down in the area but the referee was having none of it. In the seventh minute they did take the lead when Bobby Tambling played the ball to Bridges who was on the right hand side of the area, and his low shot went in off the post.

Chelsea could have gone 2-0 up soon afterwards but Lawler reacted well to block a Tambling shot that seemed to have the beating of Tommy Lawrence. A few moments later the same player had a great chance but fired the ball wide. Tambling was causing havoc amongst the Reds defence and when he beat Moran and crossed dangerously Thomson was on hand to head clear, then he hit a fierce shot that beat Lawrence but came back off the upright. Liverpool's forwards were seeing very little of the ball and the first real shot at goal came from Stevenson, who connected with plenty of power but it wasn't on target.

As Tommy Docherty predicted, Chelsea were a vastly different side to the one Liverpool had beaten at Stamford Bridge in September. Their defence was reading everything perfectly to break up attacks, and they were causing problems at the other end with Bert Murray going close with a long range effort. Frank Blunstone then had a shot parried by Lawrence but Lawler managed to get the ball clear but Terry Venables then hit a dangerous low drive that the Reds' keeper managed to hold on to.

The home crowd were now getting edgy and one of the few opportunities the Reds created came when a Chelsea move broke down. Thompson ran down the left wing but his cross was too strong and went out for a throw in, leading to cries of derision from fans in the Paddock and Main Stand. Callaghan was faring slightly better than his left wing counterpart and a good cross he put in had to be turned over for a corner by Ron Harris. The last action of the half saw Thomson, who was handling things far better than fellow reserve Lawler, head away a cross by Murray and on the whole, the Reds were glad to go back to the dressing rooms just 1-0 down.

Liverpool were kicking into the Kop for the second half and responded to the roars of encouragement. Arrowsmith had his first real opportunity when he spun and shot following a Thompson cross, producing a brilliant save by Dunn. He then tried to seize upon a sliced clearance but Dunn managed to clear before he got there. Although the Reds were now playing better than at any other time in the game, Chelsea were still dangerous and Tambling dispossessed Moran before putting in a cross that almost swerved into the net, but instead landed on top of it. Lawrence then made a hash of a low shot from Tambling, letting it go under his body, but Moran managed to get back and clear the ball off the line.

Chelsea's defence was well organised and Liverpool were on the whole restricted to long shots and trying their luck with crosses. Efforts from Hunt and Callaghan both ended up in the Kop and most of Thompson's centres were easily headed clear. On the other side of the pitch Callaghan tried a different approach and surprised everyone with a hard and low cross which John Mortimore managed to clear from the foot of the post. In the 69th minute the equaliser eventually came from what looked like an impossible position. Hunt was at the right corner of the box with his back to goal and shadowed by Frank Blunstone and Frank Upton. Somehow he managed to turn and squeeze between them before unleashing a fierce shot that Dunn didn't move for, probably because he was so surprised that the opportunity had been created.

The Reds were galvanised by the goal and Arrowsmith's low shot was spilled by Dunn but a defender scrambled it clear. Thompson then hit a brilliant drive that was turned around the post. With Lawler now far more confident at centre half there looked likely to be only one winner as the Reds attacked at will. Arrowsmith should have done better when he created a shooting opportunity but his effort was too weak and easily held by Dunn, who was now taking his goal kicks far quicker than he had at 1-0. Arrowsmith was then presented with a golden chance when Upton hit a weak backpass but his shot went wide from a tight angle.

With five minutes left the winner arrived and it was described by that night's *Liverpool Echo* as 'one of the most dramatic goals Anfield has seen for seasons.' Thompson broke clear down the left and hit a quick cross into the middle for Arrowsmith to chase. Despite the ball going past him, he somehow managed to swing his leg and volley it goalwards with the outside of his right foot at great speed. Dunn just about managed to get a hand to it but could only help it into the net to the delight of the Kop.

It had been a brilliant game played at speed with Chelsea showing they had come a long way since the start of the season and were a match for anyone on their day. Liverpool though refused to be beaten and it was capped by a sensational goal from the man of the moment. Elsewhere Liverpool's two closest rivals were in action at White Hart Lane with Tottenham beating

Blackburn 4-1. This meant that the Reds went up into second place just a point behind Spurs but with a game in hand.

Liverpool: Lawrence, Thomson, Moran, Milne, Lawler, Stevenson, Callaghan, Hunt, Arrowsmith, St John, Thompson.

Chelsea: Dunn, Hinton, A Harris, R Harris, Mortimore, Upton, Murray, Tambling, Bridges, Venables, Blunstone.

Referee: Mr A. Sparling (Grimsby).

Attendance: 45,848.

18th January 2013: West Ham United 1 Liverpool 0, Football League Division One

Immediately after the Chelsea game the players boarded a coach for Blackpool were they stayed for three nights to unwind and not kick a ball, Shankly believing the rest would reap the benefits in the long run. Apart from taking a few brisk walks and playing some golf, there would be nothing else strenuous for them to do although the injured players still underwent some light exercises and had treatment with portable equipment that was taken with the party.

As the players relaxed along with the Arsenal squad who were in Blackpool for a break as well, Alf Arrowsmith's stunning winner against Chelsea remained the main topic of conversation in the local press. In the *Liverpool Echo* on 13th January, Leslie Edwards wrote, 'How young Arrowsmith scored it only he knows' and that his teammates were 'as mystified as they were delighted.' Boss Bill Shankly wasn't surprised though, telling Edwards, 'I've seen him score quite a number of remarkable goals from half chances such as this.'

It's a joke fifty years on that supporters in the Centenary Stand like to leave early, but it was just the same for fans in what was then the Kemlyn Road in this game, much to the annoyance of a supporter identifying himself only as 'A Real Red' from Parkfield Road in Aigburth. His letter to the Echo said,

> 'I always thought that season tickets holders were keen fans. Yet fifteen minutes before the end and at the most exciting stage of the Liverpool-Chelsea match, numbers of so called supporters started to leave the new stand. How they could do this when a great game was reaching its climax disgusted me. They missed a wonderful winning goal. Let us hope they miss renewing their season tickets next season.'

On the last night of their break, Liverpool's players watched Preston take on Nottingham Forest in an FA Cup replay at Deepdale. Howard Kendall scored the winner for Preston in a game played in treacherous conditions and only restarted after half time when the snow had been cleared off the pitch. In London the pitch at West Ham United's Upton Park ground, where the Reds would be playing at the weekend, was underneath three inches of snow but the forecast for the week ahead looked good.

The Met Office moved quickly to dispel fears of another two month-long freeze like the previous winter, predicting that there would be a few further showers but nothing excessive. With the weather looking like it would clear up in time, Ron Yeats' injury appeared to be on the mend too, with Ian St John updating his fans in his weekly *Daily Post* column on the Tuesday that 'we will all be very surprised if he is not 100% fit.' The Hammers were down in seventeenth place but St John believed they would still provide a stern test as 'despite their league position they are a terribly difficult side to beat because of the tactics that they employ.'

The issue of crowd trouble at grounds seemed to be improving, with the FA acknowledging that as there had been no further incidents at Everton's Goodison Park since, they would be taking no further action regarding Chelsea's Tommy Docherty being hit by a missile the previous month. Although Everton were happy with the FA over this, they were disappointed at news reports stating that Tony Kay had withdrawn from the next England training camp scheduled for 10th February at Matlock due to injury. The club moved swiftly to phone the FA and say that their letter had been misinterpreted, as Kay had played a reserve game and would be free to join the party if he was fully fit by then. On the other hand, Bill Shankly was not in as much mood to bow down fully to the FA and sought a compromise by proposing a two day camp instead of three. With Roger Hunt, Gordon Milne and Peter Thompson all scheduled to be involved he said, 'We are not unmindful of the fact that at this stage of the season our players have restricted training. It might upset our plans if they were called upon for any undue exertions. Hard training now would be no good to our boys.'[37]

Although usually only prepared to take one match at a time, with Liverpool second in the table and looking likely to make the last sixteen of the FA Cup, Shankly admitted this week that he was contemplating the thought of playing in Europe the following season. On the Thursday he told Horace Yates of the *Daily Post*,

> 'We have come a long way already. The players are determined to keep up the pressure, continue to make progress and win a place amongst the honours. They aim to open up wider fields for next season and why not. This team of ours can be fully matured in twelve months. A year from now I calculate they will be ready and willing to take on anybody.'

If Liverpool were to compete in UEFA's prestige competition, the European Cup, Yates calculated that the Reds were well on target based on the previous season's standings at a similar stage. Liverpool now had 34 points from 24 games, compared to Everton's 34 from 23 the season before. 61 points was enough for Everton to win the league in 1962-63, meaning the Reds needed to get 27 points form their last eighteen games, eleven of which were away.

Shankly knew his side would face a tough test at West Ham who he claimed were 'capable of beating the best but falling to the worst according to their mood.' The Reds travelled to London on the Friday without Yeats, who despite having made good progress with his injured ankle wasn't going to be risked. Shankly explained that had the ground been softer he would have travelled, but he didn't want him to play on a hard pitch with so many more vital games coming up. Gerry Byrne, who hadn't played since November, was in the party of twelve but no indication was given by Shankly as to whether it would be Bobby Thomson or Ronnie Moran who would make way for him. Jimmy Melia stayed behind at his own request to play for the reserves against Barnsley to maintain match fitness and told the Post that 'I believe I can get back in and when I do it will be for keeps.'

It was Moran who made way for Byrne, with Thomson continuing at left back in a game that the Reds lost but still put in a performance that was encouraging enough. They were presented with an early opportunity when John Burkett hit a poor pass to Bobby Moore that Hunt intercepted. Hunt raced past Moore, who was then a left half, but his low shot went just wide of the post. St John then failed to meet a Thompson cross as Liverpool created the better of the early opportunities, easily absorbing any West Ham pressure. There was a golden chance for the Hammers when St John sliced a clearance to the feet of John Sissons, who crossed to Geoff Hurst but his shot went over the bar. After a quarter of an hour West Ham were gifted an even better opportunity when Lawler messed up a clearance straight into the path of John Byrne. He took the ball round the onrushing Tommy Lawrence but with Byrne and Thomson having got back to cover the line, he passed the responsibility of shooting instead to a surprised Hurst who hesitated, allowing Milne to make a last gasp challenge.

Lawler didn't let his error get to him and played with confidence, making a number of good headed clearances but he could do nothing about West Ham's opening goal in the 28th minute. Sissons crossed from the right and it went past everybody before being picked up by Peter Brabrook on the left. He crossed the ball back in and Byrne was on hand to turn it into the net. Backed by a vociferous crowd West Ham looked even more menacing, but the Reds' defence remained as steady as it had been before and denied them any clear chances. Liverpool had a great chance to equalise when the referee overruled an offside flag against Hunt and Callaghan moved into a shooting position. His shot was deflected but after being wrong-footed, Jim Standen managed to save it on the line.

The Reds had a great opportunity when Thompson centred to Arrowsmith who was impeded by Ken Brown, but he remained upright and managed to get his head to the ball, but the effort was weak and easily held by Standen. Despite having the chance, the referee still called play back for a free kick just outside the area. This was taken by Hunt but it was well saved by Standen. Soon after this, Arrowsmith moved onto the wing and crossed for St John but his header was cleared off the line by Moore. Hunt was then pushed over in the penalty area but as the incident occurred off the ball no penalty was given.

The start of the second half was delayed as police cleared a number of missiles that had been thrown from behind one of the goals, despite a loudspeaker appeal for the crowd to stop. This didn't disrupt Liverpool's rhythm and from a long goal kick by Lawrence, Hunt tried to nick the ball past Standen but the keeper managed to get his legs in the way. St John then tested the Standen from distance but he made a full length save and Brown made a frantic block when Thompson looked certain to score from close range. When Callaghan hit an almighty effort from the right side of the box Standen was finally beaten but the ball bounced off the post. Arrowsmith then played a delightful one-two with Hunt but Standen saved his shot as the Reds did everything but score.

After fending off twenty minutes of Liverpool pressure, West Ham almost added an undeserved second goal midway through the half when Sissons was presented with an open goal from a few yards but inexplicably, he put the ball wide. Brabrook was then clean through but rather than blast the ball past Lawrence he tried a lob and the Reds' keeper managed to save it. After surviving these scares the Reds looked likely to equalise again with Arrowsmith having a header from a corner saved and even Thomson getting forward, but he sliced his chance over the bar. Lawler came up for the next attack but his header was safely gathered, Willie Stevenson had a powerful shot stopped by Standen, who then held on to a ferocious drive by Hunt.

There was no way through, West Ham took both points and the Reds slipped to third, Blackburn going above them after a 1-1 draw at home to Wolves. However Horace Yates, writing in the *Daily Post* the following Monday, did not believe there was any cause for concern. Referring to Standen's outstanding performance in goal he described it as 'one man versus a firing squad' and suggested that 'it was a defeat with honour.' In that evening's *Liverpool Echo* he concluded, 'Yeats was badly missed. Here was the man who really would have made the difference to Liverpool. Don't run away with the idea that Liverpool are slipping. They are not!'

Liverpool: Lawrence, Thomson, Byrne, Milne, Lawler, Stevenson, Callaghan, Hunt, Arrowsmith, St John, Thompson.

West Ham: Standen, Bond, Burkett, Bovington, Brown, Moore, Brabrook, Boyce, Byrne, Hurst, Sissons.

Referee: Mr J. Finney (Hereford).

Attendance: 25,546.

25th January 1964: Liverpool 0 Port Vale 0, FA Cup Fourth Round

Liverpool moved quickly to reassure supporters over the fitness of Ron Yeats in the build up to this game, with Bill Shankly confirming on the Monday that he would be fit. The Reds' captain did some light training on that day and then started full sessions on the Tuesday. The defeat at West Ham was unlikely to influence team selection, with the boss saying he would have 'little trouble' in deciding who to pick for the match. This meant that Jimmy Melia, who had made three goals in the reserves 6-0 rout of Barnsley and Phil Ferns, who had scored two, would both have to bide their time a while longer before getting another chance.

Yeats had not had a free Saturday whilst his teammates were playing at West Ham. Instead he was sent to the Potteries by Shankly to watch Port Vale, leading to plenty of leg pulling that he should retire and become the club's chief scout. However on the Tuesday training was much more sombre when Ian Callaghan reported that he had been in a car accident the night before in which a girl was killed. Liverpool's midfielder escaped with just a scar on his face but was sent home by Shankly who described him as 'terribly upset'. Shankly continued, 'Training for him was impracticable. He is deeply sorry for the parents as we all are. The news of the accident left a cloud over the ground. It was so eerie you could feel it and I think we are all as upset as Ian.'[38]

The players refused to let their confidence drop after the defeat at Upton Park. Writing in his *Daily Post* column, Ian St John bemoaned the fact that 'goalkeepers reserve their top displays for our undoing'. He did believe there were positives to take, as the number of chances they managed to create would give them plenty of confidence to break down what was certain to be a stubborn Port Vale display. He believed that it was 'inconceivable that we will run into another Standen this week.'

St John also made it clear to fans that he was happy playing at inside left, saying that he was now in the game almost continuously and covering more ground than he had ever done. He also felt that although Tottenham, who were out of the cup, had moved further ahead in the league table, he would still not want to swap places with them as Liverpool were determined to fight on both fronts.

The issue of whether Liverpool could do the 'Double' was a big talking point amongst fans, but Leslie Edwards felt that only one was achievable and it was more likely to be the championship. In the Echo on 21st January he argued that if Spurs were to slip up then Liverpool 'must step into the place.' The bookmakers certainly believed that the Reds could lift their first FA Cup, shortening both theirs and co-favourites Manchester United's odds that week to 13/2. Port Vale were 1,000-1 outsiders along with Aldershot,

Bristol Rovers and Bedford, the only non-league side left in the competition.

As part of their preparations for what would be the biggest game of many of their players careers, Vale's squad enjoyed a brine bath on the Tuesday and then held a full scale practice match on the Wednesday, the first team taking on the reserves who were made to play the same tactics as the Reds. The squad then set off by coach for Anfield where Shankly had sportingly allowed them to take a look at the ground to get a feel for it. One player who would not be unfamiliar with the surroundings was centre half John Nicholson, who joined them from the Reds in 1961 for a £2,000 fee, having made just one appearance for the club in four years. Greeting them off the coach, Shankly quipped 'Hello boys, bit early aren't you? The kick off is not until three o'clock next Saturday.'

The players and manager Freddie Steele spent about forty minutes looking around but Horace Yates didn't believe there was much point to the visit. The following morning he wrote in the Post, 'If they now believe they know Anfield, how mistaken is this view! Anfield is not Anfield without the yelling, swirling, singing Kop and the great wall of concrete steps behind the goal was deserted. Still if they feel it has served purpose so well and good.'

On the Friday Shankly confirmed that Yeats would be returning to the side as he trained wearing his normal match boots and showed no reaction. Vale's scouts had watched both of Liverpool's games since the draw was made, but their captain had appeared in neither and Horace Yates predicted in the Post that 'they can have no sort of accurate idea of the problems their attack may encounter today.' Although he believed Vale would put up a 'tremendous battle,' he felt that anyone seeking a cup upset would have to look elsewhere.

A capacity crowd looked likely with Vale having sold 3,000 stand tickets and another 5,000 more expected to pay on the day for what Freddie Steele described as 'our Wembley.' When announcing which players would make the trip up to Liverpool on the Friday, Steele decided there was no room for sentiment and left out veteran Billy Bingham, who had scored in every round for Luton when they reached the final in 1959. It was a decision that was proved to be the right one as Vale held Liverpool to a draw in a game that they could well have won.

Kicking into the Kop for the first half, Vale made it clear they hadn't come to defend and created a chance in the first minute. Ron Smith completely missed his kick but the ball broke to Tony Richards whose shot was blocked. Both sides were moving the ball around well and the first chance for Liverpool came when Callaghan shot from the edge of the area but the ball was turned over the bar by Ken Hancock. Alf Arrowsmith tried his luck from a difficult angle and could only find the side netting. Stan Steele then hit a long shot that was well over the bar before putting in a dangerous cross that led to Gordon Milne dispossessing Smith who was hoping to latch on to it. Vale were performing particularly well, their defence being solid and the crowd that had been noisy at the start, was beginning to quieten down.

Steele hit a shot that led to Tommy Lawrence making a brilliant one-handed save and then Gerry Byrne had to clear a Smith header off the line. Vale's play was making Liverpool impatient and they weren't playing steady controlled football. Their movement was too hurried and the visiting defenders were able to break up play easily, with Callaghan especially having no luck in getting past Ron Wilson. The deadlock was almost broken when Willie Stevenson unleashed a fierce shot from thirty yards that Hancock couldn't hold, but he managed to gather the ball before it bounced over the line. Hunt then played in Peter Thompson but Hancock managed to block his shot at point blank range. The last action of the first half saw a neat Vale move that ended with John Rowland's low shot being well held by Lawrence.

Vale were looking just as much a First Division side as Liverpool were, each player giving 100% and all getting back when needed, but not afraid to take the game to the Reds either. After forcing two quick corners a headed clearance was only as far as Richards but his shot was gathered by Lawrence. At the other end St John had a header saved by Hancock who quickly kicked the ball upfield to Richards. He crossed but nobody was there and Lawrence was able to collect.

Midway through the half the Reds managed to get on top but Vale's defence remained solid and Arrowsmith was particularly off form. Vale were now being reduced to counter attacks but the Reds defence were catching them out most of the time by employing the offside trap. Their centre forward Richards responded by trying to barge his way through but Yeats was more than a match for him.

Nicholson had a glorious chance to give Vale the lead when he broke clear and played the ball out to Richards, who crossed into the box but the ex-Reds player missed it by inches. A great move that saw the visitors pass the ball from the back to the front led to a centre by Rowland but nobody was in the box to convert it. Jackie Mudie had a volley saved and header go just over the bar.

Vale were now dominating the game and making it clear they weren't settling for a replay, while their fans were chanting their side's name as loudly as anything the Kop could muster. When Liverpool did try to attack there was just no way through even when they had every player except Lawrence in the opposition half. Mudie then came close to getting a sensational winner with a swerving shot that was tipped around the post.

Vale were a man down for several minutes when Mudie underwent treatment, allowing the Reds to regain the upper hand, but their lack of composure was demonstrated when Thompson sliced a shot high into the Kop. St John then forced a corner when a header was saved but from it Steele was cheeky enough to pass to his keeper from four yards out rather than hoof the ball clear. Liverpool dominated the closing stages but could create just one meaningful chance which Hunt shot straight at Hancock before holding his head in his hands. When the final whistle went the visiting players cartwheeled and hugged each other and Liverpool's chairman T.V Williams admitted that the visitors had not deserved to lose. It meant the sides would replay at Vale Park just two nights later.

Liverpool: Lawrence, Thomson, Byrne, Milne, Yeats, Stevenson, Callaghan, Hunt, Arrowsmith, St John, Thompson.

Port Vale: Hancock, Whalley, Wilson, Rawlings, Nicholson, Sproson, Rowland, Steele, Richards, Mudie, Smith.

Referee: Mr H. Hackney (Barnsley).

Attendance: 52,327.

27th January 1964: Port Vale 1 Liverpool 2, FA Cup Fourth Round Replay

Chairman T.V. Williams may have been telling the press that Port Vale didn't deserve to lose, but Ian St John remained of the opinion they had played too defensive, saying that 'word seems to have got around that the only way to beat Liverpool is to bolt and bar the way to goal with a packed defence.' He admitted that he would much rather have played a First Division side as the games would have been far more open and that 'on paper, games against the lower division sides should be easy but they never are.'[39]

In his analysis in Monday night's *Liverpool Echo*, Leslie Edwards took a different stance to St John, going as far as saying that Port Vale may well have won had Jackie Mudie not been carrying an injury near the end. He wrote that Liverpool's attack had been too narrow and 'played into the hands of a well drilled packed defence' while at the other end Vale 'created more and better scoring chances.' If Liverpool were to win the replay, Edwards determined that the forwards needed to be more direct and 'less inclined to try the impossible gambit of boring through a packed defence single handed.' At least St John would have been pleased to find out on the morning of the replay that if the Reds could go through, they would be facing Arsenal in the next round.

Three trains took 1,200 Reds fans to the Potteries with many more going by coach and car, but they would be the last to travel from Merseyside on the 'football specials.' British Rail announced that day that no more specials would be run from the city following vandalism on trains bringing Everton fans home from Leeds on the Saturday. Sixty light bulbs were smashed and delays caused when the communication cord was pulled five times, leading to British Rail deciding that enough was enough.

A statement that day read, 'This is final, it will not be reconsidered. Anybody wishing to go away to football matches by train in the future will have to go by the normal services and pay the full fare.'[40] Fans queuing at Lime Street were disappointed at the news but not one of the guards, who told the *Daily Post*, 'I shall be glad to see an end to them, they have been nothing but trouble.' Prescot-based Ribble Motor Coaches were also happy, with their spokesman saying, 'I expect there will be an increased demand for coach excursions.'

An unusually large party of fifteen players left Liverpool on the morning of the game, travelling on their new 28-seater luxury coach for the first time. Bill Shankly took an extra player in each department in case there were any unexpected strains to contend with given that the first game had been just two days earlier. Trevor Roberts travelled as goalkeeping cover, Ronnie Moran was the extra defender, Chris Lawler the spare half back and Jimmy Melia an additional forward. Come kick-off time, Shankly decided to make some changes and went for experience, leaving out Bobby Thomson and Alf Arrowsmith as Moran and Melia were recalled. For Vale, Jackie Mudie failed to recover from his injury and he was replaced by Albert Cheeseborough, whose goal took the game to extra time before the Reds finally won thanks to a late, late Peter Thompson strike.

There was a huge crowd with the official attendance being 42,179, but as many as 6,000 more were estimated to have got in when the gates were rushed at the Railway End. Many fans required treatment during the game for crush injuries after being carried away on stretchers, and a man from Leek died a few days later. Astonishingly, incidents such as these were not seen as unusual at the time and did not even get reported in the Echo or Post.

Vale failed to take the game to the Reds early on as may have been expected, but instead defended deep and tackled ferociously. The return of Melia added to Liverpool's attacking options at first, but his input became more limited when he began to be man-marked by Charlie Rawlings. St John was also shackled by John Nicholson and the first real chance for the Reds came on the half hour when Peter Thompson shaved the bar with a drive from outside the area. Five minutes later the breakthrough was made when Roger Hunt broke free of his marker to latch on to a long ball from Gerry Byrne and cleverly guide the ball past Ken Hancock.

In the second half Vale continued to defend deep, as though they had accepted their big moment had passed at Anfield on the Saturday, but the Reds failed to finish them off and were too casual in attack. Vale rarely ventured forward and when they did, the three half backs did their job so efficiently that Tommy Lawrence hardly touched the ball. His first save of the game came just after the hour mark when he easily held John Rowland's low drive. However, with eleven minutes to go, Rowland beat Moran and crossed the ball into the box where it was nodded down by Stan Steele into the path of Cheeseborough who hit an unstoppable shot past Lawrence. Vale were revitalised and only the solidity of Moran and Ron Yeats prevented them creating the chances that would have caused an upset.

There were few scoring chances in extra time as both sets of players began to tire. But with two minutes left Milne hit a hopeful shot that cannoned off a defender into the path of Thompson whose volley flew into the top corner. There was delirium amongst the travelling Reds, two of whom received serious injuries when they fell through the roof of the Railway End, while a Vale fan was hit by falling debris. Vale were gone and the rest of the game was played out with little action, the huge contingent of Liverpool fans singing 'When the Saints Go Marching In' and 'We Love You Yeah Yeah Yeah' until the end. There were delirious scenes at the final whistle with several supporters invading the pitch and jumping about in celebration.

Apart from the over-exuberance, the behaviour of Liverpool's supporters had been exemplary. There was no reported damage to the three trains that carried fans home afterwards, while the behaviour of those near the ground had been praised. The licensee of the Star Hotel had said, 'I have never met a finer lot of people than I did last night. They drank well and behaved well and if they ever come to Burslem again there will always be a welcome for them and their supporters.'[41]

Liverpool: Lawrence, Byrne, Moran, Milne, Yeats, Stevenson, Callaghan, Hunt, St John, Melia, Thompson.

Port Vale: Hancock, Whalley, Wilson, Rawlings, Nicholson, Sproson, Rowland, Steele, Richards, Cheeseborough, Smith.

Referee: Mr H. Hackney (Barnsley).

Attendance: 42,179.

Top of Table

		Pl	W	D	L	F	A	GA	Pt
1	Tottenham	27	17	5	5	74	47	1.57	39
2	Blackburn	28	14	7	7	63	39	1.61	35
3	Liverpool	25	16	2	7	48	25	1.92	34

13

FA Cup Swansong

The month of February saw mixed fortunes for Liverpool as they began the month with a great victory over Sheffield United at Anfield, but then lost the derby against Everton at Goodison Park. A victory at Arsenal followed which saw them installed as favourites for the FA Cup after a favourable quarter final draw, only to succumb to a giant killing act at Anfield.

1st February 1964: Liverpool 6 Sheffield United 1, Football League Division One

Liverpool's progress in both the league and FA Cup showed that they were reaching for the stars and the Superpowers were doing the same, although their ambitions stopped at the moon as the Space Race heated up. On Thursday 30th January Ranger VI, an unmanned spacecraft, was launched by NASA to land on the moon and send back photographs of the surface. However despite the landing being a success, the camera failed and no images were sent back. On the same day that Ranger VI was launched, the Soviet Union sent two satellites, Elektron I and 2, into orbit to map radiation in the Earth's atmosphere.

Peter Thompson's spectacular goal at Port Vale didn't go unnoticed by the international selectors, who called him up for an Under-23 friendly against Scotland at Newcastle the following week. Ron Yeats, who was still awaiting his first full international cap, was given an indication that he was edging closer when he was included in a special training camp to take place at Largs on 9th and 10th February.

The Reds learned that week that they would be travelling to London for the next round of the FA Cup as Arsenal beat West Bromwich Albion 2-0 at Highbury in a replay. Bill Shankly told the *Daily Post* that it should be a good match and that he was confident, but before then there were two league games as his side looked to maintain their title challenge. First up was the visit to Anfield of Sheffield United who had inflicted on them their heaviest defeat of the season to date.Shankly confirmed on the Friday morning that the team would remain unchanged from the Port Vale match and that he was feeling on 'top of the world' due to the whole squad being fit and providing a great deal of competition for places.

The Blades were coming to Anfield on the back of an embarrassing 4-0 defeat at Second Division Swansea Town in an FA Cup replay. In his preview in the *Liverpool Echo* on the Friday, Leslie Edwards described their manager John Harris as one of the most astute in the game, and with a number of international calibre players available they would be looking to wipe the cup defeat out of their system. In the end they were hammered, their goals against tally for the week rising to ten as Liverpool hit six at Anfield for the third time that season.

The Reds came up against a defence determined to stifle them and they were undone by the offside trap four times in the opening ten minutes, leading to chants of 'We want football.' The visitors didn't heed the Kop's advice but in the thirteenth minute they tried to play an offside again but Roger Hunt managed to stay on. It surprised Alan Hodgkinson so much that he was barely ready for the resulting shot that gave Liverpool the lead. Forced to open up, Liverpool took advantage of having more space and Jimmy Melia was the orchestrator of many an attack, although he still came in for some unfair criticism from the crowd at times when he failed to control the ball. In the 27th minute Thompson, the hero at Port Vale, scored the second when he went on a run down the left, cut in and hit a hopeful shot that evaded Hodgkinson who, as with Hunt's goal, could have done more to save it.

Sheffield United were by far the worst side to play at Anfield so far that season and the Reds took full advantage with Willie Stevenson cutting their defence open with a succession of searching passes. They added two more goals before half time with Ian St John and Hunt seizing upon the poor fortune of centre half Joe Shaw who was limping around with an injury.

Ten minutes into the second half St John got the fifth with a hard low shot, but on the hour Brian Richardson pulled a goal back. For a few minutes you wouldn't have realised which side was 5-1 down as the Blades made a game of it but at the back, Ronnie Moran belied his age and Gerry Byrne was back on top form after some rustiness in previous games.

Liverpool recovered and were playing exhibition football, and with the game comfortably won they turned on the style. Gordon Milne played the ball into different channels for St John to run on to and Thompson was giving full back Len Badger a torrid time. With four minutes to go the sixth goal came, St John completing his hat-trick with a goal that was almost identical to the one he had scored earlier in the half. Remarkably, Liverpool had won the game by such a margin without having a single corner and the win lifted Liverpool up to second place, three points behind Tottenham but with two games in hand. The only complaint from the home fans was that they may not have any more goals left in the tank for the next game, the derby at Goodison.

Liverpool: Lawrence, Byrne, Moran, Milne, Yeats, Stevenson, Callaghan, Hunt, St John, Melia, Thompson.

Sheffield Utd: Hodgkinson, Badger, G Shaw, Richardson, J Shaw, Matthewson, Docherty, Allchurch, Jones, Wagstaff, Simpson.

Referee: Mr K. Howley.

Attendance: 43,309.

8th February 1964: Everton 3 Liverpool 1, Football League First Division

On the day Liverpool hammered Sheffield United, Everton won 3-0 against Sheffield Wednesday at Hillsborough to maintain their faint hopes of retaining the title. The Blues were in eighth position, three points behind the Reds, but had played two games more and realistically were looking to the FA Cup for success.

Liverpool on the other hand, firmly believed they could do the Double as Ian St John reminded everybody in his *Daily Post* column on 4th February, writing, 'We are after the Double and we mean to get it. What's more I think we will.' St John's hat-trick the previous Saturday had come at the perfect time given he had been omitted from the Scottish training camp that was to take place the following week. St John was naturally glad to get the goals as his national manager Ian McColl was in the crowd, but it remained to be seen if it would be enough to get him a recall for an upcoming match between the national side and the Scottish League. Despite St John's confidence, Everton's Roy Vernon believed he was being over-optimistic and responded in his column, published the day before the match, 'Liverpool may be able to boast eight goals against two in their last two outings but against far more difficult opposition we can boast five without reply.'

Given importance of the derby, there was not too much to report from Anfield that week but with everybody being fit and the last game won 6-1 there was no need to speculate on who would be in the team. Instead news in the press was focusing on the end of the season and Liverpool's tour of North America. Organisers had asked if they'd consider playing in a tournament but this was refused by Bill Shankly who insisted the Reds stick to their original fixed itinerary of friendly games. He said that he would rather do that than take part in something that could lead to them having to go back near the start of the season to play in a final round of matches. Chairman T.V. Williams and Director Harry Latham went to Newcastle on the Wednesday night to watch England Under-23's in action against Scotland. Although Peter Thompson was playing, the Echo reported that they were most likely there to check on Hearts left back Chris Shevlane as an eventual replacement for Ronnie Moran.

In terms of analysing the rout of Sheffield United, a major talking point was how once again the Reds had scored more goals at the Anfield Road end of the ground than the Kop. In the Echo Leslie Edwards described the

Kop as a 'two-edged weapon' and many of those who wrote to the letters section agreed. A Mr Wall from Kensington believed that the 'frantic anxiety' of the home crowd put the players off too much. His letter, published on the Thursday, said,

> 'Liverpool's splendid away record proves this and one can easily see how relaxed and confident Liverpool are away from home. I think that some members of the Kop are the biggest culprits. The main bulk of Kopites are sensible, loyal supporters, whose only wish is that their favourite team should do well. However there is a bone-headed minority who go away disappointed if one of Liverpool's players has not played sufficiently badly for them to vent their idiotic spite and abuse. Melia is proof of this. No matter how well he plays, as soon as one pass goes astray howls of derision are heard. One often gains the ridiculous notion that these fools are often watching, waiting and hoping for a mistake so that they can howl their venom. Surely this minority of fans realise that all Liverpool's players do their best. There are no shirkers in the present team. As you and other columnists have pointed out, hounding the players only worsens their play. The lack of goals at the Kop end is a warning itself. The few who cause the trouble are spoiling things for the many decent supporters who stand on the Kop and have made its name famous in football.'

There was a change to Liverpool's usual preparation for away derbies when it was decided that the players would lunch together before going to Goodison Park by coach, rather than make their own individual way there. Shankly would not give any indication of his likely tactics but did say on the Friday that form went out of the window for derbies, telling Horace Yates of the Post, 'The form team must be Liverpool but form is hardly the most reliable guide when these sides get together.' Yates himself predicted that the greatest danger to Liverpool would be down the flanks and that it would be a 'ding dong tussle' hoping for plenty of goals. An interesting battle would take place between Ron Yeats and Jimmy Gabriel, who was powerful in the air and in the past month had been moved from centre half to centre forward as part of an attacking reshuffle due to an injury to Alex Young.

With barriers in place behind the goals due to the trouble that had taken place at Goodison in previous games, the capacity was now reduced from 73,000 to 66,500 and those in the ground saw a lacklustre display from the Reds as they were reminded by their rivals as to who still held the championship trophy. The game got off to an explosive start when St John flattened Brian Harris in a challenge, leading to his every touch being booed by the home fans for the next few minutes. The first dangerous move came when Willie Stevenson played a long ball for Roger Hunt to chase and Brian Labone took no chances, hoofing it into the crowd. Everton's first opportunity came when Michael Meagan crossed to Gabriel who headed the ball down but Vernon shot wide. In the ninth minute a similar move saw Everton take the lead. Tony Kay played a high ball into the box, Gabriel out-jumped Moran to nod the ball down and Vernon hit a first time shot past Lawrence.

Everton continued to take the game to the Reds, Tommy Lawrence doing well to hold a cross from Alex Scott and then a few minutes later he saw the Blues winger hit a shot that went just past the post. Yeats then miskicked a clearance into the path of Vernon, but Lawrence was alert and made a full length diving save. In the sixteenth minute Liverpool had their first shot, Hunt trying his luck from outside the box, but his effort went wide. It was a rare foray out of their half though and Meagan then hit a shot through a crowded penalty area that Lawrence touched round the post. Everton were cleverly building from the back, with left half Kay regularly moving into the middle to spray passes out to the wings.

In the 25th minute Liverpool came closest to scoring only to find themselves 2-0 down within seconds. A corner taken by Ian Callaghan was met by Yeats and his header was goalbound, but Gordon West managed to get his hands to it. Meagan hooked the ball clear into the path of Vernon, who carried it forward out of his own half before passing to Gabriel. He went round Yeats before unleashing a shot that went into the net off the post.

Yeats was having a tough time trying to handle both Gabriel and Vernon and soon after this goal he was caught out of position, but Gabriel headed just over the bar. Yeats then atoned for this by blocking a shot from Scott, but he was static as Vernon raced past him and fired a shot that bounced off the post into the path of Moran who cleared the ball for a corner. With five minutes to go to half time, St John had only Liverpool's second serious chance of the game but his header from Thompson's cross landed on the top of the net. As the Reds trudged off into the changing rooms, it was in the knowledge that they had probably not played a poorer half of football all season.

Liverpool began the second half brightly but were stringing too many passes together rather than trying a shot on goal and sometimes even went backwards. Everton kept every player back and the Reds could find no way through, with Gordon Milne and Stevenson not getting forward enough to help put extra pressure on. St John seemed to be letting the crowd get to him and when he had a pass intercepted by Sandy Brown a long ball was played to Derek Temple who ran goalwards only to shoot wide when Yeats challenged him.

Liverpool were now looking more menacing however and forcing a few corners, all of which Yeats went up for. Brown resorted to fouling and had his name put in the referee's notebook after a lunge on Thompson. Liverpool's wingers were in fine form, but the inside forwards were not able to make headway against Kay and Labone. Hunt was virtually anonymous and when he did manage to have a run on goal after shaking off the challenges of Kay and Harris, he shot well wide. Thompson then cut inside and had an effort that was nearer the corner flag than the goal as Everton were happy to absorb the pressure given their two goal advantage and Liverpool's lack of firepower.

The Reds continued to have a tendency to present chances to Everton and when Stevenson and Moran both went for the same ball it broke loose to Stevens, who ran down the wing and put in a dangerous cross that was intercepted by Lawrence. It was Lawrence's first meaningful action of the half and came more than halfway through it, but at the other end West had hardly a touch either. With ten minutes to go St John did give Liverpool some hope, getting the better of Labone and meeting a Gerry Byrne cross with a powerful header that gave West no chance. However they were back in the game just a little more than two minutes and again Everton's goal came from a Liverpool mistake. Moran gave away a free kick when he fouled Scott and when it was crossed into the box, Gabriel rose to head the ball down to Vernon who scored from close range.

As the game drew to a close, Everton's fans taunted the Reds with chants of 'Easy,' and it ended in heated fashion when St John went in hard on West, who remonstrated with him and then went down holding his face. St John was taken over to the corner flag by the referee and Bob Paisley, who tried to intervene, was waved away. After speaking to Everton captain Vernon no action was taken but St John was booed for the rest of the game. St John later said that he had made no contact during the challenge, but after West shouted at him he did raise his hand but then thought better of it. He admitted that his own performance could have been better, saying, 'The crowd baiting me only made matters worse. I know I should have taken no notice.'[42]

It was a bitterly disappointing defeat for the Reds, as Tottenham's 4-0 loss at West Ham meant they could have put themselves in a tremendous position in the title race. As it was they slipped behind Blackburn into third, but were just three points behind Spurs with two games in hand. Other teams were closing in on them though and the Reds needed to put points on the board rather than rely on those extra games.

Liverpool: Lawrence, Byrne, Moran, Milne, Yeats, Stevenson, Callaghan, Hunt, St John, Melia, Thompson.

Everton: West, Brown, Meagan, Harris, Labone, Kay, Scott, Stevens, Gabriel, Vernon, Temple.

Referee: Mr L. Callaghan (Merthyr Tydfil).

Attendance: 66,515.

15th February 1964: Arsenal 0 Liverpool 1, FA Cup Fifth Round

There was no time to dwell on the derby defeat for captain Ron Yeats, who travelled to Largs straight after the game with victorious opponents Jimmy

Gabriel and Alex Scott for a national team training camp. For Yeats it was an important event, as he described how he had 'at last made some progress and appeared to have a chance of playing for the Scotland side against the Scottish League team.'[43]

Bill Shankly gave most of the players two days off after the Everton game. The exception was Ian Callaghan, who attended for treatment to a knock on the knee and was declared fully fit on the Monday evening. That night Yeats flew back to Liverpool after his training in Scotland but the three English players called up for Alf Ramsey's training camp in Matlock were still missing on the Tuesday. Shankly again had something to say about this, especially on hearing that Blackburn's Keith Newton injured his cartilage while away. He told the *Daily Post*,

> 'It might so easily have been one of our own players. This special training question is a matter of doing something that is going to be useful at the right time. It might have been better at the get-together to have been satisfied with talks and tactical functions without any real strenuous exertions. They actually played two games, players at this time of the season do not need extra training.'

Despite having a fully fit squad to choose from, Shankly refused to confirm early in the week that the team would be unchanged for the cup tie, which indicated that he was thinking of making a change following the poor attacking display against Everton. Certainly some fans hoped so and once more it was Jimmy Melia who was the whipping boy, with Mr Harrison from Norris Green having a letter published in the Echo on 12th February which said, 'If Liverpool are to win anything this season Melia must go. Enough of your mealy-mouthed special pleading on behalf of this Peter Pan who never quite made it. I have just witnessed the most feeble display of inside forward play I have ever seen from a Liverpool inside left. Bring back Arrowsmith by all means.' The Everton defeat, coupled with a tricky away tie, had pushed Liverpool's odds for the FA Cup out to 19/2, making them seventh favourite out of the sixteen teams left with Manchester United, away to Barnsley, having the shortest odds of 4/1.

While Liverpool had no injury worries, Arsenal were having something of a crisis. Centre forward Joe Baker was having treatment for a hamstring injury and inside forward Geoff Strong was sent home from training on the Wednesday with what was thought to be a cold but turned out to be mild bronchitis. These two players had scored fifty league and cup goals between them so far, so manager Billy Wright was naturally concerned especially when George Eastham was struck down by it too. By the Friday though, Wright announced that his sick players had recovered, as had Baker, meaning that his side would be at full strength.

The kick-off time for Liverpool's tie at Arsenal was put back by fifteen minutes to 3.15pm, something which did not please Shankly. To try and ease congestion with Tottenham being at home the same day, the games kicked off half an hour apart, with Tottenham's starting at 2.45pm. Shankly was unhappy about this with the Reds being booked to travel home on the 6pm train and he said of the switch, 'This has been done without reference to Liverpool. We shall have something to say about it. We would prefer a 2.45pm start.'[44] The authorities refused to change the times around, but the Metropolitan Police stepped in and promised to provide an escort afterwards to make sure they arrived at Euston in time.

After holding a tactical meeting at Melwood, Liverpool's party of thirteen players travelled to London on the 2pm train on the Friday. Shankly announced that Phil Ferns was travelling as reserve cover for the defensive positions, while the only choice to make was whether to recall Alf Arrowsmith, or persist with Melia who had been receiving treatment for a niggling knee injury but had declared himself fit. In his *Liverpool Echo* preview Leslie Edwards predicted that Shankly would stick with experience and play Melia as he wasn't usually one to take gambles. He wrote that although the crowd gave Melia stick, he performed better away, defences feared him, and he would gain confidence by being picked again. However, he admitted that he wouldn't have Shankly's job 'for all the money at the mint' given the decision he had to make as 'whatever move he makes will automatically be wrong if the result is wrong.' The following morning in the *Daily Post* Horace Yates didn't comment on team selection, but instead on how Liverpool's defence needed to be on top form to thwart the threat of Baker and Strong and that a draw looked the most likely result.

Those travelling by coach went overnight, with seventeen Ribble Motor Company vehicles departing from various points at around 11.30pm. As fans were leaving for their long journey, a meeting was drawing to a close at Liverpool Town Hall regarding the future of transport in the Merseyside region. Seven local authorities, backed by the Transport Minister, agreed that a new £11 million tunnel would link Liverpool with Wallasey and that construction work was likely to start in 1966. With the football special trains now axed, some Liverpool fans travelled by plane to London on the morning of the game. The Shareholders' Association chartered a 58 seater Viscount aircraft and were charging £6 for the return flight and coach to Highbury. This compared favourably with the train fare of £4 17s and with all seats being booked up more than a week in advance with twelve on the reserve list, a British Eagle Britannia was laid on as well, carrying another 110 fans.

Despite what Edwards had speculated, Shankly dropped Melia and brought in Arrowsmith, a decision that was justified as the Reds won at Highbury in the FA Cup fifth round for the second year running. The teamsheet implied that Arrowsmith would be an inside forward as he was numbered ten, but when the players took up position it was clear that he would be playing in the centre with Ian St John taking up Melia's role. This confused Arsenal as they were subjected to him chasing everything very early on, linking well with Callaghan and almost forcing Ian Ure into a short backpass.

Such was Liverpool's early pressure that Arsenal forward Eastham was spending most of the time in his own half. The Gunners looked dangerous when they did find a way forward but one quick break ended with Strong wasting the cross. Defences were well on top but Gordon Milne did play a brilliant low pass to Roger Hunt who missed the ball completely when he tried to control it. Arrowsmith was everywhere, on one occasion going down the right wing to put in a cross that was shepherded back to keeper Jim Furnell by Vic Groves, only for the Reds forward to run up and try to block the kick from his hands. While Liverpool were playing a slow build up, Arsenal were getting the ball into the box far quicker and they had a lucky let off when George Armstrong's shot from a tight angle was deflected over the bar.

Arsenal were beginning to get on top, Tommy Lawrence saving from both Strong and John Snedden and Yeats needing to be at his best to win the aerial battles. In the fifteenth minute the Reds took the lead with their first real chance of the game. Milne floated a ball into the box and St John ghosted in unnoticed at the far post to score with a low header that was greeted by pandemonium amongst the 15,000 Liverpool fans amassed on the Clock End. Less than a minute later Arsenal were almost level when Strong hit a shot that Lawrence couldn't hold but Gerry Byrne got there to clear the danger. However with the action now switching from one end to the other, Hunt carried the ball from his own half avoiding a couple of challenges before hitting a toepoke shot that just went past the post.

Lawrence had another escape when he dropped the ball from a corner and Yeats cleared but only as far as Eastham. He fired the ball low towards the goal but the Reds' keeper made up for the previous error by turning the ball around the post. Arsenal then had a huge penalty appeal turned down when Eastham's shot following a corner was blocked on the line by Ronnie Moran, with the crowd screaming for handball. Photographs later showed it had been headed away but even if it had struck Moran's hand it had been travelling so fast there was no way he could have moved it out of the way. They had two more appeals turned down in quick succession with fouls being waved away and this led to some oranges being thrown at the referee and linesman. They could only sportingly applaud Lawrence though when he made what Leslie Edwards described as the 'save of a lifetime' in that night's Echo, the Reds' keeper managing to adjust his dive in mid-air to turn away a deflected Armstrong shot.

Seven minutes before half time Baker and Yeats went down together after a foul on the Liverpool skipper. Both got up exchanging punches before Yeats went back down with a cut eye, leading to Bill Shankly coming onto the pitch to check he was alright. The referee, who had been following play, came back and promptly dismissed both men from the field and told Shankly to leave too, but not before he had quickly given some tactical instructions to players. It led to both sides having fiery tempers and St John was furious when he was denied a penalty after apparently being tripped from behind by Billy McCulloch. The Arsenal left back then turned his attentions to Callaghan, fouling him near the touchline and receiving a booking, while the Liverpool winger needed treatment. There was little more goalmouth incident before the break, the only chance of note being a Strong header that was well held by Lawrence.

Thankfully for the Reds the half time interval was good for Callaghan and he came out without any signs of limping. He was soon a danger down the flank and put in a cross for Arrowsmith but his volley was just wide. Arsenal were not playing like a team that were a goal down in a cup tie, as they passed the ball around too much and didn't try to break the strong Liverpool defence, which now had Willie Stevenson playing at centre half with St John dropping from inside left to left half. Too many times they resorted to long shots and the Reds were happy to sit back and try to catch them on the break for a second goal. Despite the beckoning of Strong, too many of the home players remained near the halfway line with only Eastham posing any real threat. Liverpool looked more likely to increase rather than surrender their lead and Peter Thompson had a low right foot shot well held by Furnell. Lawrence was first called into action when Armstrong crossed for Strong but his downward header was caught by the keeper.

Towards the end of the game, Arsenal did increase the pressure but Stevenson was doing a great job at centre half and on one occasion cleared a Snedden header off the line. Arrowsmith was by now playing as a lone striker and struggled to deal with the offside trap, but he did spring it once to round Furnell only to roll the ball wide. Liverpool continued to weather the storm, then in injury time Arrowsmith again broke clear and went past Furnell, only to be rugby tackled by the ex-Reds' keeper. This time a penalty was awarded but Hunt's kick was saved. There was no time for Arsenal to go down the other end and score and the final whistle was greeted with a pitch invasion by hundreds of travelling fans. Also with them was Yeats, who couldn't bear to watch the game after his sending off so had instead changed and gone to a local coffee bar, arriving back just as Hunt was placing the ball on the penalty spot.

It was a great victory for the Reds. They hadn't played attractive football but they had done what they needed to do and Bill Shankly said afterwards, 'We knew it would be hard, we prepared for a tough fight. I was proud of Liverpool, every man Jack of them.'[45] St John called it a 'real tonic after we were right down in the dumps after our showing against Everton.'[46] The Reds may have had a police escort to get them home but not all fans had it so easy. Twenty fans missed their coach and had to come home courtesy of British Rail, who agreed to let them travel without tickets providing they promised to pay when sent a bill. The Reds were through to the quarter finals for the second year in a row, but although the next tie was only a fortnight away there were two league games to play first against clubs from the West Midlands.

Liverpool: Lawrence, Byrne, Moran, Milne, Yeats, Stevenson, Callaghan, Hunt, St John, Arrowsmith, Thompson.

Arsenal: Furnell, Magill, McCulloch, Groves, Ure, Snedden, McLeod, Strong, Baker, Eastham, Armstrong.

Referee: Mr J. K. Taylor (Wolverhampton).

Attendance: 61,295.

19th February 1964: Aston Villa 2 Liverpool 2, Football League Division One

The issue of how long Ron Yeats would be suspended following his sending off was not going to be resolved quickly. The FA announced on the Monday afterwards that they were still awaiting a copy of the referee's report and then it would be sent to Liverpool to decide whether or not they wanted a personal hearing. This meant suspension would not be kicking-in until March, a crucial time of the season. Bill Shankly told the *Liverpool Echo* that 'we shall want to defend our man in every way'.

There was not too much sympathy for Yeats from local journalists. Leslie Edwards described it as 'one of the ugliest, most disgraceful incidents I ever saw' and that 'the referee did the right thing when he ordered them both from the field, they deserved it.' Edwards described that after the tackle by Yeats, Baker had stamped on him but Yeats then chased him and they started throwing punches. The sending off, which took place in front of Scottish officials who were also looking at Arsenal's centre half Ian Ure, didn't deter them as he was selected for the game against the Scottish League at Ibrox the following week.

The FA Cup draw which took place at the Victoria Club in London on the Monday evening, was favourable to Liverpool. They were drawn against either Stoke City or Swansea Town at home, leading to the bookmakers slashing their odds to 9/4 favourites. Shankly described it as 'a good draw from our point of view' and there was also guaranteed to be one lower division club in the semi finals, with Fourth Division Oxford United being drawn at home to Second Division Preston North End.

Shankly confirmed on the Tuesday that the team would remain unchanged against Aston Villa, who were down in seventeenth place but ten points clear of the relegation zone so in no real danger of going down. However, they had worries over the fitness of Welsh international forward Phil Woosnam, who was struggling with a heavy cold. There was a snow shower on the Tuesday but that wasn't expected to put the match in doubt because in those days they just painted the lines blue and used an orange ball. On the Tuesday night the Reds were given a massive incentive to beat Villa as Everton's 3-0 win over Birmingham City at Goodison Park lifted them above Liverpool into third, albeit having played three games more. On the same night it was confirmed that the Reds would face Swansea in the FA Cup as they beat Stoke 2-0 at the Vetch Field.

It was a bitterly cold evening at Villa Park, but Woosnam was declared fit to play in game in which Liverpool fought back from being 2-0 down in nine minutes to earn a point and go back above Everton in the table. It was a performance that saw them go behind due to individual errors but fight back superbly, and only extra caution to hold on to the point they had gained stopped them from taking both on offer.

Villa started the keener of the two sides and were closing Liverpool down every time they got the ball. The opening goal came in the fifth minute when George Graham hit a hopeful punt towards the penalty area that Willie Stevenson and Yeats both left for the other, allowing Ron Wylie to sneak in and hit an unstoppable shot past Tommy Lawrence. The second, in the ninth minute followed a weak backpass by Yeats that Harry Burrows sneaked in to intercept and lob over Lawrence.

The only good thing about being 2-0 down so early was that there were 81 minutes to put things right and the Reds didn't panic and play a rushed game. They continued to play patiently and build up their attacks slowly, as Gordon Milne and Stevenson took control of the midfield. In the nineteenth minute they got one back when Peter Thompson crossed from the left, Ian Callaghan hit the ball into the box and Ian St John headed down to Roger Hunt who scored with a scissors kick from the edge of the six yard box. Liverpool continued to dictate the play and on the half hour Alf Arrowsmith levelled, when he collected a pass from Hunt and beat his marker before unleashing a superb low shot from the right corner of the box which gave Geoff Sidebottom no chance.

Hunt had a great chance to put Liverpool ahead before half time when Callaghan crossed to him but he failed to connect with the ball, the referee dismissing appeals that he had been pushed out of the way. Just before half time the Reds had a lucky escape when Graham found himself clean through on goal, only to shoot straight at Lawrence. Early in the second half Graham missed another golden chance when he took a pass from Woosnam, only to hit the ball over the bar from seven yards out.

After the generosity of the first half, Liverpool's defence was much tighter in the second as they put the emphasis on protecting what they had rather than go all out for a win. Arrowsmith, wearing number ten but playing centre forward, was alone up front most of the time with St John dropping back.

Gerry Byrne and Ronnie Moran were impeccable at full back and Yeats made no more mistakes. The Reds did not attack too much but when they did they looked the more likely of the two sides to find the winner and received warm applause from the sparse home crowd. In the 76th minute Hunt did fine the net but he was ruled to have been a yard offside and the Reds were satisfied with the point they had picked up given their poor start. It lifted them back to third in the table, ahead of Arsenal and Everton on goal difference, but with games in hand. The title was very much in their own hands, as they were three points being Tottenham who had played two games more.

Liverpool: Lawrence, Byrne, Moran, Milne, Yeats, Stevenson, Callaghan, Hunt, St John, Arrowsmith, Thompson.

Villa: Sidebottom, Wright, Aitken, Tindall, Sleeuwenhoek, Deakin, Fencott, Wylie, Woosnam, Graham, Burrows.

Referee: Mr D. W. Smith (Stonehurst).

Attendance: 13,729.

22nd February 1964: Liverpool 2 Birmingham City 1, Football League Division One

Liverpool confirmed on the Friday that they had now received the referee's report from the FA into Ron Yeats' sending off and were considering what to do. Arsenal had already announced that Joe Baker would be seeking a personal hearing but Bill Shankly was focusing on matters immediately at hand, telling Horace Yates of the *Daily Post*, 'We have collected various statements and a case is being examined. No official action has been taken yet but we may discuss it further this weekend, possibly after the game with Birmingham.' Yeats was maintaining his innocence too, claiming that he had stud marks on his thigh for days afterwards and that he had not thrown any punches, merely held his arms up in self protection.[47]

Shankly also stated that he had not heard anything about a possible charge for entering the field of play during the game, despite suggestions that the referee had included that in his report too. The line-up for Liverpool's clash with Birmingham, he confirmed, would be unchanged with Alf Arrowsmith continuing to play at centre forward despite wearing number ten. Yates drew attention to this in his preview on the morning of the game, writing that 'both Arsenal and Aston Villa defenders experience concern trying to read intentions.' This was despite Arrowsmith clearly lining up as a centre forward at kick off. Arrowsmith's continued presence meant that Jimmy Melia, who had now recovered from a leg injury, would have to make do with a reserves outing at Sheffield Wednesday.

Liverpool's title odds were now 2/1, with Tottenham evens favourites. However the Reds were hopeful of gaining some ground in this game as Spurs had a tricky game at home to local rivals Arsenal. Birmingham had been at Goodison Park earlier in the week with Yates describing their football ability as 'limited' and although the Reds had suffered some setbacks at Anfield so far he did not expect there to be another one in this game. It would be played on a bone hard pitch with the temperature having dropped considerably in the last few days. Shankly said he hoped it would be milder for the fans' sake as on the Friday 'the weather at Melwood was cold enough to have frozen an Eskimo.'[48]

The weather was still bitterly cold at kick off with the wind chill bringing the temperatures well below zero. Leslie Edwards commented in his report for that night's Echo that he had never seen so many red and white hats and scarves in the crowd. Those that braved the cold saw another performance in which Liverpool dominated but failed to take all their chances. This time though they got away with it, eventually finding the winner with fifteen minutes remaining.

In the first minute the wind caused Trevor Smith to misjudge the ball and sliced his clearance into the path of Arrowsmith who misread it too, and it bounced out for a corner. From this the ball was headed down by Hunt into the path of Arrowsmith but his shot went over the bar. There was a scare for the Reds when a long ball down the right flank was chased by both Mike Hellawell and Ronnie Moran. The Birmingham winger managed to force Moran into hurrying his pass back to Tommy Lawrence and it was too high, but thankfully the ball cleared both the keeper and the crossbar. A dangerous cross by Jimmy Bloomfield was headed down strongly by Ken Leek but Lawrence got down to turn the ball around the post.

Neither side were able to take control of the game and plenty of passes went astray in the wind. Liverpool had plenty of possession but Birmingham were creating the better chances, one from a corner saw Leek head the ball just over the bar with Lawrence well beaten. Liverpool's only meaningful chance for a long spell was a drive from distance by Arrowsmith that went well wide aided by the wind. The first real excitement for the home crowd came from a free kick awarded when Roger Hunt was fouled ten yards outside of the penalty area. Gordon Milne floated the ball into the box but it was cleared as far as Willie Stevenson who hit a fierce goalbound drive that was headed into the air by a defender. When the ball came back down, keeper Colin Withers dropped it into the path of Hunt who somehow hit it wide from only five yards. Just a minute later Arrowsmith was clean through when he took a pass from Milne but his shot was straight at Withers.

Liverpool were totally dominant as the half drew to a close, with Ian Callaghan crossing dangerously towards the forwards and Withers coming from his line to gather. A huge goalmouth scramble then ensued when Stevenson drove the ball towards the goal and Withers failed to hold it, but Smith managed to clear the danger. Birmingham were using Leek as a loan striker but he almost gave his side a wind-assisted goal when Milne and

Yeats failed to judge the flight of the ball and it bounced in to his path, but his toepoke sent the ball just wide. Four minutes before half time, the Reds managed to break the deadlock when Hunt was fouled by Smith on the edge of the box. Moran's shot seemed to be going straight at the wall but such was its ferocity that all heads moved out of the way and the ball went into the top corner of the net like bullet. Moran celebrated not like the senior pro that he was, but as if he was a youngster scoring on his debut.

Liverpool had a great chance to double their lead before the break when Ian St John teed up Arrowsmith, but his cheeky backheel was cleared off the line by Smith. In the first minute of the second half, an Arrowsmith effort was punched clear by Withers into the path of Peter Thompson, whose shot was just wide. The Reds were then made to rue those missed chances when Birmingham found an equaliser out of nothing three minutes into the second half. There seemed little danger when Leek collected a hopeful punt upfield with Yeats standing between him and the goal, but he managed to swivel past the big centre half and hit a low shot that Lawrence couldn't get down to in time.

The Reds responded well to the equalising goal, but were guilty of rushing things a little, with Hunt wasting a chance with his back to goal when he tried a shot instead of laying off, then Arrowsmith going on to the left wing and overhitting a cross. The Reds' centre forward then fired over from only five yards after a clever run and cross by Callaghan, who followed this up with another dangerous cross that was almost headed into his own goal by Terry Hennessey. Birmingham's only real chance of getting another goal came after a fortunate refereeing decision. Moran seemed to have fairly shoulder-charged Leek, but a free kick was given which was taken by Bloomfield and well held by Lawrence. They looked most dangerous down the wings, where Stevenson was struggling, but Yeats and the full backs had the handling of the inside forwards.

Arrowsmith tried his luck from an impossible angle outside the area but the ball went predictably wide. The home crowd were now becoming increasingly anxious as the earlier hurriedness to score was turning into indecision with Yeats and Milne too often passing to each other rather than getting the ball forward and Gerry Byrne rarely crossed the halfway line. Then with fifteen minutes to go, St John created a goal out of nothing. There seemed little danger when he collected the ball near the touchline just inside the Birmingham half with his back to goal, but in an instant he hooked it over his marker and spun around him before running towards the area. He unleashed a shot that Withers got a hand to, but could only help it into the net to the delight of the crowd.

The goal gave the Reds' players extra confidence for a few minutes but with no chances created, Birmingham sensed they could still take something from the game and Dennis Thwaites had a dangerous header well saved by Lawrence. The crowd were then angry when Colin Green controlled the ball with his arm in the area before taking a shot but although the referee hadn't seen it thankfully it was wide. After riding out this brief flurry from Birmingham, Hunt had the ball in the net after a cross from St John but offside was given, leading to the linesman picking up an object from the touchline and handing it to the referee. There was then further derision aimed at the linesman when Hunt was flagged when in a dangerous position on the left wing just before the final whistle blew.

The victory lifted Liverpool into second place, as Blackburn were beaten 3-1 at home by Manchester United. Tottenham though maintained their three point lead thanks to a 3-1 home win over Arsenal. The Reds may have had two games in hand but they had to take into account they were both away and they still had to play Spurs twice. The title was in their hands but they needed to improve on this performance, with Horace Yates warning in the *Daily Post* the following Monday that the Reds 'could flatter only to deceive.'

Liverpool: Lawrence, Byrne, Moran, Milne, Yeats, Stevenson, Callaghan, Hunt, St John, Arrowsmith, Thompson.

Birmingham: Withers, Martin, Green, Hennessey, Smith, Beard, Hellawell, Bloomfield, Thomson, Leek, Thwaites.

Referee: Mr H. Wilson (Stockton).

Attendance: 41,823.

29th February 1964: Liverpool 1 Swansea Town 2, FA Cup Sixth Round

With the Birmingham game out of the way, Liverpool confirmed that they would be seeking a personal hearing for Ron Yeats in relation to his sending off against Arsenal. Bill Shankly told Horace Yates of the *Daily Post* on the Sunday, 'We have collected all the evidence now and the club are to back Ronnie's application.'

On the Monday night there was a scare involving Yeats who was injured whilst playing for Scotland against the Scottish League in Glasgow. In front of an anxious Shankly, who was accompanied by chairman T.V. Williams and vice-chairman S. Reakes, Liverpool's captain was hobbling with an injured ankle before going off in the 61st minute. After the match however, Shankly was relieved to meet up with Yeats and find out that he had only gone off as a precaution with the Swansea game in mind.

Whereas the local press would usually only begin any previews to a league game 1-2 days beforehand, the build up to an FA Cup quarter final started on the Monday. The Post reported that Swansea's leading scorer Keith Todd was suffering from a thigh strain, but otherwise the side's spirits were high. 10,000 fans were expected to travel to Anfield for the game, some on a charter flight, while as many as 3,000 would be coming from North Wales. Shankly admitted that he hadn't watched Swansea ahead of the FA Cup tie. However, given the short time between the draw and tie, and the fact that the only opportunity the previous week would have seriously disrupted his preparations for the game at Aston Villa, it was hardly a surprise. He told Yates that he had a dossier on the way they played at home and away, with them having collected just one win on the road so far.

In his weekly Post column on the Tuesday, Ian St John wrote that some fans had told him that they'd never win the cup if they couldn't beat Swansea. However he knew from bitter experience from his time at Motherwell how you couldn't underestimate anybody. In 1961 he had been part of a side that enjoyed a sensational 5-2 win over Rangers at Ibrox in the third round, only to lose 1-0 at home to Airdrie in the quarter final. St John could also point to the current season's experience against Port Vale, saying that 'they taught us a valuable lesson' and that 'in this competition it matters not to which division opponents belong, for in one game the lesser known clubs can bridge the gap successfully.'

The reason why he continued to wear the number nine shirt was also revealed, as St John wrote that he saw himself as more of a deep lying centre forward than an inside forward. He was revelling in the role, commenting, 'The more I play the better I like it, I cannot remember ever having more freedom of action.'

Shankly, a keen boxing fan, will no doubt have been interested in the upset on the other side of the Atlantic on the Tuesday night and hoped there would be no such thing at Anfield. In Miami Beach, 22-year-old challenger Cassius Clay defeated champion Sonny Liston to claim the world heavyweight title. The fight had been even until Liston retired with an injured shoulder in the sixth round and Clay (who later became Muhammad Ali) jumped about in the ring and shouted to a stunned crowd 'I am the King of the world.'

Despite the importance of the match it was still not all ticket, with the Kop and Anfield Road ends being cash at the turnstiles. Swansea sold all 4,000 of their tickets and had to return many applications due to being oversubscribed, while there was chaos at Anfield on the Wednesday as the last remaining Main Stand and Paddock tickets went on sale at 9am. Fans began queuing at 2am for the tickets that were still remaining after shareholders and season ticket holders had taken their allocation, but they had gone by 10.30am, with over 1,000 being turned away. There was anger from some fans over the selling arrangements, with Rage Red from Old Swan writing to the Echo: 'What are the chances of a member of the general public being able to obtain a stand or paddock place? When the tickets are sold on a weekday the fan must either miss a day's wages or play truant from school. The only people who benefit from this are the touts.' A Mr Williams from Bootle though had the dilemma sorted out by sending his wife down and she told the paper, 'I am not a football fan but my husband and son are. They talked me into queuing for them while they are at work.'

Swansea began their long journey on the Thursday, travelling to Buxton with Todd still doubtful. Manager Trevor Morris indicated that he was not bothered about the roar of the Kop, telling reporters as he boarded the coach, 'Just wait until those Liverpool fans hear some real music. We are bringing our Welsh choir with us and when they get going I shall be sorry for Liverpool.'[49] On the same day, the Reds' players held their usual training session at Melwood before going to Anfield where they were given a private performance by comedian Ken Dodd, who even dressed in a Liverpool strip and ran out onto the pitch. He informed the players that he was Shankly's secret weapon and would be playing 'left outside' and that 'the players too can have a body like mine if they are not very careful.'

Friday saw Swansea remain at Buxton, having a light training session at Buxton FC where Todd was still not given the green light to play. After a fitness test in the afternoon the engineering student, who had only become a full time professional the previous summer, was ruled out and Morris announced that he would be replaced by former Everton forward Eddie Thomas. Confirming his side would remain unchanged, Shankly insisted that although he believed Liverpool could win no disrespect would be shown to the opposition, saying, 'Naturally the Liverpool team have a chance against any team, anywhere. We will go into the match in the same frame of mind as against Arsenal.'

Despite Swansea's Second Division status, Liverpool's progress to the semi-final was not seen as a certainty by Leslie Edwards and Horace Yates in their previews. There had been enough surprises at Anfield so far that season to know nothing was guaranteed. Edwards wrote in the Echo on the Friday that the opening fifteen minutes of play would dictate things and that if Liverpool were 'on' during this period 'Swansea will surely go out.' In the Post on the Saturday Yates said that a 'lack of finishing accuracy' could be Liverpool's downfall and that they must 'treat every opportunity as if it were the last likely to occur.' They were right to be cautious, as a team that were facing relegation to the Third Division caused one of the most sensational cup upsets Anfield has ever seen.

Liverpool took the game to Swansea early on but there was a sense of lethargy as they didn't seize potential openings as they should have done during the first half hour. Then in the thirteenth minute Reds' keeper Tommy Lawrence touched the ball for the first time when he picked it out of the net after a snap shot from Jimmy McLaughlin. Two minutes later the visitors were 2-0 up when McLaughlin laid off for Thomas, who drilled the ball past Lawrence. Even then, the game did not look beyond Liverpool providing they could turn their dominance into clear cut scoring chances. However, there was a sign of things to come just a minute after Thomas's goal when

St John found himself one on one with keeper Noel Dwyer after springing Swansea's previously effective offside trap, only to fire the ball straight at him. Ian Callaghan then had a shot blocked by Herbie Williams and the Reds' winger furiously called for a penalty as he believed it had struck his elbow, but the referee waved play on.

Liverpool's forwards were having a serious off day and Peter Thompson, who had scored less goals than anyone else in the attacking line that season, was looking the most dangerous, giving right back Roy Evans a torrid time. In the 63rd minute he pulled one back with a great shot after an intelligent crossfield pass from Gerry Byrne. Three minutes later the post came to Swansea's rescue after Thompson had cut in from the left and unleashed a shot that bounced off the upright and away to safety.

With ten minutes remaining the Reds were given a lifeline when Williams conceded a needless penalty. Callaghan took the ball past him but it looked as though it would run out of play only for the Swansea defender to trip him, leading to the referee pointing to the spot. There was some confusion over who would take the penalty, with Roger Hunt having missed one in the last round at Arsenal. Eventually Ronnie Moran stepped forward after the Kop sang his name but there was then a delay when Thomas ran up to the line to speak to Dwyer. No doubt he had been given some local knowledge that Moran would probably aim his kick high to his right, so Dwyer stood to the left of the goal to give Moran an inviting gap. Moran took the kick just as predicted, only to miss the target altogether to the Kop's agony. It was the fourth spot kick he had missed that season.

The penalty miss did not demoralise the Reds and they went on to create some of the best chances of the game. Callaghan brought off a good save from Dwyer, who then could only block a low shot from St John with his body, but as it appeared to be looping into the net he somehow managed to get his fist up to the ball and punch it clear. With two minutes remaining Thompson unleashed a swerving drive that hit Dwyer on the elbow and went over the bar. The final whistle saw a pitch invasion by visiting fans who overwhelmed Dwyer, who had to be rescued and escorted back down the tunnel by the police. Swansea's manager Trevor Morris was in dreamland, claiming that 'we had that little bit of luck every team must have.'[50]

Yeats summed feelings up perfectly when he said 'We have to take the good with the bad. Today was bad.' Shankly was stunned, saying, 'Unbelievable, unbelievable, I have never seen the boys play better. We could have scored fourteen goals and yet we are out of the cup.'[51] Explaining the indecision over the penalty, he said that Moran was to have first choice if one was awarded but a reserve had been delegated if he didn't fancy the kick. The singing of his name and fact that he was the most experienced player seemed to have persuaded him to take the responsibility on.

In the *Daily Post* the following Monday, Horace Yates estimated that the Reds had created 24 chances and only Lawrence hadn't had a shot saved. Swansea, on the other hand, had probably only had four scoring opportunities but converted two. Dwyer, whose daughter would later marry maverick footballer Frank Worthington, so nearly a Liverpool signing in 1972, put in a display that 'hadn't been seen at Anfield for many a day.' The keeper himself was extremely modest, saying that he had only done his job, what he was paid to do.

Had Liverpool beaten Swansea, they would have faced Shankly's old club Preston in the semi final. However as Swansea turned their sights towards that game and securing their Second Division status, the Reds had just one aim now and that was to be First Division Champions. A trip to Hillsborough to face Sheffield Wednesday three days later gave them the opportunity to get the defeat out of their minds and also fend off the challenge of a resurgent Everton.

Liverpool: Lawrence, Byrne, Moran, Milne, Yeats, Stevenson, Callaghan, Hunt, St John, Arrowsmith, Thompson.

Swansea: Dwyer, Roy Evans, Hughes, Johnson, Purcell, Williams, Jones, Draper, Thomas, McLaughlin, Brian Evans.

Referee: Mr G. McCabe (Sheffield).

Attendance: 52,608.

Top of Table

		Pl	W	D	L	F	A	GA	Pt
1	Tottenham	32	19	6	7	80	55	1.46	44
2	Blackburn	33	16	8	9	73	46	1.59	40
3	Everton	32	16	8	8	59	47	1.25	40
4	Liverpool	29	18	3	8	59	32	1.84	39

14

Transfer Troubles

There was only one way to make up for the defeat to Swansea and that was to make sure the title came to Anfield for the first time since 1947. The Reds were in a favourable position in the table, being five points behind Tottenham with three games in hand, but they had to take into account they were all away from home. The title race was evolving into one of the most exciting yet, with as many as six sides believing they had a chance of glory. There was no doubting the ability of the Reds players but there was also the issue of whether they had the experience and nerve. As well as having to contend with Tottenham who had been champions in 1961, they also had to deal with a resurgent Everton, whose good run of form had given them a great chance of retaining the title. As the season entered its final two months, there was also frantic activity coming up in the transfer market as sides battled to be first over the finishing line.

4th March 1964: Sheffield Wednesday 2 Liverpool 2, Football League Division One

Having a league game on the Wednesday was probably the best thing that Liverpool could have hoped for following the Swansea defeat. It meant they had a chance to get it out of their system and Bill Shankly made it clear after training on the Tuesday that they would not be letting it get them down. Believing it was a total fluke he told Horace Yates of the *Daily Post*,

> 'They aim to get it out of their system at the earliest possible moment and make tomorrow night's game at Hillsborough a stepping stone to winning the league title. Saturday's result was the most fantastic thing that ever happened in football. We talked about the match at a players' meeting today and agreed that such a thing happens only once in fifty years. It was our misfortune that it had to happen to us. Imagine it, one of the best sides in Division One, beaten by one of the poorest sides in the game. It makes no reasoning.'

Although Shankly had total belief in his side, there were some fans who were unhappy and the letters page of the *Liverpool Echo* that week showed it. Believing that he should learn to accept defeat gracefully Mr Marshall from Netherton wrote, 'I'm sick and tired of Mr Shankly trying to find excuses for his team's failings. Results do not depend on what might have been but which team scores most goals. Any team which doesn't score from a penalty doesn't deserve another chance.'

There would be no scapegoats from the Swansea defeat as Shankly confirmed the day before that the side would be unchanged at Hillsborough. The attack would need to be at their most potent though, as seventh-placed Wednesday's home defensive record was bettered only by Manchester United. In contrast, the Reds attack had managed just eighteen away goals, the worst of the division's top fourteen sides. Wednesday's defence would have to make do without injured keeper Ron Springett, while they were also without inside forward John Fantham who picked up a knock in training on the Tuesday. His place was taken by Edwin Holliday, who scored the opening goal of a match in which Liverpool did fight back, but for the second away game running they had to be content with a point after being 2-0 down.

Wednesday were by far the better side in the first half, with Liverpool rarely able to string more than a couple of passes together as they struggled to gain any composure. Holliday's goal in the 32nd minute was no surprise. He took a pass from Colin Dobson and hit a low drive from the corner of the area that swerved away from Tommy Lawrence as he dived for it. Liverpool's first half performance had been so lethargic that in reality they had to be grateful for only being 1-0 down at the break. However two minutes after the restart Wednesday were 2-0 up when Holliday's cross from the right was met by a diving header from Mark Pearson which went in off the post.

Ian St John worked his socks off, with Gordon Milne and Willie Stevenson gaining a control of the midfield but the Reds couldn't find a way through. At the back Ron Yeats and Ronnie Moran were not troubled but Gerry Byrne was struggling to deal with Holliday and had to be spoken to by the referee on two occasions. Liverpool's first real chance of the game came when Arrowsmith had a shot blocked by Peter Swan.

With Wednesday seemingly coasting to victory, the Reds got a goal out of nothing. Ian Callaghan crossed from the right and St John broke from his marker to run on to the ball and flick it past the outrushing Roy MacLaren. Shankly then came from the stand to the dugout to give instructions and moved Arrowsmith onto the left wing to allow Peter Thompson to have a roaming role. It was a good move but despite their dominance the Reds couldn't find a way past the blanket Wednesday defence. Then a minute into stoppage time Callaghan crossed from the touchline and Stevenson met it with a powerful header that gave MacLaren no chance. It completed what Horace Yates described in the Post as a 'magnificent fighting rally' and lifted Liverpool above Blackburn and Everton into second place.

On the same night Liverpool played at Hillsborough, a stadium that would be the setting for the darkest day in the club's history 25 years later, there was a shocking indication of how poor organisation was at that time. At Roker Park, around 50,000 were locked out of the Sunderland v Manchester

United FA Cup replay. Despite the ground having a capacity of around 60,000 the official attendance was just 46,727, with another 10,000 estimated to have gained entry when gates collapsed as fans queued to get in. Over eighty fans were taken to hospital and seventeen kept in with broken limbs. Sunderland chairman Syd Collinge said the game had to be cash admission as there hadn't been time to get tickets printed, the Echo quoting him as saying, 'People don't work Saturdays and Sundays so how could we get tickets printed within 48 hours.'

Liverpool: Lawrence, Byrne, Moran, Milne, Yeats, Stevenson, Callaghan, Hunt, St John, Arrowsmith, Thompson.

Wednesday: MacLaren, Hill, Megson, McAnearney, Swan, Young, Finney, Dobson, Layne, Pearson, Holliday.

Referee: Mr W. J. Gow (Birmingham).

Attendance: 23,703.

7th March: Liverpool 6 Ipswich Town 0, Football League Division One

The day after Liverpool played Sheffield Wednesday the Football Association announced that Ron Yeats and Joe Baker would have their personal hearings in Leicester on 11th March in respect of their sending offs. This was not the only worry for Yeats as he was struggling with a stiff neck ahead of the game against Ipswich Town but on the Friday it was confirmed that he would play. The FA were quite busy on the disciplinary front that week, fining Burnley manager Harry Potts £50 for 'ungentlemanly remarks' made to match officials at half time during a recent game against Birmingham City.

Liverpool's match against Ipswich would see them on a hiding to nothing. The team that had been champions as recently as 1962, were rock bottom of the table and five points from safety. They had also endured a torrid winless run on their travels, drawing four and losing twelve of their sixteen games. On the morning of the game, Horace Yates predicted in the *Daily Post* that there will be 'howls of dismay' if the Reds fail to win, whilst warning that an all out defensive strategy had enabled Ipswich to grind out 0-0 and 1-1 draws with Everton earlier in the season. Leslie Edwards did not expect a great game, predicting in the *Liverpool Echo*, 'I fear that we are in for yet another match in which Liverpool are in command but must find their way through a packed defence. Ipswich's plan in recent weeks has been to forget about winning and concentrate on salvaging a point.'

Edwards was right as the Reds dominated the first half more than they had the second against Swansea, yet could only find the net once. After the break though, they ran riot scoring five times, for their biggest win of the season. During the first half the crowd became more agitated, as Roger Hunt missed by inches on three occasions and Alf Arrowsmith missed three sitters.

Ian Callaghan then twice got inside into scoring positions only to blast over and then hit the bar. Ipswich offered nothing in attack partly due to their ineptitude but mainly due to the solidity of the Reds defence, with Yeats easily having the measure of Gerry Baker, brother of his Arsenal nemesis Joe.

Ipswich were playing as if they were a side who knew the drop was inevitable, but as long as the Reds kept missing chances they would pick up a point that would seriously damage Liverpool's title hopes. Finally a goal came in the 41st minute in fortunate circumstances. Peter Thompson crossed from the left and Ian St John headed the ball downwards under the diving Jim Thorburn's body. It bounced off the post but crossed the line before Arrowsmith made sure by following in and slamming it into the net. At half time the Kop sang along to the Dave Clark Five's *Glad All Over* as they received an additional boost when it was announced Everton were doing the Reds a favour by leading Tottenham 2-1 at White Hart Lane.

Any nervousness that Ipswich may sneak a goal was overcome three minutes into the second half when Hunt got hold of the ball about forty yards from goal and ran through unchallenged to score. In the 53rd minute Arrowsmith made up for his earlier misses when he scored after John Elsworthy had headed the ball directly into his path. Thompson, rapidly becoming a Kop favourite due to his willingness to get inside and shoot more, twisted and turned his way past two defenders before unleashing a powerful shot that gave Thorburn no chance. Two minutes later Thompson was the provider, crossing for Hunt to nod the ball into the net from close range. Arrowsmith completed the rout with the best of the afternoon, linking well with Thompson before volleying from 25 yards into the top corner, with Thorburn rooted to the spot.

Ipswich, to their credit, were sporting in defeat and never stopped trying although only John Colrain ever looked capable of finding a way through a tight Reds back line, in which Willie Stevenson was especially outstanding. St John even said they had been a better side than Swansea, claiming that, 'They showed more guile and football idea, limited though it might have been. We did not make any more chances against this doomed side than we did against Swansea, but this time they were going in, not out.'[52] Ipswich manager Jackie Milburn believed the Reds were now favourites for the title thanks in part to the Anfield crowd. He said afterwards, 'I have not experienced such fanaticism as at Anfield for a long time. Their support is worth a goal start to them.'[53] He also felt that the club was on the verge of greatness, saying that they were the 'big noise' of English football and 'ready to resume control now.'

It had been a long trek for their supporters who had made the trip from Suffolk to see their team lose 6-0, but thirty Ipswich fans did at least have a night out to get over it. They were guests of the Liverpool Supporters' Club and had travelled up on the Friday, spent the night in a hotel, then were taken on a bus tour of the city in the morning. After lunch at the club they sat in the stands for the match before having an evening in the Supporters' Club in Lower Breck Road, finally joining their coach home at midnight.

The victory kept the Reds in second place and boosted their goal average. They were also in the title driving seat now as Tottenham went down 4-2 against Everton, meaning the gap was now two points but with Liverpool having two games in hand. If the Reds couldn't take advantage of them, Blackburn and Everton who were level on points were ready to pounce, the champions having picked up fourteen points out of the last sixteen available.

Liverpool: Lawrence, Byrne, Moran, Milne, Yeats, Stevenson, Callaghan, Hunt, St John, Arrowsmith, Thompson.

Ipswich: Thorburn, Davin, Compton, Baxter, Nelson, Elsworthy, Broadfoot, Colrain, Baker, Hegan, Blackwood.

Referee: Mr A. Luty (Leeds).

Attendance: 35,575.

14th March 1964: Fulham 1 Liverpool 0, Football League Division One

On 9th March there was a major departure from Liverpool as Jimmy Melia joined Wolverhampton Wanderers for £50,000, the highest fee the club had ever received for a player. According to Jack Rowe in the *Daily Post*, Bill Shankly's decision to rename unchanged sides following the defeat to Swansea, followed by the 6-0 win against Ipswich, had led him to conclude that his future lay elsewhere. Although he hadn't actively sought to leave, Wolves had been monitoring the situation for a few weeks and made their move, with Melia telling the Post, 'I am leaving Liverpool as the best of friends. I see no reason why I shouldn't do well at Wolves.' Shankly paid tribute to a player who had been at the club ten years, saying, 'He is a genuine player who always gives his best. He has done well for us but felt a change of club would do him good. We did not offer him for transfer.'

Given the fact that Melia had so often been made the scapegoat when things didn't go well for the Reds, there were plenty who were disappointed at his departure. In the letters page of the *Liverpool Echo* that week Mr Carter from Waterloo described him as 'one of the finest inside forwards in the country, while Miss Corrigan of Huyton said 'I hope some so-called supporters are happy.' Angry that the 'kick and rush boys have had their way,' Mr Sprall from Toxteth expressed his disgust that 'one of the best ball players the club has ever had' had been sold and that 'until they get a good replacement they won't win any honours.'

The transfer deadline was just a week away and there was speculation as to whether Liverpool would strengthen the squad or put their faith in young talent. Gordon Wallace was mentioned as a reserve player who may now get more opportunities, but Shankly was annoyed at fans who were often writing to the papers saying what players he should be buying. He told Leslie Edwards of the Echo,

'I am thinking just as hard as they are about how to better the team and don't they realise that I have travelled thousands of miles even in the last month or two to that end. We know the players we should like. It isn't our fault their clubs won't let them go. We must be patient. Surely nobody expects us to go out and buy others whom we don't rate so highly, merely for the sake of making a signing. All this talk about what we need can affect players in the team.'

The nervousness about Melia's sale with no apparent replacement lined up was emphasised the day after he joined Wolves. Everton paid £85,000 for Blackburn forward Fred Pickering, breaking the record for the highest transfer fee between two British clubs. Liverpool though, had more pressing priorities as they prepared for Ron Yeats's disciplinary hearing, with the Reds' captain travelling to Leicester on the day of the Pickering transfer in readiness for it. He was joined by director Mr L. Martindale, who would conduct his defence, Shankly and Gerry Byrne, who would be giving evidence on his behalf. Liverpool had sourced a number of photographs to use as evidence, but the one BBC television camera present had followed the ball and didn't capture the incident.

Liverpool were shocked when the disciplinary panel suspended both Yeats and Joe Baker for fourteen days, the ban coming into effect from the following Monday. This meant that Yeats would miss three games due to the Easter programme that would see away games on successive days against Tottenham and Leicester. The verdict seemed especially harsh as it was acknowledged that Baker had kicked Yeats in addition to punching him, whereas Yeats had only punched. As such, Martindale was expecting him to be given a lesser punishment than Baker. There was no leave to appeal and a shattered Yeats said, 'I thought if I got seven days I would be harshly treated but this is terrible.' A furious Shankly didn't mince his words, telling reporters that 'the way I feel I could be put in gaol for my thoughts.'[54]

On the day Liverpool's squad travelled to London for the game against Fulham, rumours swept the city that a bid had been made for Everton's Alex Young. The newsdesk of the *Daily Post* was bombarded with calls about the subject, many claiming to have heard the news on the radio. Club officials denied this, calling the claims 'absolutely groundless' while Everton manager Harry Catterick stated that no bid had been made. Dundee United though did confirm that the Reds had offered £10,000 for forward Jimmy Irvine, but they found it a 'bit of an insult.' Before boarding the train, Shankly told Horace Yates of the Post that he would only discuss transfers 'when we make a signing, not before.'

Many of the fans who made the trip to Fulham did so on Sunniways

Coaches, who left from London Road at 11.30pm, charging a fare of 37s (£1.85) for coaches that had a radio and heater. They knew on departure that they would be seeing their side unchanged for the seventh successive game, following confirmation that Roger Hunt and Peter Thompson had recovered from minor injuries that led to their withdrawal from Alf Ramsey's England training camp. Fulham were unbeaten in nine home games, a run that included a 10-1 win over Ipswich, but in his preview Yates still thought it was possible to claim both points. 'If the Liverpool attack carry over their goal thirst from last Saturday they could achieve something more profitable than a draw.' It wasn't to be the case though, as the Reds fell to defeat having gone for safety first and not having enough time to find an equaliser after going behind.

Morning rain had left the pitch in a treacherous condition. Reds keeper Tommy Lawrence was almost caught out early on when he lost his footing whilst dealing with a lob from Alan Mullery but thankfully nobody was around and he was able to recover his composure. At the other end Liverpool almost took an early lead when Tony Macedo could only block Roger Hunt's effort with his body but just as Alf Arrowsmith was closing in, Bobby Keetch managed to get the ball clear. Liverpool were in early control, Hunt almost setting up Peter Thompson, but as the rain returned and the pitch became a quagmire, Fulham took better advantage. Lawrence had to be brave to dive at the feet of Graham Leggat and Johnny Haynes had a volley that spun just wide.

Liverpool had two lucky escapes when Leggat's centre went across the face of goal with nobody there to get on the end of it, then Steve Earle's low shot was spilled by Lawrence but the ball went out for a corner. Such was Fulham's dominance that Alf Arrowsmith was now virtually playing as a lone striker, but when Yeats twice intercepted attacks and got the ball forward to him, he was unable to make any use of it. On another occasion Ian Callaghan broke down the right and got a cross in, but Arrowsmith mistimed his run on to it. Liverpool's first shot on target came when they cleared a corner and Hunt broke free, but he hit the ball straight at Macedo. The action then returned to the other end, Bobby Robson having a shot blocked by Willie Stevenson. Lawrence then had to race out of his area to charge down a Leggat shot as the Reds's players were distracted by Arrowsmith being down injured.

As the half drew to a close Fulham were awarded two free kicks on the edge of the area, the first of which was caught by Lawrence and the second punched away. Despite the pressure they were under Liverpool's defence was holding firm and they were trying to build attacks from the back. One brilliant ball by Byrne out to Peter Thompson on the left led to him getting forward and crossing to Hunt, who took too long trying to control it and was dispossessed. The last action of the half saw Earle's drive beat Lawrence but

Ronnie Moran was stood by the post and managed to clear off the line.

Early in the second half the home crowd appealed for a penalty for handball when Moran blocked a shot but the referee waved the appeals away. Thompson and Hunt then began to link well but when Hunt found himself in a good shooting position he struck the ball well wide. Fulham then took a 56th minute lead after Gordon Milne conceded a free kick just outside the area. Pat O'Connell hit a hard shot that was blocked by Ian St John, but only into the path of Reg Stratton who turned the ball into the net. Liverpool responded by driving forward, with Stevenson and Milne working well to move the ball in the right direction. However Hunt had a shot blocked by Keetch and Thompson crossed into the danger area but nobody was there to meet it. Callaghan then crossed for St John who headed it down to Hunt but he didn't respond quickly enough and the Fulham defence cleared.

St John moved to an orthodox centre forward position but Fulham's defence was holding firm. The Reds then were lucky not to be 2-0 down when Haynes played a long ball to Leggat, but his shot hit the post and bounced behind for a goal kick. Thompson came closest to equalising but his volley was wide. On the whole though Liverpool seemed unable to cope with the heavy pitch and weren't moving quickly enough on it. This was summed up when Stevenson played the ball into the path of St John but Keetch responded quickly to clear. Callaghan then took a corner that was met by nobody and went all the way out for a throw in on the other side.

In the *Daily Post* the following Monday, Jack Rowe pulled no punches in blaming the defensive tactics for the defeat. He wrote that 'Liverpool defended themselves out of a possible two points' and that 'it was a loss that might have been avoided by a more attacking spirit and adventure.' It was so tight at the top that the Reds had now slipped to fourth, although they would overhaul all the teams above them if they won their games in hand and their goal average was also superior to the top three. However, the title pendulum was swinging towards Everton, who beat Nottingham Forest 6-1 at Goodison Park to go level on points with Tottenham who were without a game that day due to the FA Cup semi finals. Club record signing Fred Pickering had scored a hat-trick and fans were anxious to see Liverpool spend the fee received for Melia to ensure their title challenge wasn't derailed. The only problem was that the transfer deadline was now just two days away.

Liverpool: Lawrence, Byrne, Moran, Milne, Yeats, Stevenson, Callaghan, Hunt, St John, Arrowsmith, Thompson.

Fulham: Macedo, Cohen, Langley, Mullery, Keetch, Robson, Earle, Leggat, Stratton, Haynes, O'Connell.

Referee: Mr G. Roper (Cambridge).

Attendance: 14,022.

20th March 1964: Liverpool 2 Bolton Wanderers 0, Football League Division One

Even as Liverpool were playing at Craven Cottage, moves were afoot to try and bring a new face to Anfield. Chairman T.V. Williams and Director Harry Latham didn't travel to London and instead were at Goodison on the Saturday, where it was speculated they made an enquiry about Alex Young. He had lost his place in the team due to Fred Pickering's arrival and played for Everton reserves at Stoke although he had not submitted any transfer request.

On the Sunday, Jimmy Irvine of Dundee United travelled to Liverpool along with his manager Jerry Kerr, after an improved bid of £25,000 had been accepted by the Scottish club. However he returned without signing, telling reporters on his return that question marks over a recent ankle injury had led to Liverpool not pressing ahead with the deal. In the *Daily Post* on the Monday morning Horace Yates predicted that Liverpool would not make a signing for the sake of it and any player that did arrive would be fit and ready to go straight into the team. There were no clues from inside Anfield whatsoever, with Bill Shankly bluntly telling him, 'If we make a signing we will let you know.'

With the Irvine deal off and no sign of Alex Young expressing a desire to leave Everton, Liverpool turned their attentions to Bolton's Freddie Hill, who had submitted a transfer request two days before. Hill had been capped twice by England in 1962 but following a cartilage operation earlier in the season managed just one goal in 21 games. Negotiations went on all afternoon but with doubts remaining over his fitness it took time for Liverpool to get the price down from £60,000 to £45,000. However, after the fee was agreed, a medical showed high blood pressure and Shankly took the doctor's advice and didn't proceed with the deal.

In desperation Liverpool turned their attentions to Jimmy Miller of Rangers, but an injury to his teammate Willie Henderson meant they were unwilling to sell. Although no players had been signed, there was no air of despondency around Anfield as Alf Arrowsmith was improving all the time. Enquiries about players were ongoing, although this was with the following season in mind, and it was felt that this would drive on those in the team to ensure there was no need to bring new faces in.

Ironically, Hill would be back at Anfield on the Friday night, playing for Bolton in a game that was brought forward due to the Grand National taking place the next day. Bolton manager William Ridding said that there were no doubts about Hill's fitness and his high blood pressure was only temporary. Hill himself said that he was disappointed and 'desperate for the opportunity to show Liverpool that they picked the right player, even if they didn't sign me.'[55] Shankly said that he was even more disappointed than Hill as he was convinced that 'here was the man who could make Liverpool's forward line even greater than it is.'

There was one change to the Liverpool line-up with Chris Lawler coming in for the suspended Ron Yeats. He was up against another youngster in twenty-year-old David Hatton who was playing at centre forward for Bolton, as opposed to his usual position of half back. Bolton were four points adrift of safety and looked set to be relegated along with Ipswich, with Leslie Edwards confidently predicting in the *Liverpool Echo* on the evening of the match, 'Hill or no Hill, Liverpool should beat Bolton who have struggled all too long.' It transpired that Hill showed some nice touches, but he had no quality around him and the Reds ran out comfortable winners without getting out of second gear.

Liverpool started off quite slowly, allowing Bolton to bring the game to them, but although Hill linked well with Francis Lee there was little threat. Jimmy Davison and Gordon Taylor both created shooting chances for themselves but their efforts were easily held by Tommy Lawrence. After a quarter of an hour Gordon Milne and Willie Stevenson took a firmer hold of the midfield while Lawler also held his own. In the 28th minute Liverpool took the lead, Ian St John playing the ball into the area and Arrowsmith hooking it over Eddie Hopkinson into the net. Two minutes before half time, Ian Callaghan crossed from the right and St John scored with a brilliant diving header.

The second half was played at almost walking pace, the Kop turning to humour to pass the time, shouting 'Doddy' every time Davison touched the ball due to his wavy hair. The main incidents were when St John had the ball in the net but Arrowsmith was ruled to be offside and Ronnie Moran had a shot from outside the area bounce off the post. Arrowsmith saw a shot spilled by Hopkinson but Bryan Edwards cleared the ball off the line. Bolton were playing like a team doomed to relegation and their only threat came towards the end when Hatton beat Lawler only to see his shot bounce off the bar and over the goal. Otherwise the teenager had been completely frozen out of the game by Lawler who had his most composed game for the senior side to date. He won every tackle and header and also distributed the ball well, even if Yeats had put in the same performance it would have been considered first class.

The win lifted Liverpool to the top of the table on goal average for 24 hours at least. The following afternoon Tottenham were beaten 3-2 at home by Manchester United, but Everton won 2-1 at Blackburn to go two points clear although they had played two games more than the Reds. The season was entering its 'business end' now and three games over four days at Easter would go a long way to decide the title. It was now win or bust for the Reds as they prepared to face fellow title challengers Tottenham at home and away as well as bogey side Leicester, who had beaten them in the last four games the sides had faced each other.

Liverpool: Lawrence, Byrne, Moran, Milne, Lawler, Stevenson, Callaghan, Hunt, St John, Arrowsmith, Thompson.

Bolton: Hopkinson, Hartle, Farrimond, Rimmer, Edwards, Lennard, Davison, Lee, Hatton, Hill, Taylor.

Referee: Mr D. Brady (Rotherham).

Attendance: 38,583.

Top of Table

		Pl	W	D	L	F	A	GA	Pt
1	Everton	35	19	8	8	71	51	1.39	46
2	Liverpool	33	20	4	9	69	35	1.97	44
3	Tottenham	34	19	6	9	84	62	1.35	44

15

Easter Rising

The Easter period saw Liverpool play three games in four days and take maximum points. These three victories, two of them over one of their closest rivals, coupled with other contenders dropping points meant they established themselves as firm favourites for the title with just six games left to play.

27th March 1964: Tottenham Hotspur 1 Liverpool 3, Football League Division One

The day after Liverpool beat Bolton, 18/1 shot Team Spirit won the Grand National at Aintree but the race was overshadowed by a light aircraft crash near Wango Lane that killed five people. The Piper-23 Apache was flying from Luton to Speke but circled the racecourse before nosediving into a cabbage field. Amongst those killed were *Daily Express* columnist Nancy Spain and Joan Werner Laurie, editor of women's magazine *She*.

Everton's run that had seen them go to the top of the table led to one fan being so confident they could secure the title that he suggested their home game against West Ham on 25th April, should double as the following season's Charity Shield. The fan, who Leslie Edwards declined to name in his *Liverpool Echo* column, was certain his side would have secured the title by then while West Ham were sure to beat Second Division Preston in the FA Cup final. Therefore, he argued, it would save the problem of having to find a suitable date pre-season if the league match was doubled up.

Everton manager Harry Catterick was not so confident however, saying that the title race was 'as wide open as ever' and that there was no such thing as an easy run in, which Everton were said by many pundits to have. 'At this stage of the season every one of them is a cup tie' he warned, as he also believed that Liverpool 'still have a good chance.'

Liverpool had nine games remaining, six of them away including at Tottenham where they had lost 7-2 the previous season, and Leicester who they had lost against four games running since promotion. At home they had fellow contenders Tottenham and Manchester United, as well as seventh-placed Arsenal. Everton and Spurs may have been there before, but that didn't mean the Reds could be written off. Despite the daunting fixture list, the title was still in their hands and Ian St John remained in buoyant mood. Describing the 7-2 defeat at White Hart Lane as a 'travesty' of a result in a game in which 'we at least deserved a draw' he predicted that the Reds would win both Easter fixtures against their rivals who were slipping, and had been beaten by both Everton and Manchester United at home.

It was essential for the Reds to secure maximum points, as Everton were expected to win all three of their Easter games against West Bromwich Albion and Blackpool at home on the Friday and Saturday, then away to West Brom on the Tuesday. Despite Ron Yeats still being suspended, Chris Lawler's performance against Bolton had helped build his confidence and previewing the game in the Post, Horace Yates did not think a win was out of the question. 'Chris Lawler has ability enough to cope with Larry Brown. He is far removed from being the accomplished centre forward.' Inside forward Jimmy Greaves was the finished article, but Yates predicted that 'if Liverpool set out to control his dynamite with the thoroughness with which they are able this match is far from being a write-off.'

As the Reds began their journey to London, the jury at Aylesbury Crown Court finally announced that after 65 hours of deliberation they had found seven of the ten men on trial guilty of the ambush in the Great Train Robbery. In addition, two others were found guilty of conspiracy while a solicitor was guilty of obstructing justice. The trial had lasted for 51 days but it still wasn't quite over, as sentencing was deferred until 15th April. Bill Shankly took thirteen players with him, Phil Ferns and Gordon Wallace accompanying the first choice eleven as a precaution, although it was confirmed that Gordon Milne had overcome an ankle injury sustained in training.

The bulk of the fans that travelled went overnight on coaches, with some even hitching a lift on the back of a Sunblest bread lorry. At a transport café at Gailey Island near Wolverhampton and Watford Gap services in the M1, bleary eyed fans piled off the coaches for refreshments and much needed toilet breaks. The previous season's games against Spurs had also been played on Good Friday and Easter Monday, although Liverpool had been at home first. On that occasion one Reds fan was warned by the police for beeping his horn outside Buckingham Palace at 6am after arriving safely following an all night drive. That was probably the most jubilant he felt all day given the 7-2 defeat, but this time Liverpool's fans were ecstatic as a magnificent display of teamwork, coupled with Roger Hunt's clinical finishing, saw him claim a hat-trick in a 3-1 win.

Knowing that defeat would almost certainly end their title hopes, Spurs tried to take the game to the Reds but the full backs easily had the measure of Greaves and fellow inside forward John White. Liverpool were clearly not settling for a point and Hunt went close in the fifth minute, his shot producing an acrobatic save from John Hollowbread. Willie Stevenson was in fine form, being the architect of many an attack and nullifying the impact of Tottenham's latest big signing, Alan Mullery who had cost £72,500 from Fulham. It was Stevenson's vision that led to the opening goal in the 28th minute when he played a long ball to Alf Arrowsmith who was running into the left wing position. Arrowsmith then crossed into the area where Ron Henry missed the ball completely, allowing Hunt a clear shot on goal and he made no mistake, hammering the ball past John Hollowbread. Winger Cliff Jones deserved an equaliser in the 37th minute when he cut inside and beat three men before hitting a powerful shot on goal, but it was tipped over by Tommy Lawrence. On the whole the first half had been a tight battle with few scoring opportunities, but the Reds were in control and didn't look like losing their grip on the game.

Just past the hour mark Hunt missed a great chance when he found himself one on one with Hollowbread, but his shot was deflected wide by the keeper's legs. Shortly afterwards Hunt made amends when he scored twice in four minutes to put Liverpool's victory beyond doubt. Arrowsmith was again the provider, running onto the ball in the 67th minute and turning it back to St John. He laid it off into the path of Hunt who beat the advancing Hollowbread with a clever lob. In the 70th minute, with Spurs leaving gaps at the back, Callaghan crossed from the right to an unmarked Hunt who headed the ball into the net.

Maurice Norman scored a consolation from a corner with six minutes remaining but there was no chance of a late rally. Liverpool had never looked like letting the game slip from their grasp with every player putting in a near perfect performance. Greaves was totally subdued by a back line that didn't give an inch. Lawler didn't look out of place at all, helped by Stevenson who provided regular back up to him in addition to his busy work down the left flank. St John worked tirelessly fetching and carrying the ball between the half backs and the front men, giving extra cover to Yeats's twenty-year-old replacement.

The two points gained in a game that saw them score three away from home for the first time since September had been a massive boost to the Reds, who were pleasantly surprised to hear that Everton had failed to win. In a dire game at Goodison Park, the Blues were booed by the crowd as they struggled to a 1-1 draw with West Bromwich Albion, meaning the Reds were just a point behind with two games in hand. Now they just had to beat that Leicester bogey.

Liverpool: Lawrence, Byrne, Moran, Milne, Lawler, Stevenson, Callaghan, Hunt, St John, Arrowsmith, Thompson.

Tottenham: Hollowbread, Baker, Henry, Mullery, Norman, Marchi, Jones, White, Brown, Greaves, Dyson.

Referee: Mr A. Holland (Barnsley).

Attendance: 56,952.

28th March 1964: Leicester City 0 Liverpool 2, Football League Division One.

Following the win over Spurs, the Reds squad headed straight to Leicester accompanied by their special electrical equipment that was used to treat injuries. Both Gordon Milne and Roger Hunt had picked up knocks to the ankle but they had finished the game strongly and Bill Shankly was confident that with treatment in the evening and on the morning of the game they would be fine. Speaking of his team's title chances, he said, 'We have a great chance, the harder the games are the better we play and if we continue to carry on like that we have a chance against anybody.'[56]

As the players slept, Alaska was struck by a massive earthquake measuring 9.2 on the Richter scale, which left over 100 dead and totally flattened several small villages. The tidal wave that was generated reached as far as Chile, while in Crescent City in Northern California, ten people were killed by a twelve foot wave.

This match was probably the most dreaded of the remaining games. The Foxes may have been plodding along in mid-table but the mere mention of them sent shockwaves down the spines of all Liverpool fans. They had beaten the Reds in all three league games since promotion and also in the preceding season's FA Cup semi final, without even conceding a goal. Leicester's blanket defence had been impossible to break down and once again there were doubts that the Reds could end the hoodoo. However Horace Yates wrote in his preview in the *Daily Post* that bogeys had to end some time and Leicester weren't as good as they were the previous season.

> Leicester have not proved themselves quite so devastatingly effective with their defensive style this season, but they will not have forgotten they have met and beaten Liverpool four times within two seasons without conceding a goal. There is no doubt that the battle plan which helped them achieve such success, pigeon holed though it may have been for several matches, will be dusted and served up anew on Saturday. Can Liverpool smash that iron curtain? Bogeys are created from time to time but they cannot last forever and Liverpool followers will need a lot of convincing that Leicester have not gone progressively nearer to defeat in the last two meetings. The onus passes fairly and squarely on the Liverpool attack.

The win at Spurs along with Everton dropping a point had lifted spirits, and left Leicester's groundsman with some re-painting to do. Exuberant Liverpool fans marked their arrival in the city on the Friday night by breaking into Filbert Street and painting the line markings, corner flags and goalposts red although rain had turned them into a runny pink. Whilst out for a walk Ian St John and Chris Lawler met some fans who told them they would be sleeping in their car for the second night running, to which St John replied, 'You are the type of true fan Bill Shankly speaks about.' Brimming with confidence following the win over Spurs and the unexpected bonus of Everton dropping a point, Liverpool had another boost when both Leicester full backs, John Sjoberg and Len Chalmers were declared unfit for the game along with centre forward Ken Keyworth. Ron Yeats was still suspended but otherwise the Reds were at full strength as they showed no signs of tiredness from the day before, winning 2-0 to put the bogey to bed.

Yeats, who had travelled from Liverpool to support his teammates, was amongst the crowd along with his national team manager Ian McColl who had hoped to be watching him. Instead he was able to run the rule over Tommy Lawrence and Willie Stevenson, as well as Leicester's Frank McLintock. On a soggy pitch the home side had the first chance when Mike Stringfellow broke down the right but his cross was headed straight into Lawrence's hands by Billy Hodgson. The Reds responded and Hunt was upended by McLintock on the edge of the area, but Ronnie Moran's free kick was deflected just wide. The game was end to end with Leicester playing much more football than they had in previous games between the two sides. Stringfellow was their most potent threat and when Lawrence slipped when running from his goal to meet one of his crosses, a goal seemed certain but Bobby Roberts prodded the ball wide.

Ian St John headed a Gerry Byrne free kick wide and Stringfellow twice played the ball across the Reds goal in dangerous fashion, but nobody was there to meet it. In the seventeenth minute Hunt gave Liverpool the lead when Peter Thompson crossed from the right and his shot took a deflection off Richard Norman to take the ball out of Gordon Banks's reach. Colin Appleton managed to get back and kick the ball against the post but it had already crossed the line and the referee pointed towards the centre circle. It was ironic that when the Leicester defence was finally breached after 377 minutes it was with the help of a deflection, but nobody cared. The spell had been broken and every one of Liverpool's outfield players ran over to Hunt, dancing with joy.

Hunt almost added another when he shot from outside the area but it went just wide of the post, but they had an almighty let off when McLintock crashed a shot against the bar from thirty yards. Byrne was getting to grips with Stringfellow but had his name taken after bringing him down, although Horace Yates's match report in that evening's *Liverpool Echo* stated that the winger had nudged him first. Thompson hit a tremendous shot that beat Banks but somehow Graham Cross managed to fling himself across the face of goal to head the ball clear, and Milne was tripped by David Gibson as he looked set to break forward, leading to the Leicester player having his name taken. The Reds had to settle for being just 1-0 up at half time but they had shown all the courage needed to break their duck and looked every bit a side determined to win the title.

Leicester started the second half dangerously but Hodgson headed over the bar after some good build up play. The Reds were then denied when Hunt's shot beat Banks only for Ian King to get in the way of the ball before it crossed the line. Leicester were now defending just in the way they had in previous games, but at least this time the Reds had scored a goal. Up front they were struggling with Gibson, who had scored in each of the previous season's league fixtures, totally ineffective. Moran and Byrne were a rock at the back and played some beautiful long passes to set up Liverpool attacks. Such was the determination shown by the Reds that even Hunt had his name taken by the referee for a rash challenge, while Stevenson although not as good as he had been against Spurs, was more than able. Milne was solid in midfield and Chris Lawler also performed like a seasoned player.

The Reds had to play the last fifteen minutes effectively with ten men after Ian Callaghan was badly shaken in a clash of heads and began wandering around aimlessly. But Leicester, who were showing no cohesion up front, never looked like equalising. They had created nothing since the hour mark when Roberts and Tom Sweenie both stood aside to allow a ball from Gibson that was played into their path run harmlessly through to Lawrence. With five minutes left the victory was sealed when Arrowsmith ran on to a through ball by Hunt and drilled the ball past Banks to the delight of the thousands of Reds fans in the ground. He almost added a third three minutes later when St John played him in and his shot rebounded off Banks back into his path, but he hit the ball wide.

The victory kept Liverpool in second place as Everton beat Blackpool 3-1 at Goodison Park, but that didn't dampen the joyous mood of both players and supporters alike. Writing in the *Daily Post* on Easter Monday, Horace Yates claimed that 'unrivalled teamwork' had led to Liverpool securing maximum points from their two tough away fixtures and that 'the stamp of champions was all over their accomplished performances. The view from the press box was clear, that there was now a unanimous willingness to regard Liverpool as the new Kings of English football.'

Liverpool: Lawrence, Byrne, Moran, Milne, Lawler, Stevenson, Callaghan, Hunt, St John, Arrowsmith, Thompson.

Leicester: Banks, Appleton, Norman, McLintock, King, Cross, Hodgson, Sweenie, Roberts, Gibson, Stringfellow.

Referee: Mr W. Holian (Chesterfield).

Attendance: 31,209.

30th March 1964: Liverpool 3 Tottenham Hotspur 1, Football League Division One

Easter Monday gave Liverpool a chance to return to the top of the league as they faced Tottenham in the return game at Anfield. With Everton not playing until the Tuesday night at West Bromwich Albion, the Reds knew they could really pile the pressure on their rivals if they could secure a fourth successive victory.

Chris Lawler had been an able deputy but there was no doubt that Ron Yeats would be returning to the side for this game, his suspension now complete. He was raring to go, telling readers of his *Liverpool Echo* column on the 28th March, 'Doing full training for five days without a match on the sixth becomes a bit irksome. I shall be raring to have a go at Spurs.' The Reds' captain also confirmed the correct pronunciation of his surname following a request from a Mr Elkes in Wrexham. He explained that it was 'Yeets' and that his ancestors were from Ireland, where the name was common in parts.

The return of Yeats was the only change that Bill Shankly made from the side that had played at White Hart Lane but for Spurs, Bill Nicholson made a number of changes as he tried to arrest his team's slide. Forwards Terry Dyson and John White were dropped to make way for Les Allen and debutant Jimmy Robertson, while at the back Peter Baker made way for Mel Hopkins. These three changes were tactical but a back injury to Jimmy Greaves sustained in the 1-1 draw at Fulham on the Saturday meant that Alan Mullery moved to inside forward, and Tony Marchi switched from left to right half with Phil Beal coming in on the left.

The two away victories meant excitement amongst Reds fans in the city reached fever pitch, and queues began to form outside Anfield at 8.30am for the 3pm kick off. Extra police were drafted in to control the crowds and queues were snaking in and out of the side streets. The Chief Constable of the Liverpool City Police, J.W. Smith, personally took control of directing the crowd and traffic, which included plenty of additional buses laid on by Liverpool Corporation. Such was the parking chaos that many fans had to leave their cars a mile from the ground, even though there were no restrictions at that time, and forty minutes before the game began the first gates started to close at the Kop end. Desperate fans tried to find another open gate but all were locked within the next ten minutes, as an estimated 15,000 fans were still outside.

Touts did a roaring trade, selling 9s stand tickets for £2 10s (45p and £2.50 respectively in today's money) and frustrated fans who hadn't been able to get in vented their anger to journalists. John Adams from Huyton said, 'It is disgusting, I have been waiting an hour and a quarter to get in. They should make these games all-ticket and save people like myself from making unnecessary journeys. Len Jackson, who had travelled from Warrington said, 'It cost me 10s just getting here, why don't they make these top games all-ticket?' It is estimated that about 3,000 fans remained outside to listen to what was going on from the roar of the crowd and their disappointment was made up for somewhat as the Reds swept Spurs aside to go top of the league.

Returning skipper Yeats won the toss meaning the Reds were kicking into the Anfield Road in the first half and they created two early chances. First Peter Thompson cut inside and hit a right footer wide before taking a pass from Alf Arrowsmith and seeing his shot saved by John Hollowbread. Ian Callaghan then crossed for Arrowsmith who headed the ball into the net but it was ruled out for a foul on the keeper by Roger Hunt. Liverpool's early attacking was creating a carnival atmosphere amongst the crowd who were cheering every move, as Spurs could barely get out of their own half in the opening stages. Their first chance came when Maurice Norman made a long clearance to Cliff Jones. He ran to the edge of the area before laying the ball off to Robertson but the forward, who had scored four goals in two reserve games over the weekend, saw his low shot saved by Tommy Lawrence.

Spurs were packing their defence and after the initial burst of attacking, the Reds started to struggle to break them down. Callaghan tried his luck with a long range shot but it was easily held by Hollowbread and a similar effort from Arrowsmith was deflected behind for a corner by Mullery. Spurs were offering nothing in return though, with only Allen and Larry Brown up front and their midfielders passing the ball between themselves rather than trying to find an opening. The only moment of alarm during the first quarter came when Mullery played a fine ball into the area for the unmarked Jones, but he failed to connect with his head. Tony Marchi was effectively playing as an additional centre back to mop up everything that Norman failed to clear, so Ronnie Moran tried to exploit the space he created on the Spurs right side by joining in the attacks. He put in one dangerous cross that was met by Hunt but his downwards header was well saved by Hollowbread.

The game was re-ignited in the last ten minutes of the half when there were two goals in quick succession, with both of Liverpool's coming from Ian St John. The first came in the 36th minute after a mistake by the previously sound Hollowbread, who jumped to meet an errant cross from the left by the Liverpool forward but mis-judged it completely, and the ball sailed over his head into the net. If there was a bit of luck over his first goal, the same couldn't be said of St John's second which came just two minutes later. The move began on the right when Hunt passed to Arrowsmith. He played a perfect through ball to St John who slotted it past Hollowbread to send the crowd wild. They had hardly calmed down though when Spurs struck back from the kick-off without any Liverpool player touching the ball. There didn't seem any danger as the players passed the ball around aimlessly, but Mullery surprised everybody with a hit and hope shot from 25 yards that dipped under the crossbar with Lawrence rooted to the spot.

There was still time before the referee blew for the end of the half for Thompson to try his luck from distance, only for Hollowbread to save, and for Mullery to see a shot blocked by Willie Stevenson. Liverpool carried on attacking when the game resumed and forced two quick corners, both of which were cleared. Callaghan then crossed for Hunt who nodded the ball down to St John, but his shot was about a foot wide. St John then took a quick throw to Stevenson who tried a shot from a tight angle, but it sailed well over the bar. The Reds were pinning Spurs in their own half and it was no surprise when Arrowsmith increased the lead in the 53rd minute, helping in a Thompson shot after Callaghan had crossed. Spurs appealed for offside but the referee waved them away.

It really did seem a case of just how many Liverpool could score as there was clearly no way back for the visitors. They still played with only Allen and Jones up front, giving Yeats an easy time in his first game after suspension. St John twice came close to a hat-trick, seeing one header go just over the bar and another tipped over by Hollowbread, who also blocked close range efforts from Arrowsmith and Hunt. There was many an occasion when every single Liverpool player except for Lawrence was in the opposition half, with even Moran getting into the centre forward position to have a header saved.

Spurs didn't have their first shot since half time until the 70th minute, when Allen fired the ball well over from distance. It was exhibition stuff from the Reds with St John being at the heart of everything and some fine ball juggling led to a pass to Arrowsmith who was unluckily just offside.

As the game drew to a close the Kop added some more songs to their usual repertoire of 'When the Reds Go Marching In' and 'We Love You Yeah Yeah Yeah.' The usual Spurs song of 'Glory Glory Tottenham Hotspur' reverted to 'Glory Glory Hallelujah' and to signify their passing as a great side, 'Auld Lang Syne' was sung. For the second season running, the North London side had blown the title after looking favourites to win it. They had been top of the league at the beginning of the month but just one point from five games had seen them slip to fourth, five points behind the Reds having played a game more. It mirrored the previous season when they led the league after Easter, only to lose three of their last six games and hand the title to Everton.

Spurs had become the first club of the 20th Century to do the Double of Football League and FA Cup in 1961, then they won the FA Cup in 1962 and European Cup Winners Cup in 1963, but now they were a fading force. In the *Daily Post* the next day Horace Yates made sure they knew it writing, 'This aged, creaking Tottenham side had seemingly thrown in the sponge long enough before the end. For so long did they leave the Liverpool end of the ground untenanted, it almost seemed they had lost their sense of direction. As plainly as can be, the era of Tottenham greatness is over.'

The balance of power had clearly shifted to the North West whose clubs occupied the top three places in the table. Yates believed that the six points gained from three testing fixtures meant Liverpool were now clear favourites and their next game was at home to Manchester United, the only other side apart from Everton that had a realistic chance of overhauling them.

Liverpool: Lawrence, Byrne, Moran, Milne, Yeats, Stevenson, Callaghan, Hunt, St John, Arrowsmith, Thompson.

Tottenham: Hollowbread, Hopkins, Henry, Marchi, Norman, Beal, Jones, Mullery, Brown, Allen, Robertson.

Referee: Mr P. Rhodes (York).

Attendance: 52,904.

Top of Table

		Pl	W	D	L	F	A	GA	Pt
1	Liverpool	36	23	4	9	77	37	2.08	50
2	Everton	37	20	9	8	75	53	1.42	49
3	Manchester United	37	20	7	10	83	54	1.54	47

16

Almost There

After the three wins over the Easter weekend put them in pole position in the title race, Liverpool took massive strides to the title by continuing their winning run in the next two games. One of these was against third-placed Manchester United who still harboured hopes of winning the title themselves. As Liverpool as good as eliminated Matt Busby's side from the running, they were also handed a massive boost when Everton imploded, leaving the Reds on the brink of the title with four games still to play.

4th April 1964: Liverpool 3 Manchester United 0, Football League Division One

Little over 24 hours after beating Tottenham, the Reds faced the prospect of dropping back down to second place as Everton had the opportunity to go above them if they could beat West Bromwich Albion at The Hawthorns. However they blew their chance losing 4-2, meaning that the Reds were now overwhelming title favourites. Four wins from their last six games would be enough to guarantee that they would be champions, but their goal average was so superior that three wins and a draw would almost certainly do.

On Wednesday 1st April it was no joke when Jimmy Greaves was dropped from the England side to face Scotland at Hampden Park ten days later. It was the first time since 1961 that he had been omitted from an England side, having missed just one of the last nineteen internationals through illness. His anonymous performances against Liverpool though couldn't be ignored and it was no surprise when Roger Hunt was selected instead of him. Gordon Milne was also chosen to play at right half meaning that Liverpool's game against Burnley, scheduled to be played at Turf Moor on the same day, was put back until the following Tuesday.

Bill Shankly had previously expressed his displeasure at international call-ups getting in the way of club preparations, but despite the stage of the season he made an exception here telling the *Daily Post*, 'We are naturally pleased. This is the number one match of the season and Hampden Park is the supreme test.' Liverpool fans were in total agreement that Hunt was deserving of his chance and that Greaves had been living on reputation and the fact he was at a London club for too long, meaning he had been given an easy ride by the press. Mr Cronin from Netherton had a letter published in the *Liverpool Echo* which said,

> 'Hunt rarely receives the praise he deserves for his whole hearted skilful play. Hunt is a valuable asset at Liverpool where the accent on teamwork means that individual genius is subordinate to a collective efficiency. Greaves is at his best in a successful side. His limitations as a team player have been exposed as Spurs have declined this season.'

Previewing the United game in the Echo on the Thursday, Leslie Edwards concluded that if Liverpool won the game 'the championship would be as good as theirs.' However if United won, the issue 'would be very open.' A potential key player in the destination of the title was the soon to be retired Stanley Matthews, whose Stoke City side still had home games to come against Everton, United and the Reds.

There were no injury worries for Liverpool but United were fretting over the fitness of keeper Harry Gregg who had a bruised thigh and would be assessed on the morning of the game. Despite Liverpool being in pole position now, Everton's Roy Vernon still refused to give up hope completely, writing in his Post column on the Friday,

> I have to admit that our championship hopes took a heavy blow at West Brom on Tuesday. Still I am not amongst those who are prepared to write off Everton's chances of retaining the title. There has been many a slip in similar circumstances and although Liverpool have matches in hand they have still to win them. We all realise that we can not afford another setback and what is more we don't intend to suffer one.

Amazingly that week, the Football League Management Committee raised the possibility of the maximum wage being re-introduced, something which Yates predicted in the Post on the Friday would lead to 'all out hostilities' between the League and players. In a document circulated to all clubs, a £20 a week maximum basic wage was mooted, with a further £10 appearance money and £2 for each year of service. Professional Footballers Association spokesman Cliff Lloyd was calm with his response, as he knew it was only at the discussion stage and would not be dealt with at that summer's Annual General Meeting. He simply said, 'It is a bridge we shall cross when the time comes.'

The proposed wage changes were not good news for Liverpool's players who were now the best paid in the country due to the crowd bonus system. There had been a capacity crowd against Spurs and further lock-outs seemed guaranteed against United and Arsenal. Peter Thompson told Horace Yates how he was out and about before the Easter weekend and was asked by a man if he was sorry he had left Preston given they had reached the FA Cup final. Before he could reply, a Reds fan chipped in and said 'Peter cries his way to the bank every week.' Thompson though was sadly the victim of crime the week of the United game when his car was broken into and a transistor radio stolen. Of far greater concern to him was a set of miniature boots given to him when he was a boy by United manager Matt Busby. They had enormous sentimental value and Ron Yeats used his Echo column to appeal for their return.

In the Post on the Saturday morning, Yates predicted that there was only likely to be one goal between the sides. He felt that Liverpool's consistency and dedication, coupled with United manager Matt Busby's insistence on playing open football rather than a blanket defence, would see the result go in the Reds' favour. It did, but by more than Yates predicted as the Reds won with ease to ensure that the title was now theirs to lose.

Queues started to form at 7.30am for entry to the ground, including some fans who had got the night boat over from Dublin. To ease congestion outside, police filtered fans down terraced streets in organisation that was described in the Echo that evening as 'first class.' The first gates to be locked were the Paddock at 1.45pm, followed by the Anfield Road ten minutes later and Kop at 2.30pm. Desperate fans started to shout that they'd pay high prices for tickets but there were no touts to be seen. Inside the atmosphere was electric, with the Echo describing how the 'Kop Choristers' had 'gone through their full repertoire to provide their own unique background to the Anfield scene.'

After losing the toss, United kicked into the Kop for the first half and took the game to Liverpool as expected, but this left them vulnerable at the back and it was Alf Arrowsmith who had the first chance early on. He broke clear and had a powerful low shot but it was well saved by Gregg who was declared fit that morning. Roger Hunt then saw a shot saved and Willie Stevenson cut in from the left and passed to Arrowsmith, whose shot was wide. United's first scoring opportunity fell to David Herd, who was set up after some good work by Denis Law but he rushed his shot and fired well over the bar.

In the sixth minute, Liverpool took the lead through Ian Callaghan. After Gregg failed to collect a Thompson corner, Hunt cleverly backheeled the ball into Callaghan's path and he drove it into the net from a tight angle before Gregg recovered his position. Soon afterwards, Maurice Setters tried to dribble himself out of danger in his own penalty area and he managed to get the ball away. He and fellow half back Paddy Crerand were being dragged all over the pitch by the lively Reds attack. Setters then made a complete mess of a free kick, slicing the ball to Ian St John who played a quick ball to Hunt but his shot was wide. United's most dangerous moment came in the twentieth minute when Bobby Charlton took a corner and Tommy Lawrence could only punch the ball to the feet of Bill Foulkes. His shot was heading for the net with Lawrence on the floor but Stevenson got in the way of the ball to deflect it for a corner.

After 22 minutes Callaghan crossed and St John collided heavily with Gregg. Both players needed treatment for several minutes, with the Reds striker hobbling and holding his knee as he got back to his feet. This disrupted Liverpool's rhythm and United began to play their best football of the game, but Lawrence wasn't troubled by a Charlton header and Yeats intercepted well when Herd played a clever pass towards Law who would have been clean through if it had reached him. Setters then played a thirty yard ball to Law but his header was wide before Charlton beat Callaghan and Gerry Byrne but his shot was blocked by Stevenson. Such was United's possession that Crerand was spending most of his time in the Liverpool half and a good ball by him to Nobby Stiles was flicked goalwards but went wide.

Just as Liverpool began to fear United were getting back into the game, they scored a second goal six minutes before half time. Callaghan hit a shot from a tight angle that beat Gregg but was cleared off the line by Law. However the ball went back to Callaghan who crossed it into the box and it was headed downwards by Arrowsmith. Gregg got a hand to the ball but couldn't prevent it going in off the post. From the restart seventeen-year-old George Best passed to Stiles who quickly laid off for Charlton, but his shot was weak and easily cleared by Byrne. Just before half time the Reds almost had a third from a free kick just outside the area. Stevenson touched the ball to St John who hit a fierce shot but it was saved by Gregg diving at full stretch.

Early in the second half a raking lunge by Setters on Hunt right in front of the Kop had the home fans furious, but the Reds wasted the free kick. Just after this, Callaghan crossed to St John who nodded the ball down to Hunt but Gregg flung himself forward to save from point blank range. Liverpool were dominant and United could have no complaints about them going 3-0 up in the 52nd minute. After a move involving five players that had been started by Gordon Milne, Hunt played the ball to Arrowsmith and despite an awkward bounce he controlled it and hit a shot past Gregg from ten yards. United were all over the place by now and spent a lot of time arguing amongst themselves, with not one player taking a grip of the situation and organising things. Law didn't have his first shot until the hour mark, but after a neat one-two with Stiles it was easily caught by Lawrence.

United were battling away in midfield but Milne and Stevenson were solid, backed up by Ronnie Moran who was playing one of his best games of the season. He nullified the threat of Best and had the Kop chanting his name in appreciation. United's players were not taking the defeat in sporting fashion and Law had his name taken by the referee after a blatant trip on St John in front of the Kop. Both he and Setters were getting booed constantly, especially as so much of the action was now taking place near the United penalty area, which had a number of coins thrown into it during the half.

Arrowsmith had a great chance to claim a hat-trick when he found himself one on one against Gregg. Despite it being far easier than the two from which he had scored, he fired the ball wide. He then went on a great run down the left wing, beating Foulkes before cutting the ball back to Callaghan whose shot was just wide. Only towards the end when Liverpool tired a little, unable to keep up the tenacity any more, did United look like they may have a chance of getting a goal back. But their desire had gone, they knew there was no chance, and they could have no complaints about the result.

There was further joy for Liverpool's fans when it was announced that Everton had lost at Stoke, meaning the Reds now needed just four points from their last five games to be confirmed as champions. The fans were singing 'Liverpool Liverpool Won The League', while there was also a moving rendition of *You'll Never Walk Alone*, which had been a feature of games since the song was number one before Christmas. Even Bill Shankly acknowledged that it was close, telling the Post, 'The title now seems to be in our grasp. The rest is up to us.' Former Liverpool player Matt Busby knew where the trophy would be heading and said afterwards,'Congratulations Bill, see that you make a good job of it now.'

Liverpool: Lawrence, Byrne, Moran, Milne, Yeats, Stevenson, Callaghan, Hunt, St John, Arrowsmith, Thompson.

Manchester United: Gregg, Brennan, Dunne, Crerand, Foulkes, Setters, Best, Stiles, Herd, Law, Charlton.

Referee: Mr H. P. Hackney (Barnsley).

Attendance: 52,559.

14th April 1964: Burnley 0 Liverpool 3, Football League Division One

Two wins would be enough to guarantee Liverpool the title, but such was their superior goal average that a win and a draw would probably be sufficient. Horace Yates felt even less would be needed, concluding in the *Daily Post* on 6th April that, 'Judging by the way that would-be rivals are slipping and sliding in the nervous finale just one more victory would probably suffice.'

That night Manchester United kept up their slim hopes of overhauling the Reds with a 1-0 home victory over Aston Villa which lifted them above Everton into second place on goal average. Despite this, even amongst the players, it was now a case of when, not if, the title would be won. Ian St John dearly hoped it could be clinched in the final home game of the season at Anfield, writing in his Post column on 7th April,

> What a wonderful ending that would be, for the title would be clinched in front of our own loyal and vociferous supporters. No stage manager could have offered a more alluring prospect. The ball is tossed firmly to our feet. Can we put it into the net? I think, and hope, we can. I shall never forget the scenes at Anfield when we clinched promotion. The memory of that will live with me forever. I am almost afraid to think ahead of a

> championship triumph. It is a very exciting prospect but we must keep calm because victory is not yet won.

The local press were convinced of where the trophy was heading too, as on the same day as St John's column a cartoon appeared depicting two fans doing their gardens, with the Liverpool fan saying: 'I reckon I'll have a right champion show here in a couple of weeks, how's yours?' The week before, which was 'bob a job week', a cartoon had shown a scout at the entrance to Goodison Park saying he had been sent by Bill Shankly to polish the championship trophy.

Liverpool's imminent title glory was not welcomed in all quarters and some stereotypical letters were sent to the London papers regarding how fans would behave when they followed their team in Europe. A cutting sent to Leslie Edwards of the Echo from an enraged fan contained the headline MERSEY MEN MAY ROCK EUROPE, accompanied by a letter which said:

> One thing is sure, they will be followed on those profitable European sorties that the title brings in its wake by a host of vociferous supporters. This would not matter much if Liverpudlians were merely noisy. But look at what they do to football excursion trains. They take them apart. Anything that can be torn off they tear off. Anything that can be smashed, shattered or splintered they feel it their duty to demolish. Mods and Rockers have nothing on Merseysiders on the spree, from all accounts. What splendid ambassadors they will be abroad – if they leave enough of their chartered airplanes alone to get there.

Edwards summarised this and other letters that had been printed, leading him to write that they showed 'further bias against all followers of the two clubs in this city' and that he found it 'incredible London should still have such a mistaken notion about the majority of followers of football in this city.'

On Tuesday 7th April Gordon Milne and Roger Hunt travelled to Troon to join up with their England teammates to prepare for the game against Scotland, which would see them train at Ayr United's Somerset Park. The only one of Liverpool's Scottish contingent called up for their country was Ron Yeats, who was cover to regular centre half Billy McNeill and didn't need to join the party until the Wednesday.

Despite the rivalry in the title race, Liverpool and Everton players came together on the Tuesday night to take part in Dixie Dean's testimonial at Goodison Park. The match was organised on an England v Scotland basis, all of Liverpool's squad being made available except for the two England players, Peter Thompson who was on Under-23 duty and Ian St John. He was receiving treatment for fluid on the knee after his collision with United keeper Harry Gregg on the Saturday and Shankly made it plain he couldn't be risked. 'This is an injury and if there is any doubt we will have to withdraw him. We want to help all we can but I would say he is very doubtful.'[57]

A healthy crowd of 36,870 turned out to pay tribute to Dean, who had scored 349 league goals for Everton, an incredible sixty of them coming in the memorable 1927-28 title winning season. Players were naturally wary of getting injured and there were few tackles made in what was described by the Post as a 'pass and run' affair. The Scottish players, which still included Yeats despite him having to travel to Scotland the next day, won 3-1 with Gordon Wallace being the only Liverpool scorer. The following night England Under-23s drew 2-2 with France in Rouen. Peter Thompson made one of the goals in a sizzling performance that drew plenty of applause form the home crowd.

There was speculation that week that Thompson's Under-23 teammate Phil Chisnall could be subject to a bid from Liverpool. Shankly refused to confirm his interest in the inside right however, telling Horace Yates, 'We know nothing about it, I wouldn't tell anybody if I was going after any player.' He also would not reveal where he was heading on the free Saturday that had been handed to him by the Scotland v England game, but Yates speculated he would most likely be watching a player somewhere. At Hampden, England were beaten 1-0 in front of 134,000 fans with Hunt missing two golden opportunities within the space of a minute in the first half.

Although Liverpool's game was off on the Saturday, Everton were in action at home to Wolverhampton Wanderers, a game that was attended by St John. He described the difference in atmosphere between Anfield and Goodison as 'striking' and that he had been surprised Everton's fans had let their side drop out of the title race without a 'supreme fight.'[58] In an intriguing twist Jimmy Melia, who was still living in Formby and training part of the week with his ex-Liverpool teammates, set up one of his side's goals in a 3-3 draw at Goodison. It had been a game in which he had the last laugh, as in the first fifteen minutes Everton were rampant and raced into a 2-0 lead. Melia hardly got a kick, falling over at one stage to the delight of the home crowd but he set up the first goal of a fightback that would see the visitors lead 3-2. Only a late Derek Temple goal salvaged a point for Everton and they could not have complained if they had lost the game.

The draw with Wolves all but ended Everton's title hopes and the following day the club was placed into further turmoil. The *Sunday People* ran a story that Tony Kay, who had signed for Everton for £55,000 from Sheffield Wednesday the previous season, had been one of three players involved in a match-fix whilst playing for his former club against Ipswich Town on 1st December 1962. The police were investigating whether any criminal offences had been committed and Wednesday acted swiftly to suspend Peter Swan and David 'Bronco' Layne on the Sunday night. Kay denied any wrongdoing, telling reporters from his Maghull home, 'I would never throw a football match no matter how much was offered to me.'[59] He then went to Sheffield but the following day met with chairman John Moores and manager Harry Catterick, where he was relieved of his match duties for as long as the investigation took place. Later that year, he was convicted of conspiracy to defraud, sentenced to four months imprisonment and banned from the professional game.

The day before the Burnley match, Manchester United won 2-1 against Sheffield United at Old Trafford to keep themselves mathematically in the hunt. On the same day the *Daily Post* published a letter which shows how the idea for Liverpool and Everton sharing a ground has not just been something that has come about in the modern area. Perhaps encouraged by the lockouts at Liverpool's last two home games Mr Yates from Thornton wrote,

> Anfield is obviously too small for a team bearing the city's name and Everton's ground, after all has been said about its capacity, is typical of the Victorian type sheds that this country struggles along with for its sports arenas. I suggest a huge new sports arena in Stanley Park that both teams can use on alternate Saturdays. It could also be used for other sporting and athletic events in the off season, like the great sporting stadia of the Continent. The support of football in this city puts it in the rank of the great European cities and I do not see how if these cities can afford it, then we can not. Why not thrown the finance open as with Sporting Club of Lisbon to those who like to watch. I am sure the numbers of folk in the Merseyside conurbation who would want to become shareholders would be enormous.

Captain Ron Yeats said that victory for the Reds against Burnley, which would mean they could guarantee the title by beating Arsenal at home, would be 'perfection.'[60] Burnley had been champions as recently as 1960 and given Liverpool two tremendous games in the FA Cup the previous season, but Leslie Edwards predicted in the Echo that they were beatable. However there were injury concerns as St John had a slight knee injury and Hunt was struggling to shake off a knock to his ankle sustained in the Scotland v England game. The Reds didn't set off until lunchtime with Shankly announcing that both forwards were fit, but shortly before kick-off Hunt suffered a reaction and it was decided to withdraw him from the lineup and play youngster Gordon Wallace instead.

Officials at Turf Moor pleaded to the thousands of Liverpool fans travelling by road to get there early and avoid congestion at the turnstiles. Burnley's manager Harry Potts knew the following would be so large and predicted that 'it will be difficult for anyone not familiar with the surroundings to be sure whether this is Turf Moor or Anfield.'[61] On their way they heard news of Chancellor Reginald Maudling's Budget, which encouraged them to have as good a time as possible that night as it would be more expensive the next day. Duties on beer, wines, spirits and cigarettes were going up 10%, while there was also a rise on fixed odds football betting. They did have a good night, as nearly 20,000 Liverpool fans in the ground saw Liverpool take a massive step to the title with a convincing victory.

There was some nervousness that Wallace, who had played seven games in 1962-63, was now making his first start of the season instead of the dependable Hunt. But nobody could have guessed this was the case as he linked with Ian St John and Alf Arrowsmith beautifully. On many occasions his control earned bursts of applause from the huge Reds following as they took control of the game. Just like Chris Lawler when he stepped into Ron Yeats's role, Wallace fitted in seamlessly and showed why Liverpool's reserves were riding high in third place in the Central League. With Gordon Milne outstanding, the Reds dominated the midfield and Gerry Byrne and Ronnie Moran mopped up everything at the back. It was no surprise on twenty minutes when they took the lead when Arrowsmith latched on to a through ball from St John and hit a shot from just outside the area that gave Adam Blacklaw no chance.

The score remained 1-0 at half time and three minutes after the restart Burnley had their best chance to equalise. Willie Morgan played the ball to Willie Irvine who was on the penalty spot, but his effort was well held by Tommy Lawrence. Then four minutes later Burnley had the stuffing knocked out of them when Blacklaw failed to hold Ian Callaghan's long range shot and St John pounced to rifle the ball into the roof of the net from three yards. Just before the hour, Arrowsmith got his second when his shot went in off the post after St John had lofted the ball over Fred Smith's head into his path. Arrowsmith then inadvertently got in the way of Peter Thompson's goalbound shot that had Blacklaw beaten and would have been Liverpool's fourth.

The huge following were loving every minute of it, singing the names of all the players as well as 'When the Reds Go Marching In' and 'We're The Best Behaved Supporters In The Land' for the last twenty minutes. The Burnley fans were sporting and applauding of Liverpool's play but there were hardly any of them left when they had two great chances to pull one back in the last minute. Brian Miller's shot was parried by Lawrence but from just a few yards, Irvine put the ball wide of the post, then a few minutes later Yeats acrobatically cleared off the line.

As the Reds supporters streamed out of the ground for their last pint before the extra penny was added to it, they did so knowing they had been at an away game they could never forget. St John had written in his *Daily Post* column that morning that he had never had so many ticket requests for an away game as this one. Somebody close to the club who wasn't there though was Shankly's wife Nessie, who was attending the 21st birthday party of the West Derby Townswomen's Guild. On hearing that the Reds had won, she told a journalist who called the club, 'What wonderful news, now I can sit down and enjoy myself.' Back at Turf Moor, her husband spoke of his pride at being so close to the title, saying, 'Fantastic, we are elated beyond words. It seems that nothing short of an earthquake can stop us now.' There were four games left and Liverpool needed just one more win, but more than anything they wanted that to be at Anfield in their next game.

Liverpool: Lawrence, Byrne, Moran, Milne, Yeats, Stevenson, Callaghan, Wallace, St John, Arrowsmith, Thompson.

Burnley: Blacklaw, Smith, Elder, O'Neil, Talbut, Miller, Morgan, Bellamy, Irvine, Harris, Connelly.

Referee: Mr K. Howley (Billingham).

Attendance: 34,900.

Top of Table

		Pl	W	D	L	F	A	GA	Pt
1	Liverpool	38	25	4	9	83	37	2.24	54
2	Manchester United	40	22	7	11	86	58	1.48	51
3	Everton	40	20	10	10	82	63	1.30	50

17

Champions

Liverpool clinched the title with three games to spare, hammering Arsenal in their last home game of the season to secure their first title since 1947. There were some of the most emotional scenes ever witnessed at Anfield as the Reds picked up the two points required to confirm their status as champions and it was all captured by the BBC for their *Panorama* programme.

18th April 1964: Liverpool 5 Arsenal 0, Football League Division One

The day after the Burnley game, Bill Shankly demonstrated how he was already thinking ahead towards the next season when striker Phil Chisnall arrived from Manchester United for a fee of £25,000. The England Under-23 international had scored six league goals for United that season but it was made clear to him by Shankly that he would be starting out in the reserves and would have to prove himself worthy of promotion to the first team. The negotiations had begun in Glasgow the weekend before when Liverpool officials met the United manager at the Scotland v England game. After a fee was agreed it was left to Chisnall to decide whether or not to sign and he did so without hesitation.

The main fitness worries ahead of the Arsenal game concerned Roger Hunt, although Chisnall would not be eligible. Shankly would not be drawn on the question when asked by Horace Yates of the *Daily Post* on the Wednesday but the journalist speculated that as he was only withdrawn from the Burnley game at the last minute, he must have a good chance. Hunt was able to train and take part in a short practice game on the Thursday, but his instep was still giving him some trouble and treatment was continuing. On that day in Aylesbury Justice Edmund Davies imposed heavy sentences on those found guilty of their involvement in the Great Train Robbery. Telling seven men, including carpenter Ronnie Biggs, that they were 'an intolerable menace to the well-being of society' he imposed a thirty year gaol tariff to ensure that the crime 'will be the last of its kind.' Four others got sentences of more than twenty years, while a solicitor who sold Leatherslade Farm to the gang but refused to give this information to the police, was given three years.

As Everton prepared to relinquish their mantle of champions, Roy Vernon wrote in his Post column on the Friday that they would be looking to win it back the following year and warned that retaining the title was the hardest thing to do. They would be doing so without Tony Kay, who was continuing to maintain his innocence over the match fixing row. On 17th April he was interviewed by Sheffield C.I.D. detectives at the offices of his solicitor. Denying all allegations, he was told that further enquiries were needed in Yorkshire.

Gordon Wallace was on standby should Roger Hunt fail to recover from his injury for what Leslie Edwards wrote in the Friday's Echo would be 'one of the greatest days in the history of Liverpool Football Club.' Bill Shankly gave fans hope when Horace Yates reported in the *Daily Post* on the morning of the game that he had said, 'Hunt's improvement is continuous, he will be at the ground on Saturday morning to do a bit of loosening up and to try out his foot. We are hopeful everything will be all right but the decision rests entirely with the boy.'

Arsenal were expected to be back at full strength, having the previous week been missing half back Jim Snedden through injury and left back Billy McCulloch being away on international duty with Northern Ireland. There would be a Liverpool connection in their side with keeper Jim Furnell making his first return to Anfield and centre forward Joe Baker having been born in the city. They were managed by Billy Wright who had former Reds forward Les Shannon on their coaching staff. They were effectively lambs to the slaughter going into what Yates called the 'hottest football cauldron in England' but manager Wright did say earlier in the week when asked for a tribute to the champions elect, 'I don't know if you are aware of it but we are playing at Anfield on Saturday and they could go down two points.'[62]

There would inevitably be a full house at Anfield for the game but it was still not all ticket. Bill Shankly expressed his disappointment that so many would miss out, telling the *Liverpool Echo*, 'The pity of it is that we cannot transport Hampden Park to Anfield for Saturday for I am sure all Merseyside will want to be there. It is a matter of real regret that so many of our fervent fans will never get near enough to see this game. I don't know what time they will start queuing but knowing them nothing will surprise me.' Leslie Edwards suggested that the club could have arranged for the game to be screened on close circuit television at the Liverpool Stadium boxing venue, or relayed to fans by loudspeaker in Stanley Park, but that, 'Football clubs are notoriously slow to move in connection with anything which hasn't been done before.'

The players were raring to go, with Ron Yeats saying in his Echo column on the day of the game, 'I have never known the boys more confident, but this does not mean over-confidence, so we approach the game in the same spirit as those Easter matches.' There was an air of inevitability amongst fans and journalists that the Reds would easily secure the two points needed to win the league, with Edwards predicting that Liverpool would win, 'maybe quite handsomely.' He was right as the Reds smashed five goals in the first hour to clinch the title and set off scenes never seen at Anfield before.

It was 10pm on the Friday night when the first fans arrived by the turnstiles, armed with flasks of coffee, transistor radios and camp beds. Seventeen-year-old Liverpool Collegiate schoolboy George Hunter was first in the queue along with his friend Alan Wilcock. As closing time approached they were joined by more fans who were leaving local pubs and the queue had risen to twenty by midnight. By 9am the next morning there were still no more than fifty outside but as fans read in the *Daily Post* of the queues having started the night before that soon changed. By midday it was chaos and Roger Hunt struggled to make his way through the crowds to get to the players' entrance. No special arrangements had been put in place, with the only change to normal being that the turnstiles would open half an hour earlier than usual at 12.30pm.

One of those fans was Peter Etherington, more commonly known as Evo who has followed the Reds far and wide over fifty years, going on to write three books recalling his experiences. He was attending Anfield for the first time, having earned his entrance fee by running an errand for his mum to the pawn shop to retrieve his dad's suit. He recalls in *One Boy And His Kop*, published by Countyvise in 2001,

> Getting off the bus at Spellow Lane and walking up to Anfield I couldn't believe what I was seeing. There were people everywhere. We queued for about two hours but I didn't mind. The sight of people going in and out of the Albert pub, the smell of onions, the sound of people in the ground singing Beatles songs, the size of the big police horses, all left me completely enthralled.

The police had been confident they could deal with the crowds, the system of having queues snaking down side streets in previous games having worked well. However this time there was chaos as no Reds fan wanted to miss seeing the Reds clinch the title for the first time since 1947 and their first at Anfield since 1923. It meant that every available officer from E Division was dispatched to Anfield where mounted police were trying to keep the lines in order and traffic was gridlocked at noon.

When the gates opened at 12.30pm, crowds in Lake Street were fifteen to twenty deep with fans singing 'When the Saints Go Marching In.' Little over an hour later the ground was heaving and turnstiles started to close, leading to more chaos as fans surged to find another entrance that was open. Those with tickets were unable to get to their turnstiles due to the sheer numbers surrounding the cash gates. By 2pm all gates had been closed but there were surprisingly few outside, with many having no doubt taken the view that if they didn't get there exceptionally early they wouldn't get in. Many of those that were locked out then headed across Stanley Park to Goodison where Everton reserves were just kicking off against Barnsley.

Inside the ground the atmosphere was unbelievable as the Kop spent the hour before kick-off going through a repertoire of songs. The fact that John Morgan was there reporting for the BBC's Panorama programme only added to the excitement. This was in the days before cameras were a feature at league matches and the fans were keen to make themselves heard for the nation. Before the game the Kop chanted 'Liverpool' in perfect rhythmic motion, gave a great rendition of *She Loves You* and swayed along to Cilla Black's *Anyone Who Had A Heart* and of course, *You'll Never Walk Alone*. Morgan reported that: 'Their rhythmic swaying is an elaborate and organised ritual. They begin singing together, they seem to know intuitively when to begin. They seem mysteriously to be in touch with one another, with "Wacca", the Spirit of Scouse.' The following Monday the *Daily Post* wrote that the singing was apparently conducted by a fan wearing a red and white suit positioned directly behind the goal who had been christened 'Sir Malcolm.' Evo remembers how he felt when he saw the Kop for the first time from the Boys' Pen, where he remained with his friend Smudge while two others, Pilch and Timmy, climbed into the Kop only to get thrown out by police.

> 'Finally I got to the front of the queue. A shilling handed over, a push and a click of the turnstile. I had entered the promised land. It was a world I had heard about but not yet seen. My first sight of 50,000 people all gathered together: 28,000 of them on a singing, swaying, all bouncing Spion Kop is something I will remember forever. "You'll Never Walk Alone" sang the masses in a moving, colourful display of togetherness.'[63]

You'll Never Walk Alone was beginning to emerge as the favourite song of the Kop, taking over from *We Love You Yeah Yeah Yeah*. It was a moving sight to see the Kop swaying slowly as they sang it and a Mr Mansell from Woolton believed its new-found prominence was down to the wording, which Liverpool's fans could particularly associate with. He said: 'We followers of Liverpool have walked through many a storm to follow the team, but on Saturday we saw the rainbow.'[64]

The teams took to the field as fans on the Kop waved scarves, rattles, hats, papers and anything else they could get their hands on. Anfield had never before heard such a crescendo of noise at the start of the match. Jim Furnell was the Arsenal captain for the day and won the toss, taking the decision to change ends meaning the Reds would be kicking into the Kop for the first half. This led to a stream of cameramen racing to that end, with just one photographer taking up position behind Tommy Lawrence in the Anfield Road goal. In a fast start both sides had chances to score in the first minute, Willie Stevenson's dangerous cross being headed away by Ian Ure then Lawrence diving at the feet of Alan Skirton after he seized on a poor backpass by Ronnie Moran. Ian Callaghan then crossed for Hunt who headed over when unmarked, before Gerry Byrne was beaten by George

Armstrong whose cross was easily collected by Lawrence.

In the seventh minute there was euphoria as Liverpool took the lead after a brilliant move involving all three inside forwards. Hunt surged into the box from the inside right position, avoiding a scything challenge by Skirton on the way, then turned the ball into the path of Alf Arrowsmith. Rather than shoot himself he edged the ball sideways to the on-running Ian St John who slid it past Furnell. Within a minute Arsenal almost had an equaliser and should really have done. Joe Baker rounded Lawrence who probably had come out of his goal too quickly, but he rolled the ball towards goal so weakly that Byrne got back to side-foot it off the line into the hands of the returning keeper.

Arrowsmith had an ambitious effort from 25 yards that went just wide and Lawrence had to be alert to save a shot from Armstrong. Furnell then made a brilliant save when he turned Arrowsmith's volley around the post before Gordon Milne intercepted a ball on the right and cut inside, but his shot had no power and was easily held by Furnell.

Arsenal though were playing good football and passing the ball well, earning a great chance to draw level in the 29th minute when they were awarded a penalty. Eastham had tried to flick the ball past Ron Yeats who handled and there were no complaints from either the crowd or players. Eastham chose to take it himself and struck the perfect penalty, low and just inside the post, but Lawrence dived to his right to push it away to the delight of the crowd and every Reds player who raced to congratulate him.

Hunt almost gave Liverpool a two goal lead when he controlled well and hit a shot that brought the best out of Furnell, but they did get their second in the 38th minute. Thompson weaved his way down the left and hit a deep cross to St John, who headed across the goalmouth for Arrowsmith to nod home from three yards. Thompson then tried to get on the scoresheet himself with some brilliant trickery but just as he was lining up his shot he was dispossessed. Arrowsmith also tried a clever backheel to create a shooting chance for St John but it was cut out. Despite being 2-0 down, just before half time there was a sporting moment from Arsenal when Terry Neill, who had a chance to attack down the right, chose to put the ball out to allow Callaghan to receive treatment for an injury.

The second half saw the Reds kicking into the Anfield Road end but the fans there were still as vociferous as the Kop. Almost from the kick-off Furnell made a great double save when he tipped Arrowsmith's cross-shot onto the bar then when Hunt came in for the rebound, the Arsenal keeper blocked it from point blank range. Soon afterwards he made a diving save from a St John shot but there was nothing he could do to prevent a third goal in the 52nd minute that put the title in the bag. Thompson cut in from the left wing and then unleashed a shot with his right foot that Furnell had no hope of reaching. The keeper almost spilled a shot from Hunt but managed to gather it at the second attempt. In the 57th minute he was beaten by Thompson again after the Reds winger weaved his way across the pitch before shooting from long range past the unsighted Furnell.

On the hour Hunt got Liverpool's fifth, shooting from distance after some good build-up play by Thompson and Gordon Milne. By now there was a carnival atmosphere and the goal was greeted by hats, scarves, papers and everything else that could be thrown into the air. In the 64th minute Arrowsmith had the ball in the net again, but the goal was disallowed and a penalty awarded instead as he had scored from the rebound after a Hunt shot had been handled on the line. Callaghan, the only one of Liverpool's five forwards not to have scored, was invited to take the kick but to everyone's dismay, his low effort was held by Furnell.

The game was then played out at walking pace. Arsenal had suffered enough and the fans put on an exhibition of singing with the best moment being when the Kop sang 'When The Saints Go Marching In' in perfect harmony with everybody rhythmically clapping along. Other's to be sung were 'Ee Aye Adio We're the Greatest in the Land,' 'We've got the Best Goalkeeper In the Land,' 'London Bridge is Falling Down,' 'We've Got the Best Eleven Players in the Land' and of course 'Champions Champions Champions.' There was humour too, with one fan near to the press box shouting out as the game neared a close 'Come on think of the goal average.'

The final whistle was met with the biggest cheer of the afternoon and a pitch invasion that was feared by the police didn't materialise, just six boys managing to make it on to the field. The players shook hands with their Arsenal counterparts then disappeared off down the tunnel, but none of the crowd were going anywhere. They soon re-appeared, holding the makeshift trophy that had been presented to Yeats beforehand. First they ran towards the Anfield Road end and then along the new Kemlyn Road stand. The noise was unbelievable and it is hard to believe that it could have got any louder, but as the players, led by St John, reached the Kop the volume increased by 50%. Horace Yates described it in the following Monday's Post as a 'step by step round of hero-worship that bordered on hysteria.' As the players ran down the side of the Main Stand and Paddock, a lady presented Yeats with a bottle of champagne and received a kiss on the cheek in return.

One person missing from the victory parade was manager Bill Shankly, who remained in the tunnel allowing the players to take the glory. Even the Kop's repeated singing of 'We Want Shankly' couldn't persuade him to come and take the applause. The players had wanted him to go out but St John later revealed that the boss had told him, 'The pitch is for the players, you are the lads they want to see. Go out and give your thanks also to the greatest body of supporters ever possessed by any club.'[65]

He stood back and modestly looked on as his players were lauded by the Kop and reminded journalists that it was not just them who should be hailed. He told Yates, 'When you hail the champions don't forget to give the best crowd of supporters in the world their appropriate place of honour.' After the players had gone back down the tunnel, the fans still wouldn't leave and to their delight they appeared again in the Directors' Box, this time accompanied by Shankly. As Yeats held aloft the champagne the supporters clapped with Shankly applauding them in return.

The players then returned to the dressing rooms and finally everybody made their way either home or to await the opening of the pubs at 5.30pm to continue their celebrations. After drinking champagne before getting changed, the players didn't engage in one big party, instead drifting off into their own groups. St John and Yeats joined fans in the *Maid of Erin* pub on Scotland Road, one of many that were demolished to make way for the Wallasey Tunnel approach roads later in the decade. In his autobiography *The Saint*, published by Hodder & Stoughton in 2005, St John recalled the special togetherness between players and fans that could never be imagined today.

> 'Anfield had throbbed in the afternoon and in the *Maid of Erin* there was a tidal flow of Guinness. Eventually our wives came to rescue us, taking us to dinner in some smart restaurant in the city centre, but for a few hours Ronnie and I were breathing the joy of the fans. I had known that intimacy before up in Motherwell, but not in such a moment of triumph and sometimes today I wonder at how much easier it was back in those days to feel part of a city, to go out on the field knowing precisely the weight of hopes and the dreams you carried on your shoulders when the referee blew the whistle to start the game.'

Too young for the pub, Evo returned home where his dad gave him two shillings for lemonade and sweets. Later that night, he was woken up by his mum and dad returning home from a night out, his dad singing 'Ee-aye-addio we won the league' and jokingly reminding his mum that if she needs to pawn his suit again, she needed to take the ticket off before putting it back in the wardrobe.

The celebrations continued all weekend, although some fans found themselves with a criminal record for their excesses. A disturbance at Walton Hospital's social club that night saw a nineteen-year-old called David Scrotten arrested for assaulting a police officer after he had been knocking over tables and chairs when asked to leave the club. When he appeared in court on the Monday morning he was found guilty and sentenced to two months imprisonment. The *Liverpool Echo* reported that he apologised for his conduct and told the court, 'If I hit the police it was because I was drunk, we were celebrating Liverpool's championship.' Also in court that morning was Wallasey man John Jamieson. Although it was not reported whether he was a Red or not his drinking had got him into trouble. On the Sunday evening he had crashed into a parked car whilst under the influence and on being arrested said to the police officer 'Please tell my wife where I am, she loves me yeah, yeah, yeah.' He was fined £25 at Birkenhead Magistrates' Court the following day and disqualified from driving for two years.

On the Monday night Liverpool and Everton reserves were meeting at Goodison Park in the semi-final of the Liverpool Senior Cup. There was speculation that the championship trophy would be presented but the Echo reminded fans that this would definitely not be the case. The trophy was still at Goodison but although Everton were very sporting about Liverpool's success, with chairman John Moores saying the Reds had 'deserved to carry off the League,'[66] club officials drew the line at presenting it to Liverpool at their own ground. In the game itself, the Reds came from 2-1 down to win 3-2, Bobby Graham netting twice in a minute near the end to set up a final against Southport.

Instead, fans would have to be content with re-living the Arsenal game on the Panorama programme which was to be broadcast on BBC1 at 9pm. It started a few minutes late though due to a power failure at the BBC's Shepherd's Bush headquarters but when it did, fans were treated to nearly five minutes of footage of the game and the Kop. The programme was compered by Richard Dimbleby at the Derby Room in the Adelphi Hotel and also focused on the city's contribution to the arts, the vitality and vigour of its people and plans for the future. It contained only the briefest of references to the Beatles, who had been victims of a burglary the day before when thieves broke into a flat that George Harrison and Ringo Starr shared in Knightsbridge, stealing £200. Liverpool Football Club, the city and its people had much to look forward to, but before that there was the matter of playing out the last three games of the season.

Liverpool: Lawrence, Byrne, Moran, Milne, Yeats, Stevenson, Callaghan, Hunt, St John, Arrowsmith, Thompson.

Arsenal: Furnell, Magill, McCulloch, Neill, Ure, Snedden, Skirton, Strong, Baker, Eastham, Armstrong.

Referee: Mr P. Brandwood (Walsall).

Attendance: 48,623.

Top of Table

		Pl	W	D	L	F	A	GA	Pt
1	Liverpool	39	26	4	9	88	37	2.38	56
2	Manchester United	41	22	7	12	87	61	1.43	51
3	Everton	41	20	10	11	82	64	1.28	50

18

Mersey-Beating All Over the World

As Liverpool and Everton were fighting it out for the league title the city's pop groups, having dominated the British charts, were now taking the world by storm. The Beatles played more concerts in Europe and then visited America for the first time where they were a phenomenon, leading to other Liverpool groups having singles released over there.

In January the Beatles made their first trip to France, performing in a run of eighteen concerts at the Olympia Music Hall between 16th January and 4th February. They were part of a nine act concert, sharing top billing with French singer Sylvie Vartan and American Trini Lopez, best remembered for *If I Had a Hammer*. The audience was different from what they were used to, consisting of the cream of French café society who were wearing evening dress. Although they received plenty of applause and fans remained in the boulevard for several hours after their first appearance, the press reaction was mixed. *Le Parisien Libre* said that they offered nothing new apart from their haircuts and that 'it is really granddaddy's rock.' *Le Figaro* was much more damning, commenting, 'There are too many hairdressers invited to Parisien galas for unkempt folk to have a triumph.' *France Soir* though was much more complimentary, describing them as having 'extraordinary rhythm' and being 'as good musicians as they are singers.'

They were joined in Paris by Gerry and the Pacemakers, who had a scare when guitarist Les Chadwick left his passport at home and a taxi had to be sent for it. They didn't play any concerts though, with Gerry Marsden telling the *Liverpool Echo* that they were going purely for a holiday and to go up the Eiffel Tower.

Whilst Gerry and the Pacemakers got on with sightseeing, the Beatles had various commitments to make. One of the tasks they had to perform was to record a special programme for members of the British Forces Network in West Germany. Despite the press not giving them the complete thumbs up, the French public couldn't get enough of them. Such was the demands on their time that for a popular television programme aimed at teenagers, Trini Lopez and three French singers donned Beatles wigs and mimed to *She Loves You* as the lads themselves were too busy to appear. However they were not met by screaming crowds everywhere they went as in Britain. After a lightning one night visit home on 28th January when they didn't have a concert, they walked unnoticed through Orly airport when they flew back to

Paris. It would be far different on their next foreign trip however.

The Beatles departed for their first visit to America on 7th February. As they boarded their flight to New York at Heathrow, hundreds of fans on the viewing balcony showered them with love letters and jelly babies. Paul McCartney told reporters he was nervous, not because of the crowds they may encounter, but in case they weren't liked by the American public. He needn't have worried because shortly before take-off a message was flashed to Brian Epstein saying that *She Loves You* and *I Want to Hold Your Hand* were joint number one in the Billboard charts. Amongst the journalists covering the tour was the ironically named George Harrison, a columnist for the *Liverpool Echo*.

On arrival at Kennedy airport at 1.16pm local time, they were met by over 3,000 screaming teenagers and were ushered into a press conference straight after going through customs. One reporter asked how they felt about so many skipping school to come and meet them, to which Ringo Starr replied, 'You can't mean they haven't been given a holiday today.'

There was some scepticism about their arrival in America, with students at Detroit University distributing stickers saying 'Stamp out Beatles,' leading to Paul McCartney saying they were looking to stamp out the university. Quickfire responses like these were loved by the journalists present, who were told by police that nobody had ever caused such a commotion at the airport, not even Marilyn Monroe at the height of her fame.

Each member of the group had a Cadillac to themselves for the journey to the Plaza Hotel on Fifth Avenue where mounted police were trying to control a 400 strong crowd. Already though the young men, none of whom had reached their 24th birthday, were showing signs of weariness with the following day's *Daily Post* saying their expressions ranged from 'pleasure to perplexity and quiet annoyance.' That night they were taken on a sightseeing tour of Broadway and the following morning they were on the front of a number of newspapers, with the *American Journal* headlining with 'IT'S BEATLETOWN USA.' As Liverpool took on Everton in the derby at Goodison Park on the Saturday, the Beatles were rehearsing for a performance on the following nights Ed Sullivan Show. The Beatles were a huge success on the primetime show, which producers claimed was watched by three quarters of the population of New York and 58% of the total population, compared to the normal 25%. The following day the *New York Times* was the only one of the papers in the city not to put them on the front page and 200 reporters attended a two hour press conference at their hotel. During this, Alan Livingstone, the President of Capital Records, told them that they were the fastest selling artists America had ever seen and presented them with two gold records, one of which was for *I Want To Hold Your Hand* which had sold one million copies.

Their haircuts and accents were a particular attraction but George

Harrison said they had no trouble being understood, telling reporters, 'You should be thankful we're not Cockneys. People tell me we're a lot easier to understand.'[67] Such was the fascination with the hair that WMCA Radio cut a lock from Ringo Starr and used it as a competition prize. The station which rebranded itself 'Beatles Headquarters USA' for the duration of the tour advised listeners on 11th February that the winning postcard would be drawn from a Beatles wig the following Sunday. That day though the weather got in the way of their plans to fly to Washington DC and they had to take the train instead. On arrival, 300 screaming teenagers were held back behind barriers at Union Station by police as the group was escorted to cars. That night they played their first concert of the tour in front of 8,000 fans at the Coliseum then attended a masked ball at the British Embassy.

The phenomenal reception the Beatles had received in America led to leading weekly magazine *United States News & World Report* interviewing David Riesman, a leading psychologist from Harvard University to see if America's youngsters were literally 'going crazy.' He concluded that it was just a passing fad and that 'one must not exaggerate and attribute to the vast majority the reactions of the minority.'

From Washington the Beatles returned to New York for a gig at the Carnegie Hall, then flew to Miami on Thursday 13th February, the day that British Prime Minister Alec Douglas-Home arrived in Washington in far less chaotic circumstances for talks with President Lyndon Johnson. Meanwhile, they literally brought Miami to a standstill. 8,000 screaming teenagers were at the airport to meet them, leading to more chaotic scenes as they were whisked away under cover without being seen. It was estimated that 2,000 extra cars had descended on the airport to take the teens there and as they all left, the biggest traffic jam Miami had ever seen was created, causing many to miss their outgoing flights.

The four lads were taken to the Deauville Hotel where armed guards were present to help prevent anybody except guests going in, while Ringo Starr joked that he hoped to take a dip in the pool with 'swimming policemen.' That night there was some tension when they were taken discreetly to a dimly lit bar and shown to a table out of the way of other customers. However when waitresses began to scream all four got up and left, leading to an argument with their road managers outside where John Lennon told one of them, 'I thought you said we were on holiday.' They ended up returning to the privacy of their hotel, knowing that their one chance of having a late night was gone as they would need to be early to bed on the Friday ready for more rehearsals followed by another television appearance on the Ed Sullivan Show on the Sunday. This show was filmed from the Napoleon Ballroom of the hotel and again attracted around 70 million viewers.

After the second Ed Sullivan Show appearance there was a day off on the Monday, when they went water skiing and on Tuesday 18th February they met Cassius Clay at the Fifth Street Gym as he prepared for his forthcoming heavyweight title fight against Sonny Liston. There were a few more days of relaxation which included a photo shoot in the hotel pool for *Life* magazine, before they began the journey home on 21st February.

When they flew out of Miami on a flight bound for New York, 500 fans were at the airport to wave them off. They flew to London aboard a Pan Am Boeing 707 that had been re-named *Clipper Beatles* in their honour. At Heathrow there was a huge police presence to try and deter youngsters from staying at the airport, with many teenage girls doing all they could to avoid being sent home on the last buses. Those that managed to stay were allowed to bed down on the floor of the Queen's building before being charged a shilling the next morning to go on the roof and view the plane arriving.

While the Beatles had been conquering America another Liverpool group, the Searchers, were continuing their rise. *Needles and Pins* spent three weeks at number one in the British charts that February, just as Everton entered a run of form that would take them from tenth to first in the league table. In a BBC radio interview the following month, Beatles manager Brian Epstein said that they were the top group of the moment, something which flattered their manager Les Ackerley who responded, 'It's very nice of him. He has said publicly that he would like to sign up the Searchers but there is no chance of this.'[68] The Searchers were displaced at number one by The Bachelors, who stayed there for one week before another of Epstein's artists, Cilla Black, hit the top with her second single *Anyone Who Had A Heart*. Black had been signed up by Epstein the previous September after he saw her performing at the *Blue Angel* jazz club in Seel Street.

The Beatles first number one of 1964 was *Can't Buy Me Love*, which hit the top at the end of March and stayed there for three weeks, so it was there when the Reds clinched the league title on 18th April. It is somewhat ironic that the song contains the line 'money can't buy me love' and Everton had failed to buy the title, the £85,000 they spent on Fred Pickering in March failing to bring success.

In April, Gerry and the Pacemakers broke America, with *Don't Let the Sun Catch Me Crying* reaching number four in the Billboard top 100. The following month they also appeared on the Ed Sullivan Show, making two appearances one of which was watched by Liverpool's players from the audience as they had arrived in New York for their football tour of North America. Prior to going to America, Gerry and the Pacemakers had been to Australia, where the Beatles went for the first time in June. This was part of a three week tour of Asia and Australasia that also took in Hong Kong and New Zealand. There were 2,000 fans to meet them at Sydney airport, where a woman threw a six-year-old disabled child at Paul McCartney, hoping he would be able to cure him. Culturally, Liverpool was the centre of the universe and subject of the BBC's Panorama programme on 20th April 1964, two days after the Reds had clinched the title. This is best known amongst Liverpool FC fans for the Kop feature, but this took up only about four minutes of a fifty minute programme about what the *Radio Times* dubbed 'the most talked about city in Europe.'

The massive growth of the popularity of the Beatles and others outside Liverpool meant they were living out of hotels and spending less and less time in their home city. In March 1964, Brian Epstein moved his operations which now included 25 staff to London, expressing his regret but saying it was a move that had to be made.

Following on from the success of their first American trip, the Beatles were back in August, spending a month there and playing in 23 cities from San Francisco to New York. This time they were playing in far bigger venues than six months earlier and often the screams of over 10,000 fans made the sound inaudible. In between crossing oceans, the Beatles had also found time to produce the film *A Hard Day's Night*, filming in March and April. This premiered at the Odeon Cinema in London Road on 10th July 1964, the Beatles making a triumphant return to the city in which they had last appeared in public in December.

The following day's *Daily Post* headlined with THE NIGHT OF 100,000 SCREAMS and reported that it was the craziest night in the city since Everton had won the FA Cup in 1933. The following year there would be another tumultuous reception in Liverpool as the Reds won the FA Cup for the first time. Just as the Beatles and other groups were taking over the world, the Reds were also about to make their mark on the international football stage, making the semi finals of the European Cup.

19

Back To Earth

Liverpool had done what their players and fans dreamed of and secured the title at Anfield, meaning the three games left to play were academic. However there would be no question of fielding fringe players in those games as Bill Shankly looked to finish the season as strongly as possible. With Phil Chisnall having arrived from Manchester United, the Reds' boss was said to be in the market for a defender so the players couldn't afford to rest on their laurels in case it was their places up for grabs. As it was though, the Reds managed to pick up just one point from the six available.

22nd April 1964: Birmingham City 3 Liverpool 1, Football League Division One

In his *Daily Post* column on the Tuesday after the title was secured, Ian St John admitted that there was a time when he wondered if the Reds were capable of becoming champions. He revealed that after the defeat to Fulham 'my heart sank to my boots' but that Bill Shankly had never lost faith in the ability of the players. He said of the boss,

> 'Match after match, he implanted his courage and confidence in us by repeating and repeating 'we can win this league, we will win this league. There's nobody left in the race as good as us. We can lick this lot.' It was mighty nice hearing when your spirits are beginning to sag and it may be an understatement of mine to say that every bit as much as any or all of the players, this title is as much a success for the boss as the team. You can travel the country through and through and you will never find a man of his spirit, drive and energy. It is infectious, you can't be in his company for five minutes without feeling your spirits uplifted. He deserves an outsize medal for what he has done. That he is the manager of the season is our view with no qualifications attached.'

It wasn't just his own players that were paying tribute to Shankly, as other managers were queuing up to give him praise. Aston Villa's Joe Mercer said, 'If ever a man deserved success it is Bill Shankly.' Chelsea's Tommy Docherty knew where the title was going early on, having seen how well Shankly's team could play. 'Personally I had no doubt at all after meeting Liverpool at Stamford Bridge early in the season that they would win the league. At the present time they have the best manager in British football.' Ex-Everton manager Johnny Carey, now at Nottingham Forest, felt that 'few people in football could argue that the title did not go to the best team in the Football League.'[69]

Although the title had been as good as in the bag since the win at Burnley, Shankly had said he wanted to see the season out by winning all of the remaining games. The *Liverpool Echo* had quoted him on 15th April, 'What are the odds against us finishing in a blaze of glory by winning all three away games as well. You can bet that will be our goal.'

It was inevitable though that attentions of the media and fans would be distracted to the future, with the Echo already speculating on who the Reds may face in European competition the following season. Cologne, Anderlecht and Benfica were certainties for European Cup participation, while with Inter Milan through to the final and AC Milan having a chance of winning the title, it was possible there would be two Italian clubs in the competition. There was also a surprise when Tommy Lawrence, Ian St John and Ron Yeats were all omitted from the Scotland squad for a forthcoming game in West Germany, with the selectors saying they did not want to impose too much travelling on them with Liverpool's American tour also looming.

Shankly made clear his intentions to treat every game with utmost seriousness when he announced the day before the match that the Reds side would be unchanged. The fixture should have taken place in October but was called off due to international call-ups. Relegation threatened Birmingham were also expected to be at full strength, with keeper Colin Withers having recovered from a bout of tonsillitis that kept him out of the previous weekend's 5-0 defeat at West Ham. They were managed by Gil Merrick who had kept goal for them in an FA cup sixth round tie on a snowy day at Anfield in March 1946-47. Albert Stubbins scored a hat-trick in a 4-1 win for Liverpool, one of the goals being a diving header that was later dubbed 'the goal in the snow.'

Liverpool may now have had nothing to play for but Birmingham's situation was dire. They were in desperate trouble at the bottom, three points behind twentieth placed Bolton with two games left to play. Only a win against the Reds would give them a realistic chance of survival given their inferior goal average, and even then they would need to go on and better Bolton's result in the final game of the season. In front of an ecstatic crowd at St Andrews, Birmingham did get the win that gave them some hope, with the Reds struggling on a slippery pitch as the excesses of the last few weeks finally caught up with them.

The home side started off brightly and were unfortunate not to be awarded a penalty when Ronnie Moran appeared to handle the ball in the area. But in the seventh minute they were given a spot kick and there could be no arguments, Gerry Byrne having fisted Ken Leek's chipped shot off the line with Tommy Lawrence beaten. Stan Lynn stepped up to take the kick and gave Lawrence no chance, leading to a small pitch invasion by some home fans who ran and congratulated him. Ten minutes later Birmingham went 2-0 up when Bobby Thomson's shot was beaten away by Lawrence but only into the path of Leek who smashed the ball into the net leading to another pitch invasion.

Shortly afterwards a fine move saw Liverpool get the ball in the Birmingham net, but scorer Alf Arrowsmith was adjudged by the linesman to be offside. This seemed to take the stuffing out of the Reds somewhat and only Peter Thompson showed any promise in attack. In the 38th minute Mike Hellawell was allowed to run fifty yards with the ball, exchange passes with Thomson, and then hit an unstoppable shot past Lawrence. This again led to sections of the crowd coming onto the pitch to congratulate the scorer and the referee was forced to issue an appeal over the loudspeakers for it to stop or he would abandon the game.

After the interval Liverpool came out much stronger and almost got one back in the 58th minute when Milne played a great pass to Roger Hunt, who shot past Withers only to see the ball rebound off the post. Despite some good play, the Reds couldn't find the net until twelve minutes from time when Thompson's shot struck Winston Foster and Hunt seized on the ball to score from a tight angle. With eight minutes left, Bertie Auld hit Ron Yeats and was ordered off, leading to Liverpool's captain being booed every time he touched the ball. Had a header from Yeats not come back off the bar the game might have enjoyed a grandstand finish, but in the end Birmingham's ten men held on for a deserved victory, their first at home in 1964.

Liverpool: Lawrence, Byrne, Moran, Milne, Yeats, Stevenson, Callaghan, Hunt, St John, Arrowsmith, Thompson.

Birmingham: Withers, Lynn, Martin, Hennessey, Smith, Foster, Hellawell, Bloomfield, Thomson, Leek, Auld

Referee: Mr S. Stokes (Nottingham).

Attendance: 22,623.

25th April 1964: West Bromwich Albion 2 Liverpool 2, Football League Division One

Although Liverpool's players may have had one eye on their forthcoming trip to North America, Bill Shankly announced the day after the Birmingham game that he would not be flying with them on 6th May. Instead he would be staying behind to scout players in Scotland where there was a summer cup taking place and he told Horace Yates of the *Daily Post*,

> 'It would have appalled me to think that I was away enjoying myself when quite possibly there were players to be seen at home who might be useful to Liverpool in the future. I could never have forgiven myself if I had missed somebody in my absence. In winning the championship we have

set standards that have to be maintained if we are to keep faith with our wonderful supporters.'

Shankly did say that he hoped to join the month long tour at the mid-way point, but even that was to be at the discretion of the Board as he said, 'If I can serve Liverpool better by staying at home, stay I certainly shall.' It meant Bob Paisley and Reuben Bennett would be looking after team affairs for the start of the tour, with chairman T.V. Williams being in charge of the overall party. As Shankly announced he would not be going, he revealed the provisional squad which included youngsters Bobby Graham, Chris Lawler and Gordon Wallace, as well as veteran Alan A'Court who hadn't featured for the first team at all in 1963-64.

Three days after the Birmingham game it was back to the West Midlands to take on a West Bromwich Albion side that had been second in the league after ten games but had fallen away following a bad run in October and November. They were now eleventh, having managed just five wins from sixteen games since New Year, but would be boosted by the return of centre forward John Kaye who had missed the last four games with an ankle injury. Liverpool had slight doubts over Ronnie Moran who had a thigh injury and Ian St John who had taken a knock during the Birmingham game. Despite some recent poor form, Horace Yates believed Albion had the ability to beat Liverpool and although the Reds would give nothing less than their best, they would 'have to be superhuman to maintain the unrelenting pressure that took them to the title.'[70] It turned out to be very much a game of two halves with the Reds cruising to victory in the first, only to find themselves clinging on to a point in the second.

The Reds put in an exhibition of passing and movement in the first half without creating too many chances as the urgency wasn't there. Albion were making mistake after mistake and looked like a third or fourth division side. The first goal came in the 29th minute when Gordon Milne passed to St John who laid the ball off for Roger Hunt to slot the ball past Ray Potter. The second goal six minutes later came in similar fashion, but this time it was Willie Stevenson making a pass to Alf Arrowsmith, who then teed up Hunt to finish.

The second half was a dull affair with Liverpool going through the motions but still remaining the better side. Then towards the mid-point Albion, backed by the wind, started to show a bit more attacking spirit and Kaye pulled a goal back out of nothing, smashing the ball past Tommy Lawrence from outside the area in the 65th minute. Albion's desire to salvage something from the game meant that the final quarter was the most exciting period of the afternoon and with five minutes remaining Ken Foggo crossed for Clive Clark to score. Foggo had been menacing down the flanks all afternoon but in his report for the *Daily Post,* Jack Rowe wrote that he wouldn't have been so effective if something was riding on the game for the Reds.

Lawrence made a couple of good saves in the last few minutes and Ron Yeats remained solid as Liverpool held on for a point. It may have looked like one dropped, but the main thing on the players minds was avoiding injuries for the forthcoming American tour and England internationals. They looked confident enough but lacked the killer touch, though Rowe felt this was excusable. He concluded in his match report, 'It is inevitable that there should be some relaxation. For when the pressure goes off so often does the complete will to win diminish. For this reason I cannot take Liverpool to task too much for their failure to win.'

Elsewhere in the West Midlands that day Birmingham completed their great escape when they beat Sheffield United 3-0. It was a result that guaranteed their First Division status for the following season, condemning Bolton who were beaten 4-0 at home by Wolves the previous evening, to the drop instead. For the vast majority of teams in the First Division the season was now over. There was just one more game to play to complete the fixture list and it involved Liverpool, who needed to travel to the Potteries to take on Stoke City the following Wednesday.

Liverpool: Lawrence, Byrne, Moran, Milne, Yeats, Stevenson, Callaghan, Hunt, St John, Arrowsmith, Thompson.

West Bromwich: Potter, Cram, Williams, FraserJones, Simpson, Foggo, Brown, Kaye, Fudge, Clark.

Referee: Mr P Bye (Bedford).

Attendance: 19,279.

29th April 1964: Stoke City 3 Liverpool 1, Football League Division One

With the exception of Liverpool's trip to the Potteries, all other First Division fixtures had been completed by the last scheduled day of the season on 25th April. This game had been scheduled for 28th December but postponed due to icy conditions, much to Bill Shankly's frustration as the Reds had beaten Stoke 6-1 at Anfield two days earlier. Stoke had been in eighteenth place in the table at the end of December, although still seven points clear of the relegation places. But with Bolton and Ipswich occupying the bottom two positions from the beginning of October to the end of March they never really looked in danger of going down.

Stoke confirmed their First Division status on 11th April with a 1-0 win at Birmingham, who had by then been dragged into the mire only to go on and stage a great escape of their own. Birmingham's escape route included a 3-1 win over Liverpool which led to some accusations that the Reds players had eased up and condemned Bolton to the drop. Ian St John reacted angrily to this in his *Daily Post* column on 28th April, writing,

> Bolton had 42 games in which to escape relegation. Surely the only team they can blame for their fate, sorry as I am to see them go, is Bolton Wanderers. We did all that we possibly could to beat Birmingham but fighting like a thousand furies they won on their merits on the night. They were fighting for their First Division lives and were ready to play until they dropped. Some teams have the temperament to pull out their best at the vital stage and so often a finishing spurt is decisive.

The week began with St John and Ron Yeats accepting an invitation from the Scottish captain to dine on board a ship that regularly called at the port of Liverpool. Fellow Scot Willie Stevenson was also invited but he was unable to attend. The following day, 28th April, Gil Merrick became the first managerial casualty of the close season with Birmingham's board looking at the whole picture of their slump in form rather than the fact they won their last two games.

For the trip to Stoke, Yeats was ruled out with a toe injury sustained in the game at West Bromwich. Gordon Milne was handed the captaincy in his absence, while Chris Lawler again was called up to deputise at centre half. Bill Shankly promised that Lawler would not let anybody down, telling Horace Yates of the *Daily Post*, 'We have all the confidence in the world in Chris. He will not let us down for already he has proved his worth. This is just more experience for him and this is what he needs. He is in the same position now as Arrowsmith was a few months ago and look what a difference it has made to Alf.' Lawler would be marking 22-year-old John Ritchie, who was prone to cause problems with his height and power and found the net once as Stoke won an entertaining encounter 3-1.

Stoke formed a guard of honour to welcome the Reds onto the field, but this was the only concession they made that evening. They began in frantic fashion, Jimmy McIlroy pinging passes around and Keith Bebbington giving Gerry Byrne a hard time down his flank. Liverpool's right back had to be spoken to by the referee for some tough tackles as he tried to quell the danger, leading to him being derided by the crowd. But his refusal to be buckled by this pressure frustrated Bebbington and he began to get the better of the Stoke winger.

Despite their possession, Stoke were unable to turn this into chances and the Reds had the better scoring opportunities. A St John header was well saved by Bobby Irvine, while Stevenson and Roger Hunt both shot wide. Peter Thompson then had a long range drive punched into the air by the Stoke keeper and when Arrowsmith came in to meet the downwards ball with his head a goal looked certain, but George Kinnell acrobatically cleared off the line. Towards the end of the half Ritchie managed to cause Lawler some discomfort, first pressuring him into a misjudgement that led to Lawrence making a point blank save. The Stoke forward then beat him in the air to nod the ball down for Dennis Viollet but his shot was straight at the keeper.

In the 48th minute the Reds were a goal down and could only have themselves to blame, Bebbington being left totally unmarked to turn in Viollet's corner. Liverpool were level on 64 minutes with a goal from nothing. Byrne took a long throw that went over Kinnell and landed at the feet of a surprised Arrowsmith who quickly composed himself and hit a well-taken shot past Irvine. Seven minutes later though Stoke were ahead again, Viollet crossing from the right and after McIlroy stepped over the ball Ritchie hammered it into the goal.

Liverpool did all they could to chase an equaliser, with Thompson a constant danger hitting a stunning drive that Irvine did well to palm away. St John also had a header that hit the inside of the post and bounced along the line amidst appeals for handball. But as the Reds threw everyone forward, Stoke broke away with two minutes left and Peter Dobing was unmarked when he received the ball and fired it past Lawrence to the delight of the home crowd. It had been a tremendous contest for an end-of-season game and meant that the Reds had finished the season on 57 points, the same total they had achieved when they last won the league in 1946-47.

Liverpool: Lawrence, Byrne, Moran, Milne, Lawler, Stevenson, Callaghan, Hunt, St John, Arrowsmith, Thompson.

Stoke: Irvine, Asprey, Allen, Flowers, Kinnell, Skeels, Dobing, Viollet, Ritchie, McIlroy, Bebbington.

Referee: Mr J Finney (Hereford).

Attendance: 32,149.

Top of Table

		Pl	W	D	L	F	A	GA	Pt
1	Liverpool	42	26	5	11	92	45	2.04	57
2	Manchester United	42	23	7	12	90	62	1.45	53
3	Everton	42	21	10	11	84	64	1.35	52

20

Conquering America

A week after their last game of the season, a Liverpool party set off for the month- long tour of North America, which had first been announced at the start of the year. It was the fourth occasion that the club had crossed the Atlantic Ocean, but the first time that they had travelled by plane.

It had been confirmed the previous month that Bill Shankly would not be going from the start. He wanted to watch games in the Summer Cup in Scotland instead and had already made an approach for the Hearts centre half, Chris Shevlane. There were also some notable absentees on the playing side. Roger Hunt, Gordon Milne and Peter Thompson were selected by England for a friendly against the United States in New York, followed by participation in a four-team tournament in Rio and Sao Paulo that commemorated the 50th anniversary of the Brazilian FA.

On 6th May, watched by Shankly and kitted out in new dark grey club suits, the players and officials boarded a British Overseas Airways Corporation jet at Manchester for a flight to New York. There would be no local journalists on the tour, with press agencies providing reports for the *Daily Post* and *Liverpool Echo*. Ian St John would still be sending updates though for his Post column, and revealed the day before departure that there was one thing that terrified him. 'Last week we had our vaccinations. It is amazing what a little needle will do. I admit quite frankly the sight of it scares me stiff. On the field I will face anybody without a quiver, but not that needle and I am not alone, believe me.'

The Reds set up camp in New York at the Governor Clinton Hotel (now the Affinia) at Seventh Avenue and 31st Street in Midtown Manhattan, just a few blocks from the Empire State Building. They spent the day after arrival sightseeing and attending the World's Fair, a major international exhibition at Flushing Meadows. One of the attractions on show there was a six-a-side football tournament which wasn't of the best standard and led Bob Paisley to rue the fact that he and Reuben Bennett didn't have Bill Shankly and Joe Fagan there with them to enter a team.[71]

On 8th May, the Reds showed no signs of jetlag or tiredness as they cruised to an 8-1 win against Boston Metros at the Everett Stadium. St John gave them a third minute lead but they took their time to keep the momentum going and it wasn't until the 28th minute that they added to their lead with Phil Chisnall getting his first goal for the club. Alf Arrowsmith made it 3-0 before half-time and after the break the squad was utilised to the full with Tommy Smith, Chris Lawler and Bobby Graham coming on as substitutes. All three of them found the net, with the other second half goals coming from Arrowsmith and St John. To their credit the home side never gave up and Ron Yeats and Tommy Lawrence had to be at their best to deny them. They scored a deserved consolation with eight minutes remaining when Oscar Sapia fired in from close range after a free kick was played into the box.

The crowd for the match was a healthy 10,000, which included four seamen from Liverpool, who had paid $90 (about £30) to fly from New York and managed to meet the players. It was the largest soccer crowd that Boston had seen, and even more impressive considering that local baseball side, the Boston Red Sox, only averaged a little over 11,000 that year. The Reds then headed straight back to New York in readiness for a game against New York All Stars on 10th May at the Downing Stadium on Randall's Island.

Chisnall opened the scoring in the fifth minute against New York, but after a quarter of an hour Paul Soane equalised from a corner. The Reds regained the lead on 34 minutes through St John, who scored another four minutes later in very fortunate circumstances. He jumped and missed a header only for the ball to drop on his heel and bounce into the net as he landed. By now, New York's confidence had dropped and Willie Stevenson added another on the stroke of half-time. Arrowsmith got a brace in the second half and the squad was again utilised, with Smith coming off the bench to get the seventh goal two minutes from time.

After the game Liverpool's players were whisked to the CBS television studios where they watched a live recording of the Ed Sullivan Show, on which Gerry and the Pacemakers were guests performing *I Like It* and new single *Don't Let the Sun Catch You Crying.* It may seem surprising that they didn't perform the song with which the group and Liverpool FC had become associated, but at that time *You'll Never Walk Alone* hadn't been released in America and when it was in 1965, it only reached 48 in the charts.

Whereas the Reds were only just starting out their American tour, Gerry and the Pacemakers were coming to the end of theirs and a week later lead singer Gerry Marsden was back at his home in the Dingle area of Liverpool. In an interview for the 22nd May edition of music magazine *Merseybeat* he said of meeting the Reds in New York, 'It was nice to have a chat with them about our home town – though most of the players seem to hail from Scotland!'

The next day the Reds party flew by TWA to St Louis, with St John taking time to write his *Daily Post* column whilst on the flight. He said that the standard of football wasn't even as good as the Lancashire Combination or Cheshire League and that 'if only this was the standard of football we had to worry about at home. I could promise you the championship, the cup and anything else you want thrown in for good measure.' Of most concern to St John was the oppressive heat which he felt was more worrying than the opposition, and made the players feel as if they had done a day's training by only walking a few blocks. St John also described how the Reds were a popular attraction and subject to plenty of media coverage, which captain Yeats dealt with aptly, never turning a hair. The only downside was the theft of cine cameras from St John and Yeats, which had included plenty of film of New York and Boston.

Despite the fact his players were enjoying America and had begun the tour with a crushing win, Bill Shankly was not bothered in the slightest that he had opted to stay behind. A *Daily Post* reporter asked him on 8th May if he had made the right decision and he replied 'without any doubt' as he told how he had taken coach Joe Fagan with him on his latest spying mission to Scotland.

St John's comments in his newspaper column came back to haunt the Reds players as they nearly had a humiliating defeat in their game against St Louis Catholic Youth Council. In front of 6,000 fans the home players, who were all amateur, equipped themselves well in defence and prevented the Reds forwards from finding a breakthrough. They also got forward on occasions and Lawler, deputising for Yeats who had an injured knee, put in a solid performance keeping them at bay. However he couldn't stop Pat McBride twice hitting the bar before they took a sensational lead with six minutes remaining when Reds defender Phil Ferns turned the ball into his own net during a goalmouth scramble. Liverpool, who were termed the 'Red Devils' by the local press, had their blushes spared two minutes later when Stevenson converted an Arrowsmith cross.

The Reds spent another couple of days in St Louis before flying to Chicago on 15th May, where the tour would begin to take a step up in terms of quality and there was no room for complacency. Their opponents at Soldier Field on 17th May would be CF Monterrey, who had just finished third in the Mexican league and been runners-up in the cup final. There were plenty of Mexicans in the 12,384 crowd who added some atmosphere to the occasion by setting off fireworks, which only added to the 80 degrees heat. The Reds coped with the conditions though, and the partisan fans were quietened down in the 18th minute when St John opened the scoring. Lawrence was a virtual spectator in goal as Liverpool took complete control of the game, St John adding two more in the second half to complete his hat-trick.

The following day the Reds returned to New York and the Governor Clinton Hotel, where they had a week's rest before the next game against Hamburg SV at Randall's Island. Some of the players took in a baseball game which St John wasn't impressed with, stating bluntly, 'What they find in that game to get excited about I cannot grasp.'

It was during this week that Bill Shankly joined the tour and his arrival was eagerly awaited by all, especially the American press who had heard so much about his charisma and enthusiasm for the game. Ian St John described his arrival as 'like a breath of home to have him with us again' and that 'I don't think he will ever talk himself out of football topics and the Americans must have learned a lot from him.'[72]

Although Shankly's arrival was welcomed, the man himself did not appear to adapt too well to American ways and some of his antics on this tour have become the stuff of legend. Those who were there have recalled how he refused to change his watch to American time saying, 'No bloody Yank is telling me the time.' This led to team sheets being pinned up on the hotel noticeboard at 6am and when he fulfilled a lifelong ambition of visiting Jack Dempsey's bar in New York, he stayed for 20 minutes before leaving at 9pm much to Bob Paisley's surprise. In Shankly's mind though, it was 2am and way too late.

In his autobiography, St John recalls that on one evening the players went out for a drink and returned to the hotel at midnight only to find Shankly up and about wanting to chat to anybody. This led to the players slipping away one by one until the boss was on his own and 'awake but with nowhere to go in a heathen place that had never heard of Tom Finney.' Shankly had been disgusted to have been asked who was Finney after he had made some comments about him at a press conference. He snapped back, 'Christ, that's it, if you don't know who Tommy Finney is you'll never have a team in this country,'[73] before storming out to the hotel lobby where he stood with his hands on his hips shaking his head.

Shankly certainly had mixed feelings over America and although he would have been glad to see Dempsey's bar, he could not have been pleased to arrive and see Yeats with his knee in plaster. However with the extent of the injury being unknown and him being the captain, he remained with the party and relied on St John to help him get dressed. Yeats was in the stands as the Reds lost 2-0 against Hamburg, bringing to an end their proud record of remaining unbeaten in America which had stretched back 34 games. In temperatures of over 90 degrees, the Reds were obviously hindered by the absence of their captain and England internationals and Hamburg were a strong side. Their star player was centre forward Uwe Seeler, a one- club man who in 1970 would become the first player to score in four World Cups (Pele joined him a few minutes later).

The day after the Hamburg defeat the Reds party flew to Detroit and took up residence at the Sheraton Cadillac Hotel. Just a few hours after Liverpool's touring party left New York, the England international squad arrived in readiness for their game against USA, which would take place on the same day that the Reds played in Detroit. Before their game, Shankly agreed that the players could give a coaching clinic to local youngsters, although he was not impressed when he saw posters advertising the match. He believed that the team name alone was enough to sell the match and the fact they came from the same city as The Beatles shouldn't have come into it. However one of the match promoters, Len Morgan, a Liverpool exile living in Detroit, told the *Liverpool Echo,* 'Unfortunately we in football are the poor relations and have to take the crumbs from the table, so to speak.'

Liverpool's game against Meidericher at the University of Detroit stadium on 27th May was the first of three that they would play against the German side over the next nine days. It ended in a convincing 4-1 win for the Reds, who led 3-0 at half-time thanks to a double from Gordon Wallace and one from Arrowsmith. After the break there was little chance of Meidericher getting back into the game with Ronnie Moran, who captained the side in Yeats' absence and Gerry Byrne outstanding in defence. Arrowsmith got Liverpool's fourth with 14 minutes remaining and Meidericher's consolation didn't come until the last minute when they were awarded a penalty which was converted by Ludwig Holden. The attendance for this game was 7,000 which, despite appearing to be low, has to be put into context with the fact that tickets were priced at $3-5 compared to the cheapest baseball seats of $1. Also, on the same day there were just 5,062 at Randall's Island in New York to watch Reds striker Roger Hunt score four goals in a 10-0 victory for England. Three days earlier Liverpool and Hamburg had attracted 13,000 to the same stadium, an indication of just how popular the foreign tourists were.

The following day it was back to Chicago on an American Airlines flight, but before leaving Shankly found he had a problem over breakfast. Being up at 6am the hotel restaurant wasn't open, but he insisted on taking two journalists from the *Daily Express* and *Daily Mail* for a walk to find some rather than wait. After eventually finding a café and ordering a full English and tea for three, Shankly was told by the huge proprietor that it was hot dogs or burgers only. When they got back to the hotel they found that all the players had eaten and were ready to set off for the airport.

On arrival in Chicago they again stayed at the Sherman House Hotel. It was not just the hotel that was familiar to the players, but also the stadium and opposition as the Reds took on Meidericher at Soldier Field on 29th May. Beforehand though, they were ordered by Shankly to take part in an impromptu five-a-side game on the very spot where Gene Tunney had successfully defended his world heavyweight title against Jack Dempsey in 1927. When it came to the match proper against Meidericher, it was a much less open affair than two days earlier and ended in a 0-0 draw.

The Meidericher game included another solid display from Lawler at the back and he was doing a good job of convincing Shankly that there was no need to enter the transfer market. At the start of the tour the *Liverpool Echo* had speculated that Shankly was looking at signing a full back, but the form of Chris Lawler in America, where Shankly watched him deal more than capably with Uwe Seeler, was making such a move unnecessary. St John's column in the *Daily Post* on 30th May had a great deal of praise for the young defender, saying that he had been 'splendid as Ronnie Yeats' deputy' and that 'he could not have discharged his duties better' against Seeler. St John's thoughts regarding Lawler did prove to be correct as he went on to play over 600 games for Liverpool, being one of only three players to win the league title in both 1966 and 1973.

Chicago may well have been Shankly's favourite place on the tour, given he visited the scene of the bout and also because of his love of the gangster movies. After the game the Reds flew west to San Francisco, while chairmanT.V. Williams returned to England with the Football League's Annual General Meeting looming. They had three nights there at the Richelieu Hotel prior to the match on 3rd June against a San Francisco Select XI at the Kezar Stadium, then the home of the San Francisco 49ers American football team and made famous by the 1971 film *Dirty Harry*.

Despite the vast distance there were no signs of homesickness as the Reds racked up their best ever victory in any type of fixture, running out 14-0 winners in a game that Arrowsmith and St John both scored four goals. Such was the Reds dominance that they were 8-0 up at half-time and in the second half, San Francisco keeper Zig Ottoboni was singled out by the press correspondent as their best player for making several spectacular saves. At the opposite end of the pitch, Trevor Roberts, who replaced Lawrence after he injured a foot in training, touched the ball just once in the first half. Lawrence's injury had meant an unexpected transatlantic dash for third choice keeper Bill Molyneux, who was flown out in the few days before the game and came on as a second half substitute.

The day after playing in San Francisco the Reds party flew to Vancouver in British Columbia, Canada for the last leg of the tour, where they would spend a week at the Devonshire Hotel and play two games. All around America they had met British immigrants but there was someone special in Vancouver for Willie Stevenson as his sister was living there. The first of the games was on 6th June against Meidericher but as the players were getting up that morning, 4,708 miles away in London (which was eight hours ahead) chairman T.V. Williams was at the Football League Annual General Meeting at the Café Royal in Regent Street. The most important thing on the agenda for Liverpool FC was the presentation of the Football League Championship trophy. Despite having been confirmed as champions six weeks earlier on 18th April, the Reds still hadn't received the trophy, the League insisting on the presentation having to wait until the AGM.

As the trophy prepared to be returned to Anfield for the first time in 17 years, the Reds played out a bad tempered game against Meidericher. The match was played at the Empire Stadium, venue for the 1954 Commonwealth Games and attracted a crowd of 19,600 who saw all the game's main talking points occur within a four minute spell in the first half. In the 28th minute Manfred Mueller badly fouled St John. He retaliated by knocking Mueller to the ground, leading to both players being sent off by referee Dan Kulak with Mueller having to be helped off due to the blow he had received. Two minutes after the sending offs, Arrowsmith burst through the defence and lobbed the keeper to put the Reds 1-0 up, but within a minute Meidericher were level when Meinz Versteeg scored from the rebound after Lawrence could only parry a free kick.

During the second half the game sometimes descended into a farce as neither looked willing to attack, play was at walking pace and officials of both sides went on to the pitch to remonstrate with the referee after challenges. Boos rang out from the spectators on several occasions and at the end of the game the Meidericher players lined up, as was their custom, to wave to the crowd only to be jeered.

In his autobiography St John recalls about his sending off, 'The German centre half decided to kick me for just about the entire first half. Eventually I snapped and gave my marker a crack. When I reached the touchline I sat next to Ronnie Yeats and told him he had been fortunate to miss the game.' The match also saw some gamesmanship from both benches who were both pumping up and letting air out of the ball every time it went near them, and on the whole it hadn't been the best advert for Anglo-German relations on the 20th anniversary of the Normandy Landings.

The Meidericher match would be the last action that Bill Shankly would see on the tour, as he returned home prior to the next and final game which was four days later on 10th June against the Vancouver All Stars at the same stadium. This game, which the Reds won 2-0, was a far better spectacle than the locals had been subjected to against Meidericher and St John atoned for the sending off with a brilliant deep lying display in which his passes created a succession of chances for Wallace and Arrowsmith. The goals both came from Arrowsmith, one in each half, and the Reds also hit the post twice.

The victory in Vancouver meant that the Reds had won six, drawn three and lost one of their 10 games and scored 40 goals. They had again been extremely popular in America breaking attendance records in several cities. The day after playing in Vancouver the Reds party flew to Toronto where they spent the night, then took an overnight flight to Manchester via Glasgow. I St John ran into trouble at Customs though and had a watch confiscated as well as receiving a fine of £20. Bob Paisley, a much more experienced traveller told him that the best place to hide things was used jock-straps as 'they don't dig around too much when they see those.'[74]

When the players got through Customs they were greeted by Bill Shankly and one fan, 45-year-old Bill Strange from Wavertree, who had been seeing his wife off on a flight and decided to stay behind to see the Reds arrive. Shankly was fairly dismissive of the tour itself telling the *Liverpool Echo*, 'They're coming home from the tour and that's all, there is nothing special in it. Everyone knows about it.' Vice-chairman Sid Reakes was much more positive though, saying that it had been 'wonderful' and they had played first class opposition but were glad to be getting home. After five weeks away, another holiday may have seemed the last thing that was wanted but many of the players had family commitments to keep, with St John taking his wife and children to a caravan in Morecambe.

21

The Legacy of 1963-64

Can't Buy Me Love by the Beatles was number one when Liverpool clinched the title on 18th April 1964. The song contains the line 'money can't buy me love' which was certainly the case with the Reds side, as the cash hadnt been splashed in the same way that other clubs had. Shankly's side had cost about £120,000, while during the last year £100,000 had been recouped in transfer fees. This demonstrated how it was a case of searching out talent and blending it together that brought success, not just writing big cheques as Everton did with Fred Pickering. The average age of the side was only 24 and all the forwards were under 25. This was a side that could only get better.

After winning the title in 1964, Liverpool followed it up with their first FA Cup the following year, which brought about scenes that the city had never witnessed before as half a million people lined the streets. Liverpool also conquered Europe, reaching the semi finals of the European Cup only to lose to Inter Milan amidst accusations of bribed referees which would be proven decades later. The following year they reached the final of the European Cup Winners Cup, losing to Borussia Dortmund. That year they also won the title again, cementing their status as the team of the mid-1960s after Tottenham had been the big side of the early part of the decade.

Arguably, the FA Cup and European Cup near miss came about as a result of the North American jaunt at the end of the season. Jaded when 1964-65 began, the players struggled and never looked like regaining the title. Instead, extra focus was put into the cups, the FA Cup hoodoo was finally broken, and the Liver Birds didn't fly away as Evertonians predicted.

Liverpool would go six seasons without a trophy after 1966 as both Manchester clubs claimed great successes and Leeds won their first title in 1968-69, but the Reds were still up there. They finished third in 1967-68, but did have an outside chance of winning the league on the last day of the season, then in 1968-69 they picked up more points than they had in their two title winning seasons. It was not until 1969-70 after an FA Cup defeat to Watford with the club way off the pace in the league, that Shankly finally broke his mid-60s side up.

He would be the first to admit that perhaps he remained loyal to those players for too long, but he put together a second great side that won the league in 1972-73 as well as their first European trophy, the UEFA Cup. This laid the foundations for even greater success abroad as well as at home, with Bob Paisley seamlessly fitting into the manager's role after Shankly retired.

There have been many great seasons in the history of Liverpool Football Club, but Shankly's first title fifty years ago set the tone for much of what was to follow. Liverpool didn't spend big in the transfer market and their most expensive players sometimes failed to live up to expectations, such as in the case of Tony Hateley and Alun Evans. Later that decade, players such as Ray Clemence, Emlyn Hughes, Alec Lindsay and Larry Lloyd were bought for modest fees and played a pivotal role in 1970s success. Such a policy continued, with Liverpool enjoying unparalleled success but rarely spending big, as players were carefully scouted and welded into the Liverpool way of playing. The only time when big money was spent was when it was received and even then profits were made. In the summer of 1977, Kenny Dalglish joined for £60,000 less than Liverpool had received from Hamburg for Kevin Keegan, and in 1987 when Ian Rush was sold to Juventus, they could still buy Peter Beardsley and John Barnes and have change.

The unique bond between club and fans also began in 1963-64. There had been chanting on the Kop before but this was the season that real singing began, with *You'll Never Walk Alone* emerging as a song that remains the club's anthem today. Bill Shankly never tired of saying how great the club's supporters were and this huge terrace, which was roofed and didn't let sound escape, was the talk of English football. It was this season that led to the Kop establishing itself as the most famous terrace in the country and arguably, in time, the world. This was aided by the Panorama programme and more coverage from the next season with the BBC's Match of the Day being aired for the first time.

Liverpool Football Club had won five titles before, but within seven years of their fifth one they were in the Second Division. However, after this sixth title there was no danger of such a repeat. They had a charismatic manager who believed his team's supporters were the best in the land and deserved to have the best. In his own words he would have 'conquered the bloody world' if he had Napoleon with him and wanted to create a side so great they'd have to send a team from Mars to beat them. These factors together meant that Liverpool Football Club were destined for greatness and it all started off with that title-winning 1963-64 season.

Appendix

The Players and Coaching Staff

Gordon Milne (42 league games, 5 FA Cup)

Gordon Milne was the son of Jimmy Milne, a former teammate of Bill Shankly at Preston in the 1930s. A forward as a schoolboy, he joined Preston North End at the age of 17 and switched to right half. He joined Liverpool in the close season of 1960 for £16,000 and was an ever-present in the promotion season of 1961-62 before making the transition to the top division with ease, earning his first England cap in May 1963. In 1963-64 he played in every league and cup game, scoring two goals, one of which was the only goal of the game at home to West Bromwich Albion in October. Milne did not do the spectacular, instead he did the simple things with unerring efficiency and without complication. He was skilful, rarely misplaced a pass and was very unselfish in his play, creating plenty of opportunities for others and also linking well with the right back when he needed to defend. Milne was unlucky to miss the 1965 FA Cup final through injury, and in 1965-66 missed two months of the season that saw him fall down the pecking order for the World Cup squad. Milne left for Blackpool in 1967 and went on to enjoy a long and successful managerial career with Coventry, Leicester, Besiktas and as a director of football with Newcastle.

Ian Callaghan (42 league games, 5 FA Cup)

A right half as a schoolboy, Dingle's Ian Callaghan thought he was on his way to becoming a heating engineer before Bill Shankly persuaded him to sign professional forms with the Reds. He was soon switched to the wing and made rapid progress through the ranks, making his first team debut in place of Billy Liddell after just six reserve appearances. 1963-64 saw him play in every game, creating numerous chances for the forwards. Although just five feet seven inches tall, he had great pace and liked nothing better than to beat the defender and get to the by-line to put in a cross. He also chipped in with goals, his total of eight being more than double his tally for the previous two seasons combined. His most memorable moment of the season was his double against Everton, including an incredible shot from outside the box, that gave the Reds their first derby win since returning to the top flight. 'Cally' went on to enjoy a long and distinguished Anfield career, playing more appearances for the club than anyone else. He reinvented himself as a central midfielder after an injury in 1970-71 saw Brian Hall establish himself on the right wing, meaning that when the Reds won the title in 1973, he was the only player to appear in all three of Shankly's title winning sides. It is unlikely his 857 appearances will ever be beaten, and he is the only player to have played for the club in both the Second Division and a European Cup final.

Peter Thompson (42 league games, 5 FA Cup)

A former Carlisle, Cumberland and England schoolboy, winger Peter Thompson joined Preston North End at the age of just 15 and broke into the side in 1960-61 as a left winger. He was a regular for three seasons and caught Bill Shankly's eye when he scored the winning goal for Preston against Liverpool in the second replay of an FA Cup fifth round tie in 1962. An Under-23 international, his signature was the final piece in the jigsaw of Shankly's title-winning side. Coming into the team at the expense of veteran Alan A'Court, he played every game of 1963-64 and showed amazing trickery down the flank, sometimes not giving his own teammates any clues as to what he was going to do. As well as numerous assists, he also got six league goals himself including a double in the title-clinching game against Arsenal. He played sixteen times for England and survived Bill Shankly's team rebuilding of 1969-70, coming on as a substitute in the 1971 FA Cup final. However the next two seasons saw him struggle with a knee injury and he finally left for Bolton in December 1973. He enjoyed four and a half seasons at Burnden Park, retiring after they had won promotion in 1978. Thompson later went into the caravan park and hotel trade and is now living in retirement in Portugal.

Roger Hunt (41 league games, 5 FA Cup)

Spotted playing for Stockton Heath in the Mid-Cheshire League, Roger Hunt joined Liverpool as a twenty-year-old in 1958 after completing his National Service. He scored on his debut against Scunthorpe in September 1959 and retained his place in the side, scoring goals with incredible regularity. In 1961-62 he netted 41 league goals in 41 games as the Reds were promoted, a record that still stands today and which earned him a place in England's World Cup squad that year. Hunt made the step up to the First Division with ease, scoring 24 league goals in 1962-63 then 31 as the Reds won the title. He was not an out and out centre forward, instead playing in the inside right position. This meant he was getting knock-downs, rebounds and creating his own chances from outside the box. He was quick, strong, had great skill and a powerful shot and never gave up working for the team. In 1966 he was the only Liverpool player in England's World Cup winning side and was the club's top scorer eight seasons running up unto 1968-69. His final tally of 286 goals in all competitions has only been bettered by Ian Rush, but Hunt still managed more in the league – 245 compared to Rush's 229. In 1969-70 Hunt lost his place to Phil Boersma and joined Bolton Wanderers, but it's a measure of how well he was thought of that 55,214 turned out for his testimonial when he retired from playing in 1972. Hunt then went into his family's haulage business.

Tommy Lawrence (40 league games, 5 FA Cup)

Born in Dailly, Ayrshire in 1940, Tommy Lawrence joined the Liverpool groundstaff at the age of 16 and signed professional forms a year later. He had to wait patiently for his chance though, finally getting an opportunity in the 14th game of 1962-63 after Jim Furnell got injured. Lawrence performed so well that he made the number one shirt his own and played 40 games in 1963-64, making many a crucial save including a penalty from George Eastham in the title-clinching game against Arsenal. At six feet tall and 13 stone he got the nickname the 'flying pig' due to his agility and made three appearances for Scotland. As the decade went on he also became known as the 'sweeper keeper' due to his tendency to play almost as an extra defender in days when keepers usually didn't go further than the six yard line. Lawrence missed just two more matches over the following five seasons before losing his place in 1969-70 to Ray Clemence. After leaving Liverpool in 1971 he joined Tranmere Rovers and later played for Chorley before working in a wire factory as a quality controller. He now lives in retirement in Warrington.

Ian St John (40 league games, 5 FA Cup)

Born in Motherwell in 1938, Ian St John started out with his home town club for whom he scored a hat-trick in two and a half minutes against Hibernian in 1959. In the summer of 1961, Liverpool smashed their transfer record and paid £37,500 for a player who Bill Shankly described as 'the only centre forward in the game.' He made an immediate impact scoring a hat-trick on his debut against Everton in the Liverpool Senior Cup final, then developed a brilliant understanding with Roger Hunt, contributing eighteen goals in the promotion season. St John started out in 1963-64 as Liverpool's centre forward, but he moved to inside forward following the emergence of Alf Arrowsmith. St John revelled in his new role which led to him covering far more areas of the pitch than previously and creating plenty of chances. He still found the net regularly though, his total of 21 being his best tally for the season at Liverpool. St John scored the winning goal in the 1965 FA Cup final and remained a key player at Liverpool until 1969-70. St John was one of the casualties of the FA Cup defeat to Watford that season and he played just four more times for the Reds before joining Coventry and later playing for Tranmere. After retiring from playing in 1973, St John spent four years as a manager with Motherwell and Portsmouth before carving out a successful media career. He is currently a pundit for Liverpool commercial station Radio City.

Willie Stevenson (38 league games, 5 FA Cup)

Born in Edinburgh, midfielder Willie Stevenson played for Scotland schoolboys and signed professional for Rangers at the age of 17, playing against Eintracht Frankfurt in the European Cup final in 1960. A lack of further first team opportunities led to him playing in Australia for a while, but after returning to Ibrox he was granted a transfer request and snapped up by Bill Shankly in October 1962 when Liverpool were struggling to adapt to life back in the First Division. Stevenson went into the side in place of Tommy Leishman and helped the team climb up the table to an eventual eighth place finish. In 1963-64 a groin injury and the form of Phil Ferns kept him out of the side for four games early in the season, but on being recalled he was an ever present. His only goal of the season was a vital last minute equaliser at Sheffield Wednesday in March, but he created many more. He had plenty of skill on the ball and also a good eye for a pass, while off the pitch he was known for his liking of smart suits and cognac. In 1964-65 Stevenson scored a vital penalty as Liverpool beat Chelsea 2-0 in the FA Cup semi-final, and after losing his place to Emlyn Hughes he joined Stoke in 1967. After six years there he had spells with Tranmere and Vancouver Whitecaps before going into the pub trade on retirement. He also ran a contract cleaning business in Macclesfield where he still lives.

Ron Yeats (36 league games, 5 FA Cup)

A former slaughterhouse worker in Aberdeen, Ron Yeats' first taste of success was helping Dundee United to promotion in Scotland. In the summer of 1961 he joined Liverpool for a club record fee and was immediately dubbed 'Colossus' by Bill Shankly due to his height and fourteen stone frame. Midway through 1961-62 he was handed the captaincy and went on to lead Liverpool out of the Second Division. Yeats never shirked a tackle and would build many an attack after he had won the ball. He was limited in the goalscoring stakes though, finding the net just sixteen times in 454 games, the first of which was away to Manchester United on 23rd November 1963. A year after winning the title Yeats became the first Liverpool captain to lift the FA Cup, and he led the side to another title in 1966. After losing his place to Larry Lloyd in 1970, he had a brief stint at left back then became player manager of Tranmere in 1971. In 1986 he returned to Liverpool as chief scout, a role he held for twenty years before retiring after the 2006 FA Cup final.

Ronnie Moran (35 league games 4 FA Cup)

A former schoolboy player for Bootle and Crosby, defender Ronnie Moran was recommended to Liverpool in 1949 by the postman who delivered letters to the club chairman. Initially combining his job as an apprentice electrician with playing for Liverpool's C team, he signed professional forms on his eighteenth birthday in February 1952 and made his first team debut at Derby the following November. He played thirteen games in the relegation season of 1953-54 and missed only six league games during five Second Division seasons until 1959. Club captain when Bill Shankly arrived as manager, he spent fourteen months on the sidelines through injury from October 1960, but came back to play enough games to win a championship medal in the promotion season. Moran was a no-nonsense left back but by 1963-64 his place in the side was vulnerable and Phil Ferns kept him out of the team in October. He also had bad luck with penalties, missing four in a row including in the shock defeat against Swansea in the FA Cup. In 1964-65 he didn't feature at all in the league, losing his place to Chris Lawler, but he did return to the side at the end of the season and played both legs of the European Cup semi-final against Inter Milan after Gerry Byrne broke his collar bone in the FA Cup final. He remained at the club in the reserves, finally retiring in 1967, and went on to become a vital part of the coaching staff for the next 32 years, which included a caretaker management role in 1991 prior to the appointment of Graeme Souness. Since retiring in 1999, Ronnie has continued to live in Crosby and made occasional local media appearances. His grandson Ian has played semi-professional for AFC Liverpool, Bootle and Burscough.

Gerry Byrne. (33 league games 4 FA Cup)

As a schoolboy, Gerry Byrne wasn't overly keen on pursuing a professional football career but after being spotted playing left back for Liverpool Catholic boys he was persuaded by a Liverpool scout to sign for them upon leaving school in 1953 at the age of 15. His debut in September 1957 saw him score an own goal in a 5-1 defeat at Charlton and he hardly got a look in over the next three years. However an injury to Ronnie Moran in 1960-61 gave him a chance and he played 33 games at left back that season, retaining his place for the promotion season in which he was an ever-present, although he switched from left to right back in February when Moran was recalled in place of Dick White. Most of Byrne's 33 games in 1963-64 were at right back, although when he returned from two months out through injury in January it was at left back to briefly accommodate Bobby Thomson. He had a good partnership with Moran at the back and linked well with Gordon Milne down the right side. Byrne's tough tackling went down well with the crowd, although he left the shooting to others and managed just four goals in 333 appearances for the Reds. He was best remembered for his bravery in the 1965 FA Cup final, when he continued to play with a broken collarbone. He was a non-playing member of England's 1966 World Cup winning squad but by the end of the following season his knee problems began that eventually forced his retirement in 1969.

Jimmy Melia (24 league games, 1 FA Cup)

One of family of ten children from the city's Scotland Road area, Jimmy Melia captained Liverpool schoolboys and signed professional forms for the Reds on his seventeenth birthday in November 1954. In 1956-57 he became a regular in the side and was the top scorer with 21 goals in 1958-59. Bill Shankly tried to play him on the wing in 1959-60 but the next season he was restored to his original position of inside forward after the emergence of Ian Callaghan. Melia was an ever-present in the promotion season of 1961-62 and his performances in the top flight led to him being picked to play for England against Scotland in April 1963. A good passer of the ball and industrious worker, he sometimes frustrated by keeping hold of it too long and was often the subject of harsh criticism from the crowd. An injury in December 1963 saw him lose his place to Alf Arrowsmith and although he was recalled for three games at the end of January and early February, he was dropped after the 3-1 defeat at Everton. Too good for the Central League, he was sold to Wolves for £50,000 in March but his 24 games was still enough for a championship medal. He later managed Aldershot, Crewe and Brighton, guiding them to a FA Cup fifth round victory at Anfield in 1982-83. He has also coached in the Middle East and North America.

Alf Arrowsmith (20 league games, 4 FA Cup)

Born in Manchester, forward Alf Arrowsmith played for Ashton Town in the Lancashire Combination before joining Liverpool in 1960 when he turned 17. He made just four appearances for the first team in his first three seasons but did manage 81 reserve goals in that time. He got his first chance in 1963-64 against Wolves in September. Replacing the injured Ian St John, he scored in a 6-0 win and kept his place the following week away to Sheffield United. However the return to fitness of St John meant he had to wait until Boxing Day for another opportunity when he replaced the injured Jimmy Melia at inside forward against Stoke. Arrowsmith scored in this game, and then in the FA Cup third round tie against Derby County he was tried in an experimental centre forward position and struck four times in a 5-0 win. Arrowsmith's immediate impact, coming into a side that had been struggling to score, meant he retained the centre forward position with St John moving to inside left, although Arrowsmith still wore the number ten shirt. He had pace and power, as well as the ability to get shots on target from acute angles, and his goal against Chelsea at Anfield was one of the best the ground has ever seen. He finished the season with fifteen league goals in twenty games and a bright future beckoned, but he picked up a serious knee injury in the following season's Charity Shield against Manchester United. After this he was never the same again, being unable to twist and turn as he had done previously. He made 24 more appearances scoring five goals, before leaving in December 1968 for Bury. Arrowsmith later played for Rochdale and remained a keen Liverpool supporter until he died after a short illness in 2005.

Phil Ferns (18 league games, 1 FA Cup)

A versatile player who was captain of the reserves where he played as an inside forward, Phil Ferns signed professional forms for Liverpool in March 1958 at the age of twenty. He did not get his first team debut until 1962-63, when he made five appearances covering for Tommy Leishman or Ronnie Moran. His ability to play in a number of positions meant he played eighteen times in the league in 1963-64, initially at left half where he was keeping Willie Stevenson out of the side. He then covered for both Gerry Byrne and Ronnie Moran at the back, but by New Year his form was dipping and his confidence waning due to some negative press coverage. His last game of the season was against Derby in the FA Cup on 4th January and he was left out in favour of Bobby Thomson the following week. In 1964-65 he played four games and joined Bournemouth & Boscombe at the end of that season. Ferns still lives in Dorset and his son, also called Phil, played for Blackpool in the 1980s.

Chris Lawler (6 league games)

A former skipper of England schoolboys, defender Chris Lawler joined Liverpool in 1960 at the age of 17. He was included in a tour party to Czechoslovakia in the summer of 1961, but on arrival found out he could not play as rules there at the time barred anybody under 18 from playing in organised matches. On the occasions he was asked to stand in for Ron Yeats at centre half due to injury or suspension he did commendably and was given further opportunities during the post-season American tour. Such was his ability that Bill Shankly abandoned plans to sign a new full back and in 1964-65 he made the right back position his own, with Gerry Byrne switching to left back at the expense of Ronnie Moran. As well as being an excellent defender, Lawler had an eye for goal and notched an impressive 61 goals in 549 games. He survived Shankly's cull of 1970 and won the title in 1972-73, but a cartilage injury sustained the following November was the beginning of the end of his Anfield career. In October 1975 he left to join Portsmouth but was back at the club in the 1980s as reserve team manager. He later managed Cemaes Bay in Wales and is still involved in the game, working as a scout and youth coach in Skelmersdale.

Bobby Thomson (2 league games, 1 FA Cup)

Signed for £7,000 from Partick Thistle in December 1962 at the age of 23, Bobby Thomson played four games that season when Gerry Byrne was out injured. In January 1964 he played three successive games, firstly coming in for Phil Ferns who suffered a loss of form, and then retaining his place at the expense of Ronnie Moran. However after the 0-0 draw with Port Vale in the fourth round of the FA Cup, Shankly went for experience in the replay and Moran was recalled. Thomson never played for the Reds again, moving to Luton Town in August 1965 and later settling in Australia.

Jim Furnell (2 league games)

Born in Clitheroe in 1937, Jim Furnell spent eight years in Burnley's junior and reserve sides before coming to Liverpool in February 1962 after turning down an approach from Everton. Although the Reds were on their way to promotion, Bill Shankly knew improvements were needed if they were to succeed in the First Division and Furnell went straight into the side at the expense of Bert Slater. After thirteen games of the 1962-63 season he broke a finger in training and failed to get his place back due to the form of Tommy Lawrence. He played two games when Lawrence was injured in 1963-64, at home to West Ham and Wolves in September, but when the chance came to become number one at Arsenal in November he couldn't turn it down. Furnell was back at Anfield as captain of the Gunners on the title-clinching day and he stayed at Arsenal until 1968. He then played for Rotherham and Plymouth, retiring in 1976, and went into coaching at his last club, before moving to Blackburn in 1981 to oversee the reserves and junior sides. He retired in 1998

Gordon Wallace (1 league game)

Born in Lanarkshire, Gordon Wallace grew up in Llanelli where he developed a Welsh accent and played rugby more than football. After being spotted playing for Carmarthenshire boys he was invited for a trial at Huddersfield in 1959 while Bill Shankly was manager. After Shankly took over at Anfield he remembered Wallace and invited him to join the Reds instead in July 1961. Wallace played seven games in 1962-63 but in 1963-64 was overtaken by Alf Arrowsmith in the forward line pecking order. He managed just one appearance, away to Burnley in April, when Roger Hunt was injured. The following season a serious knee injury to Arrowsmith gave Wallace another opportunity and he scored Liverpool's first European goal away to KR Reykjavik, as well as netting two against Arsenal in the opening league game, the first match to be shown on *Match of the Day*. They were to be his last two league goals however, and he lost his place in September to Bobby Graham. He left for Crewe in 1967 and later ran a garage in the Anfield area.

Bill Shankly (manager)

Born in Glenbuck, Ayrshire in 1913 and a player with Carlisle and Preston, Bill Shankly went into management in 1949, returning to his first club in the Third Division North. He went on to manage Grimsby and Workington in the same division before going to First Division Huddersfield as assistant manager and reserve team coach in 1955. The following year he became manager after their relegation and gave a debut to sixteen-year-old Denis Law, who would go on to greatness with Manchester United. Liverpool's directors were impressed with his management style, a 5-0 win over the Reds in October 1958 doing him no harm at all. In December 1959 Shankly was appointed after Phil Taylor resigned and immediately set about revamping the club, doing away with long runs in training and introducing more ball-work on grass. Although the players welcomed his methods, persuading the board to part with the money necessary to build a team capable of promotion was another matter. It was only with the help of director Eric Sawyer that he was able to persuade them that the club couldn't afford not to sign Ian St John and Ron Yeats in the summer of 1961. Promotion followed and within two years the Reds were champions. This was followed by the club's first FA Cup success and another title in 1966. It was seven years before the next title, won with almost a completely new side in 1973, when the UEFA Cup was also added to the trophy cabinet. Shankly stunned the football world by retiring in 1974 but Bob Paisley continued to build the dynasty he created. Shankly died after a heart attack in September 1981.

Bob Paisley (trainer)

Originally from Hetton-le-Hole in County Durham, Bob Paisley was rejected by Wolves for being too small and signed for Bishop Auckland instead, winning the FA Amateur Cup with them. He joined Liverpool in 1939 but World War Two meant he did not make his debut until 1946-47 when he won a championship medal. After retiring from playing at the end of 1953-54 he took over the reserve side, guiding the Reds to the Central League title for the first time in 1955-56. Under Bill Shankly, Paisley was the first team trainer and the one who would also run onto the pitch to treat any injured players. He could read the game brilliantly and provided invaluable advice to players, remaining a loyal assistant to Shankly until 1974 when he was promoted to manager following Shankly's shock resignation. Paisley enjoyed unparalleled success, winning seven league titles and three European Cups in just nine years in charge. He remained a board member until 1992 when he left for health reasons and died of Alzheimer's Disease in a Woolton care home on 14th February 1996.

Reuben Bennett (trainer)

Born in Aberdeen, Reuben Bennett began as a junior there and was signed by Hull City after playing in a friendly match against them. A goalkeeper, he later played for Queen of the South and Dundee, where he became a trainer after his playing days finished. After a spell coaching at Third Lanark, he moved to Liverpool in 1959 where he was heavily involved with the juniors but also assisted with first team training sessions. With Bill Shankly demanding high levels of fitness Bennett, a former sergeant major and physical training instructor in the army, was perfect for this role. He believed the best way to deal with grazes was to rub them with brillo pads and also advocated rubbing kippers on bruises. Shankly and Bennett had a close bond and they often went on scouting missions together. Despite his regimental nature, Bennett enjoyed a lot of banter with the players and was forever saying Scotland were the best team in the world, always having a novel excuse for a defeat. He had no fear, standing around in shirt sleeves in temperatures well below freezing and also drinking anybody under the table on summer tours, before getting up at the crack of dawn for a swim the next morning. Bennett remained at Anfield under Paisley and died in December 1989 at the age of 76.

Joe Fagan (reserve team trainer)

A former Liverpool Schoolboys player, Joe Fagan signed for Manchester City where he helped them win promotion to the First Division in 1947-48. After retiring from playing he became manager of Nelson in the Lancashire Combination then joined Football League side Rochdale as a trainer. He moved to Liverpool in 1958 as an assistant trainer, overseeing the reserve side. Fagan helped develop players such as Tommy Lawrence, Ian Callaghan, Alf Arrowsmith, Roger Hunt who would all play a key part in the 1963-64 success. He also brought along Tommy Smith and Chris Lawler who would enjoy success later in the decade. Although his main role was with the reserves, he did accompany Shankly on scouting missions and stood in for Paisley when he was ill for the Everton home game. In 1971 he was promoted to the first team picture and Shankly's departure in 1974 led to him becoming assistant manager. Fagan then managed the club between 1983 and 1985, winning an unprecedented treble of Football League Championship, League Cup and European Cup in 1984. A humble man, Fagan continued to live at his home in Lynholme Road, very close to Anfield right through his coaching and managerial career. He died of cancer in 2001, aged eighty.

Albert Shelley (stores/treatment room)

Albert Shelley was a player with Southampton in the 1920s who came to Liverpool in 1936 to join George Kay's coaching staff. He remained as a trainer under Don Welsh and Phil Taylor, but after Reuben Bennett arrived in 1959 he was moved to the general staff, having responsibility for overseeing the treatment room. In what were very primitive days when it came to treating player injuries, he was unseen to the fans but well regarded by all the players. Ron Yeats revealed how his method of treating sore feet was to dip them into boiling wax, while he was also a good masseur and knew how to get rid of stiffness and other aches and pains.[75] He was still working for the club when he died in 1971 at the age of 72.

Endnotes

1 *Liverpool Echo* 14th May 1963.
2 *Liverpool Echo* 14th June 1963
3 *Daily Post* 17th July 1963.
4 *Liverpool Echo* 20th June 1963
5 *Liverpool Echo* 24th July 1963
6 *Liverpool Echo* 24th July 1963
7 *Liverpool Echo* 31st July 1963
8 *Liverpool Echo* 6th August 1963
9 *Liverpool Echo* 31st August 1963
10 *Daily Post* 27th August 1963
11 *Daily Post* 26th August 1963
12 *Daily Post* 27th August 1963
13 *Liverpool Echo* 31st August 1963
14 *Liverpool Echo* 10th September 1963
15 Ron Yeats column, *Liverpool Echo* 21st September 1963
16 *Daily Post* 30th September 1963
17 *Liverpool Echo*, 9th October 1963
18 *Daily Post* 7th October 1963
19 *Liverpool Echo*, 12th October 1963.
20 *Daily Post* 1st November 1963
21 *Daily Post* 4th November 1963
22 *Liverpool Echo* 9th November 1963
23 *Daily Post* 8th November 1963
24 *Daily Post* 25th November 1963
25 *Liverpool Echo* 30th November 1963
26 *Liverpool Echo* 25th November 1963

27 *Liverpool Echo* 30th November 1963
28 *Daily Post* 9th December 1963
29 *Daily Post* 13th December 1963
30 *Liverpool Echo* 21st December 1963
31 *Liverpool Echo* 14th December 1963
32 *Daily Post* 19th December 1963
33 *Daily Post* 21st December 1963
34 *Daily Post* 7th January 1964
35 *Liverpool Echo* 9th January 1964
36 *Daily Post*, 11th January 1964
37 *Daily Post* 16th January 1964
38 *Daily Post* 21st January 1964
39 *Daily Post* 28th January 1964
40 *Liverpool Echo* 27th January 1964
41 *Daily Post* 28th January 1964
42 *Daily Post* 11th February 1964
43 *Liverpool Echo* 8th February 1964
44 *Daily Post* 1st February 1964
45 *Daily Post* 17th February 1964
46 *Daily Post* 18th February 1964
47 *Liverpool Echo* 22nd February 1964
48 *Daily Post* 22nd February 1964
49 *Liverpool Echo* 27th February 1964
50 *Daily Post* 2nd March 1964
51 *Daily Post* 2nd March 1964
52 *Daily Post* 10th March 1964
53 *Liverpool Echo* 14th March 1964
54 *Daily Post* 12th March 1964
55 *Daily Post* 20th March 1964
56 *Daily Post* 28th March 1964
57 *Daily Post* 6th April 2013
58 *Daily Post* 14th April 2013

59 *Daily Post* 13th April 1964
60 *Liverpool Echo* 11th April 1964
61 Burnley v Liverpool 1963-64 match programme p5
62 *Liverpool Echo* 17th April 1964
63 Peter Etherington: *One Boy And His Kop*, Countyvise 2001.
64 *Liverpool Echo* 22nd April 1964
65 *Daily Post* 21st June 1964
66 *Daily Post* 21st June 1964
67 *Daily Post* 11th February 1964
68 *Liverpool Echo* 24th March 1964
69 *Liverpool Echo* 22nd April 1964
70 *Daily Post* 25th April 1964
71 Letter from Ian St John, *Daily Post* 12th May 1964.
72 Letter from Ian St John, *Daily Post* 30th May 1964
73 Ian St John: *The Saint*, Hodder & Stoughton 2005 Page 131
74 Ian St John: *The Saint* Hodder & Stoughton 2005. Page 140
75 *Liverpool Echo* 31st August 1963

About the Author

Steven Horton was born in Liverpool in 1971 and has been attending Anfield regularly since he was seven years old, holding a Kop season ticket since 1986. In 1987 he saw a clip of the *Panorama* programme that featured the Kop during the final game of 1963-64 against Arsenal, leading to a fascination with that season which culminates in this book. Steven has written for the *Liverpool Echo*, *Times* and official club website, as well as various fanzines and unofficial sites. This is his third book about the club he loves, following on from *Ending the Seven Year Itch* (2012) and *Red All Over the World* (2013). He lives in the Childwall district of Liverpool and is married with one son.